CYCLES O

CYCLES
OF
DESTINY

*Understanding
return
charts*

RONALD C. DAVISON

THE AQUARIAN PRESS

First published 1990

British Library Cataloguing in Publication Data

Davison, Ronald C. (Ronald Carlyle)
Cycles of destiny: understanding return charts. —
(Aquarian astrology handbook series).
1. Astrology
I. Title
133.5

ISBN 0-85030-768-6

The Aquarian Press is part of the Thorsons Publishing Group, Wellingborough, Northamptonshire, NN8 2RQ, England

Typeset by Harper Phototypesetters Ltd, Northampton, England

Printed in Great Britain by Mackays of Chatham, Kent

1 3 5 7 9 10 8 6 4 2

CONTENTS

EDITOR'S FOREWORD

Thirty-five years separate this book, the author's last, from its companion and complement, *The Technique of Prediction*, which was his first. In between come just two others, one of which, simply titled *Astrology*, may possibly have taught more people how to draw up and interpret a horoscope than any other. That 35 year span also contains most of his 25 years as President of the Astrological Lodge of the Theosophical Society, and the whole of his 23 years as editor of the Lodge's highly respected journal, *Astrology*. It is most unlikely that anyone will be able to hold these posts for so many years again.

Nor will there be astrologers like him again: he belonged to an earlier era, and when he died in early 1985 that era, in which astrology had closer links with philosophy than psychology, died with him.

Ron Davison's writing had an easily recognizable and quite inimitable style. For that reason, very few changes have been made to the manuscript, so that its old-fashioned niceties and dashes of salty humour may be enjoyed by all. The order of the chapters has been changed a little and the calculation procedures, which were previously either done 'long-hand' with logarithms or by 'ready reckoner' methods, have been replaced by those which use calculators or computers, as most astrologers do today.

Finally, astrologers and admirers of Ron Davison the world over owe a huge debt of gratitude to his widow, Marian, whose tremendous effort in retyping the entire manuscript after her husband's death played a large part in bringing this work to its eager audience.

BERNARD FITZWALTER

Note

A major feature of this book is the careful study of a single event, measured with virtually every astrological time-measure imaginable. The event chosen is the marriage of Ann Harding, who also featured as an example horoscope in the earlier book, *The Technique of Prediction*. With such concentrated attention being paid to one event, readers might be curious as to who Ann Harding was, especially if they are too young to remember her. She was a film actress, popular in the 1930s, and a full biography of her, plus stills from her films, is given in James Parish's *The RKO Gals* (Ian Allen, 1974).

PREFACE

In recent years, astrologers have paid an increasing amount of attention to the Solar Revolution, or Solar Return, and its auxiliary, the Lunar Revolution, or Lunar Return, as a means of prognostication, but for various reasons the popularity of this predictive method is still not as widespread as it deserves to be. This is no doubt due in part to the labour involved in calculating a whole series of lunar figures in order to determine whether the major effects indicated by the Solar Revolution are likely to take place, to the uncertainty as to whether any reliable method of progressing the revolutional figure exists and to the emphasis of some astrologers on the use of the Sidereal Zodiac rather than the Tropical Zodiac as a basis for the Solar Revolution. Many astrologers prefer to work in the Tropical rather than the Sidereal Zodiac and perhaps feel reluctant to abandon the Tropical Zodiac that they have successfully used as a basis for all kinds of astrological work. This volume is designed, therefore, with several ends in view: to introduce a new approach to the whole concept of the Solar Revolution, to suggest a new method of interpreting these horoscopes, to show how they may be progressed in a simple and effective manner, to examine whether better results are obtained when an allowance for the amount of precession elapsed since birth is taken into account, and to present the results of some original experiments with other types of revolutional figure.

The introduction of these additional figures, all based on the same general principles, makes it possible also to undertake a demonstration of the wonderful variety of means by which a probable pattern of events may be gained, a demonstration which should serve as a valuable testimony not only to the efficiency of the methods themselves but to the whole fabric of astrological truth.

Because a certain amount of new ground has been covered it has occasionally been necessary to coin a new term. The reader is, for instance, introduced to the 'Composite Solar Revolution' and the 'Composite Lunar Revolution' and the manner in which they are contrived may remind him of the 'Complete System of Secondary Directing' which appeared in *The Technique of Prediction*. Because many of the basic principles used in secondary directions are, in the present work, applied to the progression of revolutional figures, this book may properly be regarded as a companion volume.

Some of the ideas put forward in relation to the progression of revolutional figures require a rather more flexible application of the nature of time than is usual. For this reason, a chapter on the nature of time has been included in the hope that it may encourage those who have not already done so to make a deeper study of this very complex subject, which contains within it keys to many of the technical problems of astrology.

Finally, I should like to acknowledge my indebtedness to the many astrologers past and present, too numerous to mention individually, whose writings have provided a source of inspiration for the thesis presented in the following pages.

R. C. DAVISON

INTRODUCTION

The directional systems of prognostication used in Western astrology can be classified, broadly speaking, under four main headings: Primary Directions, Secondary Directions, Solar and Planetary Revolutions and Symbolic Directions. In Primary Directions the progressed and converse angles and planets are considered to move at a speed determined by the rotation of the earth upon its axis. In Secondary Directions the angles and planets are progressed at the rate of a day before and after birth for each year of life. Solar and Planetary Revolutions are calculated for the periodical return of the Sun, Moon or planet to the exact place which it held at birth, or to some other significant point in the radix. All directional systems are in a sense symbolic but the term Symbolic Directions is usually applied to all those systems by which the positions of the angles and planets in the natus are progressed by the addition of a fixed increment or a predetermined variable increment dependent upon the actual motion of the Sun or a planet over a period of days.

Primary directions have now fallen largely into disuse, not because of any inherent weaknesses in the system but because there are so many other systems which involve less protracted computations and yet give equally satisfactory results. I have no wish to suggest that excellent results cannot be obtained through the use of primaries, properly computed and interpreted but I believe that secondary directions, used according to the system explained in *The Technique of Prediction*, are in no way inferior to primary directions, as the terminology might appear to imply; nor is the one dependent on the other. In primary directing, a year is represented by four minutes of time, while in secondary directing the time-unit equivalent to one year is the True Solar Day of approximately 24 hours. (In actual practice it is sufficient to use the Mean Solar Day, as explained in *The Technique of Prediction*.)

Those who are familiar with the works of Ouspensky or similar explorers in the realm of metaphysics will be acquainted with the idea that the phenomenon of time owes its existence to the fact that ordinary human consciousness cannot comprehend the happenings of everyday life except as a sequence of events. To a more all-embracing consciousness, past, present and future would appear to exist simultaneously, and what to ordinary consciousness would appear to be 'time' would be recognized as a fourth dimension. By taking four minutes to represent the passage of a year, the astrologer who uses primary directions is employing a time-measure equivalent to the speed at which an individual possessing a very high level of consciousness would be able to experience the events of his life. The heightened consciousness of a drowning man, for instance, enables him to witness all the events of his life in a panoramic flash. By taking 24 hours to represent one year, the astrologer using secondary directions is employing a time-measure equivalent to the speed at which an individual functioning on a lesser level of consciousness would live his life. Alan Leo, in *Casting the Horoscope*, has suggested that primary directions are related to that level of consciousness which in theosophical terminology belongs to the Buddhic plane, while secondary directions are related to that level of consciousness that belongs to the Devachanic plane. In other words, primaries represent the speed of perception in the intuitive world; secondaries, the speed of perception in the mental world. Solar Revolutions and similar figures, calculated in terms of the planetary positions actually occurring on the native's successive birthdays, must therefore relate to the normal speed of perception in the everyday physical world and to man's ordinary waking consciousness.

The object of the present volume is to suggest a new approach to the handling and interpretation of Solar and Lunar Revolutions, to introduce several new types of revolutional figure and to present a new method of progressing such figures. This method is the same as that proposed in *The Technique of Prediction* as an extension of a-day-for-a-year or secondary directions and it can in fact be applied, with appropriate modifications, to any type of horoscope. In the course of our survey we shall have occasion to consider the respective merits of revolutional figures cast with and without an allowance for precession and the opportunity will arise to consider the merits of the Prenatal Epoch.

Revolutional figures are cyclic figures and we shall show as our investigations progress that events coincide with the simultaneous arrival of a 'peak' in several interlocking cycles. The establishment of such a pattern, arrived at by the application of unvarying formulae to the horoscope of birth, should provide fresh evidence of the validity of astrology for those who wish to impress the sceptic.

The first concern of this work, therefore, is not with the presentation of a simple time-saving method by which the astrologer in a hurry may get quick results. In fact, I believe that accurate results often demand painstaking and sometimes protracted investigations. Rather, it is the intention to survey in as much detail as possible, the whole field relating to Solar and Lunar Revolutions, so that the student may select for his own use those particular methods and revolutional figures that appeal to him most. If he should require a check upon the testimony of one particular figure, he will then have in reserve a second or third method with which to confirm or refute his original findings.

PART I:
BASIC PRINCIPLES

1.

PRELIMINARY SURVEY — PART 1

Prognostication by means of the Solar Revolution is a well-established astrological practice. The Solar Revolution is a figure cast for the return of the Sun each year to the exact degree, minute and second that it held in the natal horoscope. Such a return of the Sun to its own place marks the start of a new cycle and seems to supply the whole horoscope with a fresh charge of energy. the nature of this fresh influx of energy depends to a great extent upon the aspects received by the Sun on the day for which the Solar Revolution is cast and also upon the position of the Sun in the new figure. The Solar Revolution is, in effect, a summation of all the transits that fall due on the birthday, these transits having a more potent effect than those occurring at other times of the year.

My experiments have also led me to the conclusion that a horoscope cast for the Sun's yearly return to the place of the Moon at birth produces results equally as effective as those obtained from the figure cast for the Sun's return to its own place. This yearly conjunction of the Sun with the position of the radical Moon may be regarded as an 'Annual New Moon'. Students of astrology will not need to be reminded of the significance of New Moons in mundane astrology nor of their importance as transits in all branches of astrological practice. Although, in one sense, the Annual New Moon is a 'synthetic' phenomenon, there seems to be little doubt that there is a very real connection between the Annual New Moon horoscope and the fortunes of the native to whom it refers.

Further experiments using the radical Ascendant as the point of yearly return for the Sun also produced convincing results. The moment of such a return is equivalent to an 'Annual Sunrise' horoscope. The significance of the rising Sun, signalling the birth

of a new day, should be obvious to the astrological student and
there is no doubt that the arrival of the Sun at the place of the
radical Ascendant is, from the point of view of the native, an
extremely important moment in its annual journey round the
zodiac.

At this point it is opportune to emphasize that, in order to erect
any revolutional figure, it is necessary to know the exact degree,
minute and second of longitude occupied by the luminary or
point of return which forms the basis of the revolution. A
variation of four minutes in the birthtime will make a difference
of 10 seconds to the Sun's position or a difference of about 2 to
2½ minutes to the Moon's position. But it can make a difference
of about 2¾° to the Ascendant, if it is in a sign of short ascension.
Unless, therefore, the birthtime is known to within a quarter of
a minute or so, it is possible under such circumstances, to be as
much as two whole days out in the calculation of the Annual
Sunrise Horoscope. This emphasizes the necessity of ensuring
that the ascending degree of the natal horoscope is determined as
exactly as careful calculation, observation, research and testing
will allow. Should the exact Ascendant be in doubt, although
known to be within a few degrees of arc, it may be possible, by
manipulating the Annual New Moon and Annual Sunrise
figures, to arrive at a more exact estimate of its position. The use
of revolutional figures in rectification will be discussed in greater
detail later.

The rising degree at birth bears a closely defined relationship
to a horoscope cast for a moment in time some nine months prior
to birth, the precise moment being determined by a horizon–
Moon interchange according to the rules of the Prenatal Epoch.
The degree held by the Moon in the Epoch horoscope becomes
the rising or setting degree of the natal horoscope and the degree
held by the Ascendant or the Descendant of the Epochal figure
will be the degree occupied by the Moon in the Natal figure. It
is thus possible, if the moment of birth is known within a few
minutes and if the correct Prenatal Epoch has been identified, to
arrive at the true Ascendant of the nativity. It is possible that, as
the Moon's position at Epoch determines the Ascendant–
Descendant axis of the birth horoscope, the Annual Sunrise
horoscope is the most effective in those cases where the place of
the Moon at Epoch rises at birth. When the place of the Moon at
Epoch sets at birth, an 'Annual Sunset' horoscope may produce
better results. It will be appreciated that in both cases the figure

thus produced may be regarded from the standpoint of the Prenatal Epoch as an Annual New Moon.

It will also be evident that such a figure will either prove or disprove the validity of the Epochal figure selected, for if the Annual Sunrise horoscope does not indicate the timetable of events during the year to which it relates it will be because it has been computed from wrong data. In a subsequent chapter it will be explained how Solar Revolutions and similar figures can be progressed day by day. If the configurations arising from these daily progressions do not agree in essence with the nature of the daily experiences, it can safely be assumed that the given birthtime is incorrect and that the Epochal figure from which the birth Ascendant has been derived is a false one. The fact that it is possible to construct a horoscope based on the exact moment of the Sun's annual return to the precise position of the birth Ascendant as determined by a correctly ascertained Prenatal Epoch and the fact that such an Annual Sunrise horoscope, when progressed day by day, produces indications in accordance with the daily trend of events throughout the year will no doubt prove of great interest to those students who have been reluctant to accept, for one reason or another, the doctrine of the Prenatal Epoch.

The usual method of forecasting the general trend of events during a given month is by calculating a figure for the periodical return of the Moon to its own radical position. Such a figure is known as a Lunar Revolution or Lunar Return. As the lunar month consists of just over twenty-seven days, it follows that during the span of a year it will be necessary to erect thirteen or fourteen Lunar Revolutions, according to the age of the native, because the period of a lunar month does not divide exactly into the period of a year.

It is also possible to calculate a series of monthly figures based on the Moon's periodical return to the place of the radical Sun. These figures are the equivalent of a monthly 'New Moon' and are also valid as a basis for monthly prognostication. They stand in the same relationship to the ordinary Lunar Revolution as the Annual New Moon horoscope to the Solar Revolution.

A monthly horoscope may also be cast for the moment of the Moon's conjunction with the radical Ascendant. This monthly 'Moonrise' figure is the lunar equivalent of the yearly Sunrise figure. The three types of lunar figure are useful adjuncts to the three types of solar figure already mentioned and help to determine when the main events of the year indicated by the major figures are likely to come to pass. It is also possible, as we shall see later, to progress the major figures themselves in such a way as to enable an effective interpretation to be made without recourse to such lunar figures.

In addition, we may apply another method to the yearly Solar Revolutions to obtain a series of twelve minor solar figures for the twelve months of the year. In mundane astrology a figure cast for the return of the Sun each year to 0° Aries is held to be of great significance in relation to the nature of events to be expected during that year. This figure is also a Solar Revolution although it cannot be related to and compared with a particular nativity as is the case with a Solar Revolution in natal astrology. Nevertheless the principle involved is the same and just as the Aries Ingress, as the mundane Solar Revolution is called, can be judged to a considerable extent on its own merits, so in the realm of natal astrology, the Solar Revolution can also be judged, although it is advisable to consider it as part of a 'composite horoscope' including the nativity, as we shall show later. In mundane astrology the Aries Ingress is not considered as the sole horoscope of reference for the whole year. In fact, some authorities regard the Capricorn Ingress as having more weight. Each cardinal ingress is usually considered and, sometimes, the intermediate sign ingresses as well. Using this as a precedent we can construct for each nativity a series of twelve 'personal ingresses' during the year for the times when the Sun arrives at successive distances of 30° from its radical position, each of which may be considered as indicating the trend of events for the month to which it relates. It is proposed to call these intermediate horoscopes 'Duodecimal Solar Returns'.

In the same way it is possible to construct a series of intermediate monthly horoscopes based on the arrival of the Sun at successive distances of 30° from the radical Moon and another series based on the same elongations of the Sun from the radical Ascendant. The same process may be applied to the Lunar Return horoscope, with special emphasis upon the 'first quarter' 'full moon' and 'last quarter' positions, when the Moon will be 90°, 180° and 270° removed from its radical position. Comparable figures, based on similar elongations of the Moon from the radical Sun and Ascendant may also be constructed as extensions of the Monthly New Moon and Monthly Moonrise horoscopes. It will not be possible, within the compass of the present volume, to make a detailed examination of all the minor figures mentioned here but enough ground will be covered to enable the student who wishes to do so to make his own further investigations.

There are two classes of further revolutional figure which are also dealt with in later chapters. These differ from the types of revolution already mentioned by virtue of the fact that they are used symbolically, in the time sense, to represent a much greater span of time than they actually cover in the calendar.

The first of these is the Synodical Return, cast for the exact moment each month after birth when the Sun and Moon arrive once more at the same longitudinal elongation from each other as they were at the moment of birth. Each successive synodical lunation is regarded as being equivalent to one year of life so that this measure is, in fact, a synodical month for a year. The same type of figure, when cast for the actual month under review, can also be used as a current horoscope in the same way as other lunar figures.

The Lunar Revolution is used by the Church of Light as an auxiliary to secondary directions. In this case, each successive lunar revolution, or lunar month after birth is equated to a year of the native's life. As we have already noted, the same type of figure is also equated exactly to its own length of time, i.e. used as a current figure, and employed as an extension of the current Solar Revolution. There is thus every reason to suppose that similar current lunar figures, such as the proposed monthly New Moon and monthly Moonrise figures, can also effectively be equated to the passage of a year of life.

Although the scope of the present volume does not allow for the consideration of planetary returns, it may be mentioned in passing that a further series of annual Solar Returns can be computed, using as starting-points the position of each planet in the nativity. In order to construct these figures accurately it would be necessary to calculate the zodiacal longitude of the planet concerned to the precise degree, minute and second. Horoscopes may thus be drawn up for the annual conjunction of the Sun with Mercury, Venus, Mars and so on.

The return of a planet to its own place is also an important moment in time, especially when the planet concerned is one of the heavier bodies. The more frequently such a conjunction occurs, the less significance it is likely to have in relation to the native's affairs. Mercury returns to its own place in approximately one year (always being found within 30° of the Sun). Jupiter, however, only completes a circuit of the zodiac in about 12 years, while the cycle of Saturn is completed in about 30 years. It follows, therefore, that the Saturn Return is potentially a more important figure than the Jupiter Return, which in turn, carries greater weight than the Mars, Venus and Mercury Returns, which occur more frequently.

Because Uranus does not return to its own place until a period of approximately 84 years has elapsed, and because the cycles of Neptune and Pluto last proportionately longer, there can be no practical application (as far as natal astrology is concerned) of horoscopes cast for the moment of the return of Neptune and Pluto to their original positions in the nativity. Only in the case of Uranus is it possible for such a return to take place during the human lifespan, though not everyone survives to experience their Uranus Return. The conjunctions of Uranus, Neptune and Pluto with other planets and sensitive points in the nativity may, however, occur well within the span of a lifetime and there is good reason for believing that figures cast for the exact moment of such conjunctions may provide valuable indications of the native's psychological attitudes and the type of experiences he is likely to encounter at the time in just the same way as the figures cast for the solar conjunctions with significant points in the nativity reflect the native's fortunes in the corresponding periods.

As the cycles of the three outer planets are of such long duration, it is permissible to subdivide the cycles (in the same way that the Solar cycle may be subdivided to produce Duodecimal Solar Returns). The quarter cycle of Uranus would then occur at about 21 years of age, a time already acknowledged as being of exceptional importance in the development of the individual. It is in mundane astrology, particularly in relation to the horoscope of dynasties and kingdoms that remain in being over the centuries, that figures for the periodical return of the three outer planets to their own places will have their most effective application.

2.

PRELIMINARY SURVEY — PART 2

The Solar Revolution is a horoscope cast for the annual return of the Sun to the exact position which it held in the birth horoscope. As the apparent motion of the Sun through the zodiac is about 1° per day or 1″ of arc every four minutes of time and as 1° of Right Ascension passes over the Midheaven in four minutes, it follows that it is not possible to construct an accurate Solar Revolution horoscope unless the birthtime is known within fairly narrow limits. Until the turn of the present century it was apparently supposed by later-day astrologers that Solar Revolutions should be calculated on the basis of the Sun's radical position measured in terms of the Tropical Zodiac. But in the December 1902 issue of *Modern Astrology* there appeared an article by H. S. Green suggesting that the Solar Return should be calculated on the basis of the annual return of the Sun to its 'true position' at birth. Owing to the fact that the Earth's polar axis appears to wobble in space, rather in the manner of a top which is losing momentum, the phenomenon known as the Precession of the Equinoxes takes place, causing the First Point of Aries in the Tropical Zodiac to retrogress slowly through the zodiac of the constellations at the rate of about 50″ of arc per annum. A Solar Return calculated in terms of the Tropical Zodiac does not take into account the fact that this zodiac is constantly shifting its position in relation to the Sidereal Zodiac. The retrograde motion of the Equinoctial Point through the Sidereal Zodiac means that with every passing year the difference between the First Points of Aries in each zodiac increases. Therefore, as the native grows older, there will be an ever greater discrepancy between the position of his radical Sun calculated in terms of the Tropical Zodiac and the exact position in the heavens (in terms of the Sidereal Zodiac) which the Sun held at birth. In order to compensate for this discrepancy the natal position of the Sun in the Tropical Zodiac has to be corrected by adding an increment of 50.2572" for each year of life and the horoscope for this more advanced position of the Sun in the Tropical Zodiac calculated, still in terms of the Tropical Zodiac.

More recently, Cyril Fagan suggested that in ancient times the Solar Revolution was always calculated in terms of the radical Sun's position in the Sidereal Zodiac. Some astrologers who prefer to work with the Sidereal Zodiac have maintained that it is illogical to correct the Sun's position in terms of the Tropical Zodiac by adding a yearly increment to counteract the effects of precession and then to continue to cast the horoscope in terms of the Tropical Zodiac, as advocated by H. S. Green. They maintain that once the Sun's position has been adjusted by the appropriate precessional increment, consistency then demands that the position of this luminary, together with all the other horoscopical factors, should be expressed in terms of the Sidereal Zodiac.

Although this argument has considerable weight in its favour and has the merits of tidiness and consistency, there is also a school of thought which maintains that it is equally valid to continue to refer the corrected positions of the radical Sun, Moon and planets to the Tropical Zodiac, since both Sidereal and Tropical Zodiacs are merely convenient devices for charting the relative positions of the luminaries and planets in the ecliptic, the former with reference to a fixed point in the constellations, the latter with reference to a moving point determined by the intersection of the plane of the Earth's Equator with the plane of the ecliptic. It may also be said in favour of this second method that the majority of astrologers are more used to interpreting horoscopes cast in the Tropical Zodiac. In order to transpose planetary longitudes from the Tropical into the Sidereal Zodiac it is necessary to know the Ayanamsha, or the exact number of degrees, minutes and seconds of arc between the First Point of Aries in each zodiac. At the present time not all astrologers are agreed as to the exact location of the Equinoctial Point in terms of the zodiac of the constellations, though I agree with Cyril Fagan's estimate that the two zodiacs coincided in AD 221.

Alan Leo mentions another class of Solar Revolution in his excellent survey of the various techniques of predictive astrology, *The Progressed Horoscope*. Here it is suggested that a Solar Revolution figure may be cast for the moment of the Sun's yearly return to the place of the secondary progressed Sun on the day that is known as the 'Progressed Birthday'. This day falls as many days after birth as the native is years old. The astrological purist may be temped to regard such a blending of methods as suspect. It may, however, be argued in support of such a procedure that since the annual return of the Sun to its radical position brings a fresh charge of energy to the natal horoscope, so the Sun's yearly return to any significant point is similarly important. The secondary progressed Sun is an extension of the position of the radical Sun. It was pointed out in *The Technique of Prediction* that transits over the positions of progressed planets and angles were particularly effective in precipitating events. As the Solar Revolution can be regarded as a kind of composite transit map, it is logical to suppose that it may be equally effective when linked with the progressed Sun. In any case the examples given by Alan Leo are sufficiently convincing to warrant attention being paid to this type of revolutional figure.

The point now arises as to whether it is valid to calculate such a revolutional figure for the progressed birthday, at the same time making a correction for precession to the place of the progressed Sun, in the same way that it is possible to apply a precessional differential to the position of the radical Sun and draw up a figure for the Sun's return to that point. Thus, besides there being two possible Solar Revolutions for the 'radical' birthday anniversary, there would also be two possible Solar Revolutions for the 'progressed' birthday. In a subsequent chapter will be set forth comparative examples of Solar Revolutions computed according to these various methods, so that readers may have the opportunity of assessing for themselves the merits of each type of solar revolutional figure.

If a Solar Revolution horoscope based on the position of the secondary progressed Sun accurately reflects the fortunes and experiences of the native during the course of the year over which it holds sway, the point must inevitably arise as to whether a similar figure based on the position of the secondary converse Sun is not equally valid, since converse secondary directions are as effective as progressed secondary directions, as I demonstrated in *The Technique of Prediction*. Furthermore, as I suggested there, transits can, in effect, be regarded as 'day-for-a-day' directions and the exact number of years, months and days that make up the native's age on a given date can also be measured backward in time from the day of birth to provide converse 'day-for-a-day' directions. It follows, therefore, that if the Solar Revolution calculated on the Sun's return each year *after* birth to the place of the radical Sun (whether or not an allowance has been made for the precessional movement of the Tropical Zodiac) owes its particular significance to the fact that it is a summation of the transits or 'day-for-a-day' directions on the birth anniversary, then a similar Solar Revolution may be calculated for an equal number of years *before* birth, representing a similar summation of the converse 'day-for-a-day' directions.

In addition, if it can be demonstrated that a figure cast for the Sun's return each year *after* birth to the position of the secondary progressed Sun (whether or not an allowance has been made for the precessional movement of the Tropical Zodiac) bears an exact relationship to the affairs of the following twelve months, then it would appear that a similar figure cast for the Sun's return each year *before* birth to the position of the secondary converse Sun should also bear a similar relationship to the year's happenings.

From the foregoing it will be seen that it is possible to distinguish two main types of Solar Revolution, those calculated with reference to the position of the radical Sun and those calculated with reference to the position which the Sun has reached by secondary direction, whether progressed or converse, on the days measuring to the birthday in question. For every Solar Revolution based on the Sun's yearly return to its radical position *after* birth, a corresponding and complementary Solar Revolution may be erected for as many years *before* birth as the native is years old. For every Solar Revolution based on the Sun's yearly return *after* birth to its place on the secondary 'progressed birthday', a corresponding and complementary Solar Revolution may be erected for the Sun's yearly return *before* birth to its place on the secondary 'converse birthday'.

Thus it is possible to construct four separate Solar Revolutions having a bearing on the events of any one year. They may be tabulated as follows:

Postnatal Solar Revolution (Radical)
Postnatal Solar Revolution (Progressed)
Antenatal Solar Revolution (Radical)
Antenatal Solar Revolution (Converse)

By applying the appropriate precessional differential to the place of the radical, progressed and converse Sun, it is possible to obtain the 'true position' of the radical progressed and converse Sun. By calculating the Solar Revolutions for the Sun's annual return to these 'true positions' a further four figures having a bearing upon the events of the year may be added to those already listed above. It is convenient to refer to this latter group as Precessional Solar Revolutions.

At this stage the student may well be excused for protesting that if a similar series of horoscopes is to be based on the Annual New Moon horoscope and the Annual Sunrise horoscope there will be such a vast array of possible charts all having a bearing upon a relatively short period of time that the year will probably have elapsed before he is able to erect and interpret them all! And although it is scarcely practicable to propose a converse and progressed Annual New Moon and a progressed and converse Annual Sunrise horoscope, even without these, the number of figures eligible for consideration would be appreciably augmented by taking into account the additional horoscopes to allow for precession and the 'day-for-a-day' antenatal transits. The main purpose of this survey is not so much to present the student with a compact and ready-made system of easy prognostication, as to demonstrate that from the nativity there may be derived many different revolutional horoscopes, each calculated on the basis of different points of return yet subject to the same general principles and each confirming and elaborating the testimony of the other, converging inevitably upon a common point of focus. Such a demonstration must furnish valuable proof of the truth of astrology, showing that the horoscope of birth is an entity and its various parts the source of a number of derivative horoscopes, giving the same general indications in much the same way as the number of rings in a tree trunk may be exposed to view at no matter what point the trunk is sawn through and thus providing in each case, for those who are able to read it, evidence of the age of the tree.

Once the possibilities of the various types of revolutional horoscope have been studied the student will be able to choose for himself which class of Solar Return he prefers.

PART II:
THE SOLAR REVOLUTION

3.
THE CALCULATION OF SOLAR REVOLUTIONS

In order to be able to calculate correctly the time of the Sun's annual return to the place which it held at birth it is necessary to determine the longitude of the radical Sun to the nearest second of arc and to know where the native was living at the time of the Sun's return to its own place. The daily position of the Sun at noon is given in Raphael's Ephemeris in degrees, minutes and seconds of longitude. Tables of the Sun's daily motion are also included so that it is a comparatively simple matter to calculate the Sun's position by a straightforward proportion sum. Once this has been done the Solar Revolution for any desired year may be calculated according to the method used in the following example.

Let us suppose that it is required to calculate the Solar Revolution for Ann Harding's 24th birthday. She was born on 7 August 1902, 9.09.35 p.m. GMT, at Fort Sam Houston, Texas, and was living in Chicago in 1926. The method is as follows:

From the longitude of radical Sun (7 August 1902)	14°23′33″ ♌
Subtract noon position of Sun on 7 August 1926	14°12′40″ ♌
Difference (+ or −)	+ 10′53″
Daily Motion of Sun on 7 August 1926	0°57′32″

The problem is now to find how long the Sun will take to cover an arc of 10′53″, travelling at a speed of 0°57′32″ in twenty-four hours. This amount of time, added to noon, GMT, will give the actual moment of the Sun's return to the position it held at birth. Any pocket calculator which has scientific functions will make easy work of such calculations. The angular difference must be divided by the daily motion, and then multiplied by 24. The resulting figure is the amount of time, in hours, after the ephemeris datum (noon) at which the Sun returns to its natal position.

In this case, 0°10'53" divided by 0°57'32" is equivalent to

0.18138 divided by 0.95888;

this gives 0.18981657, which when multiplied by 24 gives 4.5399768 hours, or 4 hours and 32 minutes p.m.

Had the native then been living in London we could have set up the horoscope without any adjustment to this time. As in this case we have to cast the horoscope for Chicago (longitude 87°W39'), we must make a correction of four minutes for every degree of longitude:

Longitude of Chicago	87°W39'
Turn into time at 4 minutes per degree	5 hours 51 minutes
From GMT of Solar Return	4.32 p.m.
Subtract	5.51
Local Time at Chicago	10.41 a.m.

It now remains to turn Local Time into Sidereal Time so that the house cusps at Chicago may be determined.

Subtract from	12 noon
Local Time of Solar Return	10.41 a.m.
Difference	1 hour 19 mins
Add correction for Sidereal Time	
(10 secs per hour)	13secs
	1 hour 19mins 13secs
From Sidereal Time at noon, 7 August 1926	9°01'00"
Subtract	1°19'13"
Sidereal Time at Chicago	7°41'47"

The Midheaven corresponding to this sidereal time is 23° Cancer and the Ascendant at Chicago is 19° Libra.

Exactly the same methods may be used to calculate the time of the Antenatal Solar Revolution for Ann Harding's 25th year. Her 24th birthday measured backwards in time from her date of birth falls on 7 August 1878. In this case the calculation is as follows:

Longitude of radical Sun (7 August 1902)	14°23'33" ♌
Noon position of Sun on 7 August 1878	14°47'47" ♌
Difference (+ or −)	− 24'14"
Daily Motion of the Sun on 7 August 1878	0°57'31"

0°21′14″ divided by 0°57′31″
is equivalent to 0.4038888/0.9586111
                 or 0.4213271;
multiply by 24 to obtain 10.111852, or 10 hrs 6 mins 42 secs.
10 hrs 7 mins to nearest minute.

Subtract 10 hours 7 minutes from Noon =	1.53 a.m. GMT
Subtract correction for Chicago Longitude	5.51
Local Time, Chicago (6 August)	8.02 p.m.

Turn into Sidereal Time:

Sidereal Time at noon, 6 August 1878	8 59 34
Add	8 02 00
Plus increment of 10 secs. per hour	1′20″
Sidereal Time at Chicago	17°02′54″

The Midheaven corresponding to this sidereal time is 17° Sagittarius
and the Ascendant at Chicago is 5° Pisces.

If it is required to calculate the Solar Revolution making an
allowance for the precessional movement of the Equinoctial Point,
the appropriate increment must be added to the radical position
of the Sun in the case of Solar Returns calculated for the birthdays
measured forwards in time from the day of birth, and subtracted
in the case of birthdays measured backwards in time from the day
of birth. The Equinoctial point moves backwards through the
zodiac of the constellations at the rate of 50.2572″ per year. A
table of increments covering the span of a normal lifetime is given
in Appendix 1 and the cumulative amount of precession for any
number of years can thus be seen at a glance. In the case of Ann
Harding's Solar Revolution for 1926 the calculation is as follows:

Longitude of Radical Sun (7 August 1902)	14°23′33″ ♌
Add Precessional Increment for 24 years	0°20′26″
	14°43′59″ ♌
Longitude of Sun at noon on 8 August 1926	15°10′12″ ♌
Longitude of radical Sun + precessional increment	14°43′59″ ♌
Difference (+ or −)	− 26′13″
Daily Motion of Sun on 8 August 1926	0°57′32″

0°26′13″ divided by 0°57′32″
is equivalent to 0.4369444/0.958888
                 or 0.4556778;
multiply by 24 to give 10.936262 or 10 hrs 56 mins 10 secs
(before noon).

Convert to Chicago Local Time by subtracting 5 hours 51 minutes = 7.12.50 p.m. on 7 August 1926.

To Sidereal Time at noon, 7 August 1926	9	01	00
Add	7	12	50
Plus increment of 10 seconds per hour		1	10
Sidereal Time of Postnatal Precessional Solar Return	16	15	00

The Midheaven corresponding to this Sidereal time is 5° Sagittarius and the Ascendant at Chicago is 16° Aquarius.

In order to calculate the Antenatal Precessional Solar Revolution it is necessary to *subtract* the appropriate increment from the Sun's radical longitude. The corresponding Antenatal Solar Revolution for Ann Harding should therefore be calculated as follows:

From longitude of radical Sun (7 August 1902)	14°23′33″ ♌
Subtract Precessional increment for 24 years	0°20′06″
	14°03′27″ ♌
Subtract longitude of Sun at Noon on	
6 August 1878	13°50′16″ ♌
Difference (+ or −)	+ 13′11″
Daily Motion of Sun on 6 August 1878	0°57′31″

0°13′11″ divided by 0°57′31″
is equivalent to 0.2197222/0.9586111
          or 0.2292089;
multiply by 24 to give 5.5010142 or 5 hrs. 30 mins. 3 secs.

Convert to Chicago Local Time (subtract 5 hours 51 minutes)
= 11.39 a.m.

Convert to Sidereal Time:

Sidereal Time at noon, 6 August 1878	8	59	34
Subtract hours and minutes before noon of Local Time	0	21	00
Subtract correction for Sidereal Time at 10 secs per hour		00	03
	8	38	31

The Midheaven corresponding to this Sidereal Time is 7° Leo and the Ascendant at Chicago is 1° Scorpio.

Solar Revolutions for the Progressed Birthday

The time-measure used in secondary directions is one day,

measured forwards or backwards in time from the date of birth, for every year of life. Thus when the native is 24 years old, his 'progressed birthday' will be 24 days after his date of birth and his 'converse birthday' will fall 24 days before his date of birth. A horoscope may be set up for the Sun's annual return to its position on the corresponding progressed or converse birthdays. Once again, it is necessary to determine the exact position of the Sun so that the time of its return to this point may be accurately calculated. In this case, everything will depend on the method used to determine the yearly progress of the Midheaven by secondary direction. As explained in *The Technique of Prediction* I favour the 'Solar Increment' system, by which the Midheaven is made to progress at the exact rate of the Sun's motion, so that the distance between the progressed Midheaven and the progressed Sun remains constant. Exactly the same method is used to determine the position of the converse Midheaven, the arc travelled by the Sun between noon on the converse birthday and noon on the day of birth being subtracted from the radical Midheaven. In order to calculate the exact position of the Sun on the progressed or converse birthday it is first necessary to determine the position of the progressed or converse Midheaven. The following example illustrates the method of calculation:

It is required to calculate the Progressed Solar Revolution for Ann Harding's 24th birthday:

From the noon position of the Sun on 31 August 1902 (24 days after birth)	7°07'46" ♍
Subtract the noon position of the Sun on 7 August 1902	14°01'35" ♌
Difference	23°06'11"
Add position of radical Midheaven	27°00'00" ♍
Position of progressed Midheaven	20°06' ♎
When 20°06' Libra culminates the Sidereal Time is	13 14 13
Subtract Sidereal Time at noon on 31 August 1902	10 34 55
	2 39 18
Add correction for GMT	27
Local Time at Fort Sam Houston, Texas (95°W20') (Birthplace)	2 39 45
Convert Local Time to GMT by adding 4 minutes for every degree of longitude birthplace is West of Greenwich	6 21 20
GMT	9 01 05

Calculate the Sun's position at 9 01 05 p.m. on 31 August 1902.

9 hrs. 1 min. 5 secs. becomes 9.0180556; divided by 24 this gives 0.3757523, the fraction of a day required. Multiplied by 0.9683333 (the Sun's daily motion, 0°58′06″), the figure for the angular distance travelled in the time is 0.3638534, or 0°21′49.8″.

Then

To Sun's position at noon on 31 August 1902	7°07′46″ ♍
Add	0°21′49″
Position of Secondary Progressed Sun	7°29′35″ ♍
Subtract position of Sun at noon, 31 August 1926	7°18′46″ ♍
Difference (+ or −)	+ 10′49″
Sun's daily motion on 31 August 1926	0°58′04″

Then
0°10′49″ divided by 0°58′04″
is equivalent to 0.1802777/0.9677777
                  or 0.1862801;
multiply by 24 to give 4.4707233 or 4 hrs. 28 mins. 14 secs.

Subtract 5 hours 51 minutes (correction for Chicago longitude)
  = 10.37 a.m. local time

Turn into Sidereal Time

Sidereal Time at noon, 31 August 1926	10	35	38
Subtract amount of time by which local time falls short of noon (+ correction of 10 secs. per hour)	1	23	13
	9	12	05

The Midheaven corresponding to this Sidereal Time is 15° Leo and the Ascendant at Chicago is 7° Scorpio.

This horoscope is cast for the return of the Sun to its progressed position for the 24th birthday but no allowance has been made for precession. If it is required to adjust the longitude of the progressed Sun in order to allow for precession, it will be necessary to extract from the table of precessional increments in Appendix 1 the appropriate arc for 24 years and 24 days and add this to the position of the progressed Sun already calculated. The time of the Sun's return to this new position can then be calculated in the usual way.

If it required to calculate the Solar Revolution based on the position of the converse Sun for the 24th birthday, the position of the converse Midheaven must first be calculated so that the exact position of the converse Sun may be determined. The calculation is made as follows:

Noon position of Sun on 7 August 1902	14°01′35″ ♌
Noon position of Sun on 14 July 1902	
(24 days before birth)	21°05′20″ ♋
Difference	22°56′15″
From radical Midheaven	27°00′ ♍
Subtract	22°56′
Converse Midheaven	4°04′ ♍
Sidereal Time when 4° ♍ 04′ culminates	10 23 50
Subtract Sidereal Time at noon, 14 July 1902	7 26 40
	2 57 10
Subtract 10 secs per hour	30
Local Time at Fort Sam Houston, Texas (95°W20′)	
(Birthplace)	2 56 40
Convert Local Time to GMT. Add	6 21 20
	9 18 00

Calculate Sun's position at 9 18 00 p.m. GMT, on 14 July 1902.

Daily Motion of Sun on 14 July 1902	0°57′13″

9 hrs 18 mins 0 secs becomes 9.3; divided by 24 this gives 0.3875, the fraction of a day required. Multiplied by 0.9536111 (the Sun's daily motion, 0°57′13″), the figure for the angular distance travelled in the time is 0.3695243, or 0°22′10″.

Then

To Sun's position at Noon on 14 July 1902	21°05′20″ ♋
Add	0°22′10″
Position of Secondary Converse Sun	21°27′30″ ♋
From position of Sun at noon on 14 July 1878	21°51′05″ ♋
Subtract position of Secondary Converse Sun	21°27′30″ ♋
Difference (+ or −)	− 23′35″
Sun's daily motion on 14 July 1878	0°57′13″

Then
0°23′35″ divided by 0°57′13″
is equivalent to 0.3930555/0.9536111
            or 0.4121759;
multiply by 24 to give 9.8922225 or 9 hrs 53 mins 32 secs.

Subtract 5 hours 51 mins to convert to Chicago Local Time 8.16 p.m. (13 July)

Turn into Sidereal Time	
Sidereal Time at noon, 13 July 1878	7 24 56

Add hours and minutes after noon
(+ 10 secs per hour)   8 17 23
Sidereal Time of Solar Revolution   15 43 19

The Midheaven corresponding to this Sidereal Time is 28° Scorpio
and the Ascendant at Chicago is 5° Aquarius.

This horoscope is cast for the return of the Sun to its converse
position for the 24th birthday but no allowance has been made
for precession. If it is required to adjust the longitude of the
converse Sun in order to allow for precession it will be necessary
to extract the appropriate arc for 24 years and 24 days from the
table of precessional increments in Appendix 1 and subtract this
amount from the position of the converse Sun already calculated.
The time of the Sun's return to this new position can then be
calculated in the usual way.

4.

THE INTERPRETATION OF SOLAR REVOLUTIONS: PRELIMINARY CONSIDERATIONS

To a certain extent the Solar Revolution horoscope may be judged on its own merits but before doing so it is wise to make a thorough study of the nativity. However promising or threatening the configurations in the Solar Revolution, it should always be remembered that nothing can come to pass that is not shown in the nativity. Thus, in order to corroborate the testimony of the Revolution, and to refine interpretations made on the basis of this figure, it is necessary to relate it to the nativity, observing the cross-aspects between the two horoscopes.

As a first step, regard the Solar Revolution as a figure to be judged in its own right. One of the cardinal rules of astrology is that a planet which is exactly rising or culminating, or in opposition to these two positions, is thrown into great prominence by virtue of being so placed. A Solar Revolution which marks an important year of the native's life will nearly always contain one or more planets within a degree or two of the horizon or meridian of the chart. These planets will indicate the main trend of events during the year, according to their intrinsic nature, the signs they occupy and the aspects they receive from other planets. Although, generally speaking, benefics on angles coincide with favourable events and pleasant experiences, and malefics with unfavourable events and difficult experiences, this is not invariably the case, since an afflicted benefic on an angle may prove to be the indicator of much discomfort if there is little support from other parts of the figure, while a well-aspected malefic in the same position in a horoscope containing a preponderance of harmonious configurations need occasion little cause for alarm. Nevertheless, if two of the so-called malefics are on the angles of the Solar Revolution, the nature of the aspect between them will do little to modify the stresses indicated, so that if Saturn is on the Midheaven of the figure in trine to Uranus on the Ascendant, a difficult period may be anticipated.

Planets in close square or trine to the angles of the Solar Revolution often appear to act with great power. Any planet within 12 or 15 degrees of an angle on either side will also exercise a dominant influence during the year. Planets in cadent houses, as long as they are within the specified distance of the major angles, do not seem to lose power on that account. The closer a planet is to the exact conjunction of an angle, the more powerful it is likely to be. If the Nodes of the Moon are close to the angles the year is likely to be marked by some important happening.

As the Sun is the all-important factor in determining the precise moment for which the Solar Revolution is cast, aspects to this luminary are most important and it is not overstating the position to say that a well-aspected Sun in the revolutional figure can go a long way to counteract the adverse effects of angular malefics. Conversely, much less good will result from angular benefics if the Sun is much afflicted in the figure.

Any prominent planetary groupings and configurations should also be noted, especially in relation to the signs occupied. House position, while sometimes highly significant, is not invariably so, and principal attention should be paid to planets in, or fairly near, the cusps of the first, fourth, seventh and tenth houses. Nevertheless, any house strongly tenanted, and especially that holding the Sun, merits special attention in the light of all the other factors operative during the period. It is not recommended that any special attention should be paid to accidental house rulerships and it will be sufficient to consider each planet in terms of its own essential nature, the sign and house it occupies in the nativity and in the Revolution, and the aspects it receives in both.

A careful study of the various groups of interplanetary aspects in the figure sometimes provides a valuable clue as to the main trend of the year's events. The next chapter contains examples of Solar Revolutions covering periods in which certain definite types of event occurred and it will be seen that certain horoscopical factors, involving a combination of angular planets, solar aspects, lunar aspects and interplanetary configurations recur very frequently, according to the nature of the event.

The next step is to compare the revolutional figure with the nativity. Any radical planets falling within two or three degrees of the angles of the Solar Revolution, or any planets in the Solar Revolution falling within two or three degrees of the angles of the natus, are especially powerful and may be regarded as equal in potency to any planets in the Solar Revolution that are similarly close to the angles of that figure.

Planets in the Solar Revolution in strong, close aspect to radical planets place a strong emphasis on those things signified by the radical planets, for good or ill, according to the nature of the planet and aspect.

Any solar or planetary indications in the Solar Revolution which repeat contacts present in the natus are extremely important and indicate a strong likelihood of the precipitation of such events as are foreshadowed by the radical planetary complex. It is not necessary for the exact aspects at birth to be repeated but only for the same group of planets to be once more linked together, irrespective of the type of aspect.

It is sometimes useful to pay particular attention to the sign on the Ascendant of the Solar Revolution and to the house of the nativity in which the revolutional Ascendant falls and to the house of the Revolution in which the natal Ascendant falls. Events of the nature of the signs and houses thus emphasized may occur, provided other indications agree. If the rising degree of the Solar Revolution is within two or three degrees of a radical house cusp or if a house cusp of the Solar Revolution is within two or three degrees of the radical Ascendant, this is likely to accentuate more strongly the type of event denoted by that house.

Aspects from planets in the Solar Revolution to intermediate house cusps in the nativity, provided they are within a degree or two of exactitude, also place a strong emphasis upon the affairs of that house. In this connection, the Placidean system of house division appears to yield very satisfactory results and in all cases subsequently, where intermediate house cusps are referred to, their positions have been calculated according to the Placidean system.

When the angles of the Solar Revolution repeat the angles of the natus, an important year is signalled.

A further point of emphasis is derived from the aspects received by the Part of Fortune. I have found that more spectacular results may be obtained by modifying the usual procedure for calculating the longitude of Fortuna, as far as the revolutional horoscope is concerned, and this is dealt with in Chapter 8.

Although, in many respects, the converse Solar Revolution will be found to resemble the more widely recognized Postnatal Revolution, it is a wise plan to compare the indications of the

Antenatal Revolution with the nativity and also with the Postnatal Revolution, especially in so far as the angles of all the figures are concerned. Antenatal planets on postnatal angles and postnatal planets on antenatal angles are just as important as any other angular planets thrown up by a comparison of either revolution with the nativity. As we shall see later, 'event configurations' often arise from a combination of radical, postnatal and antenatal angles and planets. It is therefore recommended that a final interpretation be drawn up on the basis of the 'Composite Solar Revolution' in which the natus and the postnatal and antenatal revolutions are considered together as three parts of one whole.

Summarizing briefly, these are the important factors on which interpretation should be based:

(1) Planets in close conjunction with and in opposition to the Midheaven and Ascendant. These fall into four classes:
   (a) Solar Revolution planets (both antenatal and postnatal) on the angles of the Revolution itself.
   (b) Solar Revolution planets (both antenatal and postnatal) on the angles of the natus.
   (c) Radical planets on the angles of the Solar Revolution figures (both antenatal and postnatal)
   (d) Postnatal Revolution planets on antenatal Revolution angles and antenatal Revolution planets on postnatal Revolution angles.

   (Include also planets in close square or trine to the angles. These are less powerful than planets exactly on angles but are still important.)

(2) Solar aspects. (For all practical purposes the Sun's position may be regarded as a constant, even when an allowance for precession has been made. Antenatal and postnatal aspects can thus be considered together.)

(3) Lunar aspects. These may be divided into four classes:
   (a) Aspects to the Solar Revolution Moon from planets in the Revolution itself (whether antenatal or postnatal).
   (b) Aspects between Solar Revolution planets (both antenatal and postnatal) and the radical Moon.
   (c) Aspects between radical planets and the Solar Revolution Moon (both antenatal and postnatal).
   (d) Aspects between postnatal Revolution planets and antenatal Revolution Moon and between antenatal Revolution planets and postnatal Moon.

(4) Interplanetary aspects. These may be divided into three classes:
   (a) Aspects among planets in the Solar Revolution itself. (Whether antenatal or postnatal.)

     (b) Aspects between Solar Revolution planets, (both antenatal and postnatal) and radical planets.

     (c) Aspects between postnatal Revolution planets and antenatal Revolution planets.

  (5) Sign emphasis. Give special consideration to:

     (a) The sign on the Ascendant of the Solar Revolutions.

     (b) The sign positions of any natal planets that are closely aspected by planets in the Solar Revolutions.

     (c) Any sign strongly tenanted in the Solar Revolutions.

  (6) House emphasis. This may be shown in several ways:

     (a) By the house position of the Sun in the Solar Revolution.

     (b) By a concentration of planets in one or more houses of the Solar Revolution.

     (c) By a concentration of planets in one or more houses of the nativity.

     (d) By a concentration of natal planets falling in one or more houses of the Solar Revolution.

     (e) By the degree of the natal Ascendant falling on or close to a cusp of the Solar Revolution (or to a lesser extent by the house in the Solar Revolution in which the radical Ascendant falls).

     (f) By the degree on the Ascendant of the Solar Revolution falling on or close to a natal house cusp (or to a lesser extent by the house in the nativity in which the Revolutional Ascendant falls).

At this stage it is appropriate to mention briefly the main significations of the luminaries and the planets when they appear prominently in the Solar Revolution:

The Sun

Honour, authority, prestige, limelight, enjoyment of patronage, establishment of settled conditions, individual consciousness, creative power, pride, the male element, the father, the husband (where applicable).

The Moon

Change, publicity, feelings, instinct, sensitivity, cherishing propensities, restlessness, the female element, the mother, the wife (where applicable), domestic life, the home.

Mercury

Travel, movement, reading, writing, speaking, propagation of ideas, intelligence, opportunism, study, detailed work, ability to correlate ideas, brothers, sisters, relatives, children and young people.

Venus
Romance, pleasure, love and marriage, preferment, financial gain, the emotional life, harmony-seeking propensities, aesthetic sensitivity, conciliatory instincts, young women, the wife (where applicable).

Mars
Energy, passion, enterprise, initiative, hard work, impatience, fire, inflammatory conditions, quarrels, antagonism, destructive tendencies, young men, the husband (where applicable).

Jupiter
Expansion, increase, honour, advancement, enjoyment of patronage, financial gain, joy, charitable instincts, travel, legal matters, matters connected with religion and philosophy.

Saturn
Contraction, consolidation, crystallization, loss, delay, hindrance, limitation, death, disappointment, lack of appreciation, hardship, integrity, hard work, responsibilities, selfishness, the father, old people.

Uranus
Sudden and unexpected changes, upsets, unusual developments, new departures, cutting adrift from old connections, strong tensions, dynamic impulses, awakening of new interests, mental stimulus, repolarization, enlightenment.

Neptune
The broadening of horizons, the loosening of bonds, the removal of barriers, long distance travel especially by sea or air, emotional stimulus, ecstasy, restless dissatisfaction, bitter disappointment, deceit, treachery, abandonment, self-sacrifice.

Pluto
Transformation, new beginnings, rebirth, reorientation, destruction, elimination, intensification, compulsion, refusal to compromise, death.

Unless the traditional benefics, Venus and Jupiter, are overpowered, when angular, by the malefics, a good year may be anticipated.

When Mars, Saturn, Uranus or Pluto are angular a troublesome period is likely to follow unless strong benefic indications are present elsewhere.

When the Sun or Neptune is angular a great deal will depend upon the support which either body receives. When well aspected, each can signify much happiness and contentment but a preponderance of adverse aspects can be a warning of sorrow and misfortune to follow.

The Moon and Mercury are convertible influences, depending a great deal upon external contacts for their conditioning. Either body, well aspected and in a congenial sign, can denote much success during the year but if either be weak by sign and much afflicted, emotional upsets (Moon) and worrying circumstances (Mercury) may predominate.

An approximate guide to the probable effects of any two angular planets in combination may be gained by referring to the readings given in *The Technique of Prediction* for an aspect formed by the same two planets by secondary direction. In this connection it cannot be too strongly emphasized that a badly placed and poorly aspected benefic in the nativity will not act strongly for good in any subsequent Solar Revolution and that a well-placed and well-supported malefic in the nativity will not prove particularly disastrous in any later revolutional figures.

5.
THE INTERPRETATION OF SOLAR REVOLUTIONS: EVENT CONFIGURATIONS

The angles of the Solar Revolution, which will vary from one year to the next, tend to fall successively on or near the positions of the luminaries and planets in the nativity, accentuating first one body and then the other, thus heralding events which not only correspond to the nature and general condition of the planets so stimulated but which are also related to the things signified by the signs and houses occupied by those planets in the radix. As a first step towards the interpretation of any Solar Revolution, therefore, it is necessary to have a clear picture in the mind of the type of event that each planetary configuration in the nativity is likely to portend.

In addition, it will generally be found that one or more planets in the Solar Revolution itself falls on or close to the angles of that figure, thus placing a special emphasis on those planets in relation to the type of experiences likely to be encountered during the succeeding twelve months. Strong close aspects between planets in the Solar Revolution and the radical angles and planets appear to derive considerably greater power from the fact that they occur at the time of the Sun's yearly return to the exact place that it held at birth. The Solar Revolution can, in fact, be regarded as a frame of reference for all the transits occurring during the year, producing a temporary but none the less definite reorientation of all the native's forces during the period.

As there are so many different types of possible planetary combinations, both in nativities and revolutions, not to mention cross-aspects between the two types of horoscope, which need to be taken into account when making an analytical survey of the probable effects likely to be experienced during the year, it may be more helpful to present a series of 'event configurations' common to a group of Solar Revolutions typical of one specific type of event, rather than to attempt to examine in isolation all possible combinations and groupings of planets in order to make a theoretical assessment of what they might portend.

It is not possible, however, to postulate the existence of certain invariable constants in connection with each special type of event, for just as every witness of a street accident, because of his own personal prejudices and limitations, is apt to give an account of it that conflicts in greater or lesser degree with the testimony of every other witness, so the mental, emotional and physical reactions of each individual to certain types of experience are also likely to vary, in accordance with his own unique approach to the problem of living as shown by the special features of his own nativity. Such varying personal reactions will be indicated by differing configurations in the Solar Revolutions (as well as the nativities) and such indications will depart more or less from the normal according to the degree in which the native's predispositions tend to deviate from what may be regarded as the average.

In spite of the existence of such variations, an attempt has been made to identify and tabulate some of the main horoscopical factors which appear to denote the likelihood of certain types of events occurring during the year, so that the student may have the opportunity to become conversant with the general pattern and texture of the planetary influences in force at the time of such happenings. It should be clearly understood that unless all, or nearly all, of these special features associated with a given type of event are present in the Composite Solar Revolution, an event of that nature is unlikely to occur during the year.

Many of the special features involved will consist of two or more planets linked by aspect. Such planetary groupings may be considered effective when they occur in the Solar Revolution itself, when they occur as a result of the combination of radical and revolutional planets, between planets in the Antenatal and Postnatal Solar Revolutions or between the natal planets themselves, one or more of which have been stimulated by a close aspect from a planet in the revolution. Wide orbs by no means rule out the effectiveness of such configurations and any attempt to assess planetary groupings on a 'precision' basis may well lead to the ignoring of some important configuration, although the closer an aspect is to exactitude the more likely it is to play an important part in determining the planetary climate of the year.

In the same way that planetary combinations may be built up

through the interaction of radix and revolution, so a planet may become angular in a variety of ways (see examples 1a, b, c and d later), each of which appear to act with equal effect. Sign and house emphasis may also be indicated in a similar number of ways but in this connection it should be noted that for all general purposes 'house rulerships' may safely be ignored, so that when assessing the probable significance of each planet, attention should be given only to the basic principles that it represents. In certain cases, however, the planet ruling the radical Ascendant and the revolutional Ascendant may merit special consideration.

Aspects between planets have been traditionally classed as benefic or malefic. This concept has now largely been abandoned by modern astrologers when dealing with the nativity from the point of view of character analysis, and probably rightly so, but from the standpoint of events there is not so much justification for throwing overboard the traditional classifications. Directional astrology demonstrates repeatedly that a preponderance of favourable aspects forming by direction will indicate events of a nature that are likely to bring joy and pleasure to the native, while a majority of unfavourable progressed aspects will herald the approach of difficult conditions, sorrowful experiences and sometimes calamity. Theoretical considerations as to whether calamitous happenings are likely to prove beneficial in terms of 'soul growth' are not likely to afford much comfort to the sufferer! In no branch of predictive astrology is there a more effective demonstration of the sharp distinction between the effects of benefic and malefic configurations than in the series of horoscopes included under the general classification of Solar Revolutions. A strong preponderance of favourable aspects in the revolution, linked by benefic aspect to planets in the nativity, will always signify welcome experiences and pleasurable events. Severe afflictions, on the other hand, will always indicate the possibility of upsets and reverses. Once again, it must be stressed that a well-supported malefic on an angle is usually favourable in its action, while an afflicted benefic will indicate the likelihood of events which disturb the emotional harmony or interfere with material comfort or physical well-being.

In the paragraphs that follow will be found an analysis of the principal features of Solar Revolutions for the year in which some specific event occurred, together with a few illustrative examples for each type of event. Revolutions with and without an allowance for precession are included and it will be noticed that both types of figure appear to produce equally significant indications. This applies, of course, only to the positions of planets on or near angles and to the lunar aspects (as the difference in time between the two types of figure begins to increase as the years progress).

Marriage

Apart from the fact that people do not all marry from the same motives, there are so many secondary effects connected with the occurrence of an event of this nature, such as the setting up of a home, the acquisition of relatives-in-law, the possible loosening of old ties, the development of new friendships and the probability of new financial commitments, that several rather variable factors are likely to be encountered in any group of Solar Revolutions cast for the year of marriage. Nevertheless, certain indications recur with considerable frequency, making it possible to regard them as normal factors in the marriage Solar Revolution.

Each factor has been numbered and these factors are used as group headings in the table of examples below, so that the reader can see at a glance how each factor is represented in the example horoscopes.

(1) Either Venus or Mars, or both, will be angular or in strong close aspect to another angular planet, usually Uranus or Pluto. Mars represents the masculine and Venus the feminine side of life and the institution of marriage is intended to symbolize the harmonious linkage between these two great principles. The action of Mars stimulates the passions and sexual instincts, while Venus acts to develop the native's ability to live in harmony with others. Mars and Venus, therefore, are usually the most active planets at the time of marriage and even when there is no strong emotional tie between the two partners it will still be found that Venus is prominent because marriage is an exercise in maintaining harmony.

Both Uranus and Pluto indicate radical change and new beginnings and when in aspect to Venus and Mars they are likely to stir up all the native's most romantic impulses.

(2) Jupiter will be very frequently found on an angle. Jupiter is the symbol of joy and happiness and represents opportunities for expression through those mutual experiences and interests that arise through sharing the life with another.

(3) Venus will often receive aspects from Jupiter and Neptune. Occasionally these aspects will occur instead of the more usual aspects to Mars, Uranus and Pluto, but they occur quite frequently in addition to these contacts. Such configurations are indicative of great joy and rapture. Aspects from Saturn to Venus are likely to promise lasting affections. It almost goes without saying that if the native marries during a year when the Solar Revolutions contain heavy afflictions to Venus and there are, at the same time, other awkward stresses present in these figures, the success of the marriage is likely to be in jeopardy.

(4) The Sun will frequently be in aspect to Saturn. This is a symbol not only that marriage is intended to be a permanent partnership but that it brings with it considerable responsibilities. The setting up of an independent domestic establishment, even if this does not always entail moving into a new house, will also be represented by this contact. Sometimes Venus or Mars, or both, will be in aspect to the Sun.

(5) The sign Libra will nearly always be accentuated. Planets in Libra (the sign of partnership) are nearly always active at this time and the sign will often be found on one of the angles of the Revolution. The domestic sign Cancer is often similarly stressed.

There does not appear to be a strong Sun–Moon emphasis unless the luminaries are in aspect in the radix.

The above indications are likely to be found irrespective of the sex of the native. The following additional indications are usually present in the case of a man:

(6) Venus or the Moon is often angular (sometimes both are) and there will frequently be a benefic aspect between the revolutional Venus and the radical Moon or between radical Venus and revolutional Moon. Sometimes both contacts occur. These aspects suggest that the domestic environment (Moon) will be made a centre of joy and harmony through the gentle influence of one of the opposite sex. Other aspects to the Moon and Venus will depend largely upon the type of partner to whom the native is attracted, as shown by the natal horoscope. A

preponderance of favourable aspects to the Moon and Venus may be expected.

(7) The Moon will often be well aspected by Mars and Jupiter. These contacts indicate that the native's domestic and home-making instincts receive a considerable stimulus and that he becomes more zestfully aware of the feminine side of life and all that it stands for.

In the case of a woman the following additional features are likely to be present:

(8) The Sun will frequently be well aspected by Mars and Jupiter or by Mars and Uranus. This symbolizes a strong accent on the masculine side of life and the tonic effect which a particular member of the opposite sex will have upon the native.

(9) Mars will very often be well aspected by Jupiter, Uranus or Pluto. Mars is the principal significator of the male element in a female horoscope and the aspects to Mars will depend largely upon the type of man to whom the native is attracted, as shown by the condition of Mars in the nativity.

In the Solar Revolutions of both sexes there will always be a strong emphasis upon the benefics and a great preponderance of favourable aspects.

Examples of typical configurations in the Solar Revolutions covering the year of marriage will be found in the horoscopes listed below. The necessary data for their calculation are given in Appendix 4.

Case No. 1	Nativity No. 1 (Male)	Postnatal Solar Revolution (Non-precessional)	No. 1 a
		PNSR (Precessional)	No. 1 b
		Antenatal Solar Revolution (Non-pr.)	No. 1 c
		ANSR (Pr.)	No. 1 d
Case No. 2	Nativity No. 2 (Male)	PNSR (Non-pr.)	No. 2 a
		PNSR (Pr.)	No. 2 b
		ANSR (Non-pr.)	No. 2 c
		ANSR (Pr.)	No. 2 d
Case No. 3	Nativity No. 3 (Female)	PNSR (Non-pr.)	No. 3 a
		PNSR (Pr.)	No. 3 b

		ANSR (Non-pr.)	No. 3 c
		ANSR (Pr.)	No. 3 d
Case No. 4	Nativity No. 4	PNSR (Non-pr.)	No. 4 a
	(Female)	PNSR (Pr.)	No. 4 b
		ANSR (Non-pr.)	No. 4 c
		ANSR (Pr.)	No. 4 d

As an example of the way in which the various factors occur in specific cases, the planetary positions in the horoscopes comprising Case No. 1 (Male) are set out opposite in tabular form.

Should the birth horoscope suggest that marriage would be unlikely or would not occur until fairly late in life and many of the above indications appear in a Solar Revolution while the native is still relatively young, a romantic attachment may result, bringing happiness or the reverse, according to the predominant trend of the aspects, especially those involving Venus and Mars. If these two planets are angular and much afflicted, unfortunate love affairs or emotional distress are nearly always indicated.

Not all marriages are blessed with perfect harmony nor, in every case, does the union meet with the unanimous approval of the families involved. An affliction in the Solar Revolution between Saturn and Neptune shows the possibility of a marriage for the wrong motives, while the presence of adverse aspects between Saturn and Uranus seems often to indicate a marriage contracted against the parents' wishes. If Mars is afflicted by Uranus or Neptune the native, being carried away by his passions, may make an unwise choice of partner. Marriage hastily contracted or undertaken in the face of advice to the contrary is often shown by an adverse aspect of Mars to the Moon, together with an emphasis on the headstrong signs, Aries and Scorpio, and a prominently placed Uranus. If in addition Pluto is angular, an element of inevitability seems to be present, suggesting a preordained partnership, for good or ill, brought about in accordance with the workings of some inscrutable karmic law.

If the native marries in spite of severe afflictions in the Solar Revolution, the marriage may not last long. The following examples are illustrative of cases where marriage was contracted during the year, to be followed in the space of a year or two by separation or divorce. The necessary data for setting up the horoscopes are to be found in Appendix 4.

Case No. 5	Nativity No. 5	PNSR (Non-pr.)	No. 5 a
	(Male)	PNSR (Pr.)	No. 5 b

Case No. 1 (Male)		MC	Asc.	☉	☽	☿	♀	♂	♃	♄	♅	♆	♇
Nativity No. 1	1a	7°♓	12°♍	23°♍	7°♒	5°♍	6°♍	20°♏	12°♋	22°♌	24°♒℞	8°♌	6°♋
PNSR (Non-pr.)	1b	24°♍	29°♏	23°♍	12°♍	8°♍	16°♎	12°♎	11°♍	9°♋	13°♓	3°♎	9°♌
PNSR (Pr.)	1c	6°♒	11°♓		16°♍								
ANSR (Non-pr.)	1c	23°♒	28°♓	23°♍	23°♋	6°♍	7°♉	8°♒	23°♈	2°♎	4°♏	11°♓℞	9°♓
ANSR (Pr.)	1d	12°♎	11°♐		18°♋								

Factor 1

♇ p.n. (☍MC p.n. Pr.)✶♂ p.n. ☍♀ a.n. ☍♂ a.n.

♅ p.n. (☌Asc. p.n. Pr.) △♂ p.n. △♀ p.n.

♀ p.n. (☌MC a.n. Pr.) ☌☽ p.n.

♆ a.n. (☍Asc. a.n. Pr.) ☌♇ a.n. ✶♀ a.n. △♂ a.n.

♆ a.n. (☌ Asc. p.n. Pr.) ☌♇ a.n. △♂ p.n. △♀ p.n.

☿ a.n. (☍MC r.)✶☍♀ a.n. △♂ a.n.

♅ r. (☍MC a.n. Non-pr.) □☍ r. △♀ p.n.

Factor 2

Asc. r. ☌♃ p.n.

Factor 3

♀ p.n. ☍♃ a.n. △♆ a.n.

♀ a.n. ☌♆ r.

♀ r. ☌♃ p.n.

Factor 4

☉ r. 30°♄ r. stimulated by 150°♃ a.n.

☉ r. ☍♂♄ a.n.

Factor 5

♀ p.n. ☍MC a.n. Pr. ☍♂ p.n.

♄ a.n. ☌♆ p.n.

Factor 6

☽ r. (☍MC p.n. Pr.) ☍♀ a.n.

♀ p.n. (☍MC a.n. Pr.) □☽ a.n.

☽ p.n. Non-pr. (☍Asc. r.) ☌♀ r.

Factor 7

☽ p.n. ☍♃ p.n.✶☍ r.

☽ a.n. Pr. ☍♃ r. △☍ r. □☍ p.n.

☉ r. (☍ M.C. p.n. Non-Pr.)✶☽ a.n.

		ANSR (Non-pr.)	No. 5 c
		ANSR (Pr.)	No. 5 d
Case No. 6	Nativity No. 6	PNSR (Non-pr.)	No. 6 a
	(Female)	PNSR (Pr.)	No. 6 b
		ANSR (Non-pr.)	No. 6 c
		ANSR (Pr.)	No. 6 d

Birth of Children

The principal indicators of this event are Mercury and Uranus. The restless activity of the very young and their constant demands for attention bring a strong Mercurial influence into the life, while the novel experience of caring for an infant, the alteration of outlook that a newcomer to the family circle can bring and the changes of plan that often follow upon the child's arrival, especially if it is not of the sex hoped for, all partake of the nature of Uranus.

The main features are as follows:

(1) Mercury is nearly always angular or in strong close aspect to the Ascendant or to an angular planet. It is often well aspected in the revolution itself or receives aspects from a strongly benefic configuration in the nativity. Uranus, too, is often angular.

(2) The Moon will almost invariably be angular. This is the case irrespective of the sex of the native. In the horoscope of a woman the Moon has a particular connection with the bearing of children, so that a special emphasis on this luminary might be expected in the case of a woman about to become a mother. As the Moon appears to be equally prominent in the case of fathers-to-be it must be assumed that its significance in these horoscopes derives mainly from its connection with the cherishing propensities in general, its accent on the family and the domestic side of life and the fact that the wife's role takes on a new dimension through her additional role of mother. Nevertheless, the particular connection of the Moon with parturition must not be overlooked and a much-afflicted Moon in a woman's Solar Revolution at this time does not promise easy childbirth.

(3) A benefic will usually be angular, signifying the happy event.

(4) Pluto will often be angular, but not invariably so. Pluto has a special connection with changes from one state into another (particularly in relation to states of consciousness) and no changes of this nature are more far-reaching in effect than the phenomena of birth and death. Hence Pluto is apt to be particularly active when events connected with the beginning and ending of human life are heralded.

(5) Both luminaries will usually be in aspect with one or both benefics. The Moon will frequently be found square to Venus, possibly as an indicator of the extra financial outlay involved! Neptune may be present instead of Venus or Jupiter.

(6) In addition, one or both luminaries will often be well aspected by both Jupiter and Mars, or by Uranus and Mars and it is by no means unusual for there to be a close configuration involving the Moon, Venus, Mars and Jupiter.

(7) The fifth house cusp of the Solar Revolution will often be in aspect to a radical planet or well supported by planets in the revolution itself or in the complementary revolution.

(8) Planets in the positive signs ruled by Mercury and Uranus, and the signs opposite them — Gemini, Leo, Sagittarius and Aquarius — will nearly always be accentuated. The fact that Gemini and Leo are signs traditionally regarded as unfruitful does not prevent them from appearing as significators of young life in the revolution. Naturally, the possibility of parenthood must first be determined, by reference to the number of factors indicating fertility present in the nativity.

(9) In the case of the birth of a male child there will be a tendency for Mars–Uranus contacts to be accentuated. In this connection the condition of Mars appears to be much more important than that of the Sun, for Sun–Mars contacts are sometimes present in the revolution preceding the birth of a daughter.

(10) Also in the case of a male child, there will probably be a strong accentuation of the radical Mars.

(11) The child will probably be female when Venus–Uranus contacts are accentuated. In this connection the condition of Venus appears to be much more important than that of

the Moon, for Moon–Uranus contacts are sometimes present in the revolution preceding the birth of a son.

(12) Additionally, in the case of the birth of a daughter, there is likely to be a strong accentuation of the radical Venus.

(13) Mercury will very often be afflicted by Mars or Saturn. A new arrival in the family will often be the source of minor upsets in the domestic routine and may occasion a certain amount of worry and inconvenience. These contacts suggest that the celestial intelligences are fully aware of this side of the picture and that careful planning and thoughtful attention to detail will be a necessary feature of this rather crucial period!

A careful examination of a number of revolutional horoscopes of both sexes failed to disclose any marked differences between the main features of each. The foregoing factors, therefore, may be expected to occur with equal prominence and frequency in the Solar Revolutions of both sexes. Examples of typical configurations in the Solar Revolutions covering the year in which offspring were born will be found in the horoscopes listed below. The necessary data for their calculations will be found in Appendix 4.

Case No. 7	Nativity No. 7	PNSR (Non-pr.)	No. 7 a
(Birth of	(Female)	PNSR (Pr.)	No. 7 b
Son)		ANSR (Non-pr.)	No. 7 c
		ANSR (Pr.)	No. 7 d
Case No. 8	Nativity No. 8	PNSR (Non-pr.)	No. 8 a
(Birth of	(Female)	PNSR (Pr.)	No. 8 b
Daughter)		ANSR (Non-pr.)	No. 8 c
		ANSR (Pr.)	No. 8 d
Case No. 9	Nativity No. 9	PNSR (Non-pr.)	No. 9 a
(Birth of	(Male)	PNSR (Pr.)	No. 9 b
Son)		ANSR (Non-pr.)	No. 9 c
		ANSR (Pr.)	No. 9 d
Case No. 10	Nativity No. 1	PNSR (Non-pr.)	No. 1 e
(Birth of	(Male)	PNSR (Pr.)	No. 1 f
Daughter)		ANSR (Non-pr.)	No. 1 g
		ANSR (Pr.)	No. 1 h

Change of Residence

Such an event may be a matter of choice or it may be dictated by circumstances outside the native's immediate control. When the native deliberately chooses to make many changes of residence this is probably due to an inherent streak of restlessness either in himself or in those around him. The principal factors present at the time of changing house are these:

(1) Moon–Mercury, Moon–Uranus or Moon–Pluto contacts in the nativity will be stimulated. Inveterate house-movers nearly always have such aspects, for the Moon symbolizes the domestic environment and Mercury and Uranus are both planets of restlessness and change. Such aspects will always be stimulated when a move is due to take place. Any change of domestic environment will usually find these bodies in aspect in the Solar Revolution even if there are fairly static indications in the nativity.

(2) Mercury is frequently in aspect to Uranus, Neptune or Pluto.

(3) One or more of the planets of movement and change, Mercury, Uranus, Neptune and Pluto, also the Moon, are likely to be on or near an angle.

(4) The natal Uranus is nearly always likely to be stimulated, especially if in aspect with the radical Moon.

(5) The Sun will frequently be aspected by Uranus, Neptune or Pluto. The Sun indicates the establishment of settled conditions, while Uranus, Neptune and Pluto symbolize the revitalizing effect (or the reverse) of a totally new domestic environment.

(6) The Moon will often be afflicted by Mars. This is probably an indication of the upheaval and turmoil attendant upon moving.

(7) Saturn will often be angular or in aspect to an angular planet, especially Uranus or Pluto. Saturn is the planet of property and also of roots and foundations and the contacts with Uranus or Pluto denote the change of focus brought about by moving house.

(8) Planets in Cancer or Capricorn will nearly always be active at this time.

(9) It is not unusual to find the Sun, Saturn or the ruler of the radical Ascendant in the fourth house of the revolution.

(10) The Gemini–Sagittarius polarity will usually be emphasized. This is probably due more to the fact that these signs are associated with neighbours rather than

with journeys, for the helpfulness or uncooperativeness of neighbours plays a large part in establishing the environmental atmosphere of a new home. This is also another reason for the prominence of Mercury at this time.

The preponderance of good or bad aspects present may very much depend upon whether the move is a congenial one or whether it was made reluctantly. Changing house, too, can result in profit or loss. The new house may be more or less comfortable than the old. If the new residence is far removed from the old, friendships may become more difficult to maintain, and so on.

When the native first sets up home on his own after leaving the parental home or lodgings, the Sun is likely to be found in good aspect with Saturn and one or both bodies may be angular, signifying the acquisition of property and the establishment of settled domestic conditions. Because such a state of affairs promises opportunities for expansion and removes many restrictions that would otherwise be present, Jupiter is often angular also.

Examples of typical configurations in the Solar Revolutions covering the year in which the native changed residence occur in the horoscopes listed below. The necessary data for their calculation are given in Appendix 4.

Case No. 11	Nativity No. 10	PNSR (Non-pr.)	No. 10 a
	(Male)	PNSR (Pr.)	No. 10 b
		ANSR (Non-pr.)	No. 10 c
		ANSR (Pr.)	No. 10 d
Case No. 12	Nativity No. 11	PNSR (Non-pr.)	No. 11 a
	(Male)	PNSR (Pr.)	No. 11 b
		ANSR (Non-pr.)	No. 11 c
		ANSR (Pr.)	No. 11 d
Case No. 13	Nativity No. 9	PNSR (Non-pr.)	No. 9 e
	(Female)	PNSR (Pr.)	No. 9 f
		ANSR (Non-pr.)	No. 9 g
		ANSR (Pr.)	No. 9 h
Case No. 14	Nativity No. 12	PNSR (Non-pr.)	No. 12 a
	(Female)	PNSR (Pr.)	No. 12 b
		ANSR (Non-pr.)	No. 12 c
		ANSR (Pr.)	No. 12 d

Change of Occupation

Some of the factors present at the time of a change in the native's occupation will, to a certain extent, be dependent upon the nature of that occupation and upon whether there is any drastic change in the type of work undertaken and in the circumstances under which that work is performed. The following general factors are likely to be prominent in the Solar Revolution covering a year in which the native changes his occupation:

(1) Mercury is nearly always angular or in aspect to an angle and frequently configured with the Moon, Uranus, Neptune or Pluto. Such contacts not only indicate a certain restlessness but also show the mental stimulus afforded by a new job when the native is required to familiarize himself with new techniques or new sets of circumstances.

(2) A Mercury–Mars aspect will often be present. This probably represents the output of mental energy required to cope with new details and, in the first place, strengthens the native's resolve to make changes.

(3) The radical Mercury is nearly always accentuated, and the radical Uranus too, especially when the latter planet is also in aspect to the radical Midheaven.

(4) Any radical planet in aspect to the radical Midheaven is likely to receive a special emphasis at this time.

(5) The Sun will very often be aspected by Mars, Neptune or Pluto. Aspects to the Sun from Mars and Pluto particularly, act to stimulate the native's ambition and desire to succeed.

(6) There will frequently be a Moon–Uranus contact. This suggests the acquisition of a new set of habits and a change of environment.

(7) There will probably be aspects from Uranus to Saturn. These will indicate a breaking away from old conditions and a stimulus to the ambitions and security drives of the native.

(8) The signs Cancer and Capricorn will frequently occur on the angles of the Solar Revolution and planets in these signs will be specially active.

(9) If the change is beneficial, bringing financial improvement and more congenial conditions, good aspects from

Venus and Jupiter to the luminaries are likely.

(10) Should a change of occupation be dictated by some form of external compulsion and entail certain factors that the native is unable to appreciate, an afflicted and angular Saturn will often figure prominently in the configurations. In such circumstances, Pluto and Neptune also may afflict key planets or angles.

Examples of typical configurations in the Solar Revolutions covering the year in which a change of occupation took place will be found in the horoscopes listed below. The necessary data for their calculation are given in Appendix 4.

Case No. 15	Nativity No. 1	PNSR (Non-pr.)	No. 1 i
	(Male)	PNSR (Pr.)	No. 1 j
		ANSR (Non-pr.)	No. 1 k
		ANSR (Pr.)	No. 1 l
Case No. 16	Nativity No. 12	PNSR (Non-pr.)	No. 12 e
	(Female)	PNSR (Pr.)	No. 12 f
		ANSR (Non-pr.)	No. 12 g
		ANSR (Pr.)	No. 12 h
Case No. 17	Nativity No. 2	PNSR (Non-pr.)	No. 2 e
	(Male)	PNSR (Pr.)	No. 2 f
		ANSR (Non-pr.)	No. 2 g
		ANSR (Pr.)	No. 2 h
Case No. 18	Nativity No. 13	PNSR (Non-pr.)	No. 13 a
	(Female)	PNSR (Pr.)	No. 13 b
		ANSR (Non-pr.)	No. 13 c
		ANSR (Pr.)	No. 13 d

Travel

Long-distance travel is primarily connected with Neptune and the sign Pisces. The Neptunian vibration encourages the transcending of boundaries and all vast expanses of space are related sympathetically to the planet Neptune. This means that both sea travel and air travel also come under the sway of Neptune. The following factors are likely to be prominent in the Solar Revolutions covering a year that is notable for travel:

(1) Neptune or planets in Pisces will often be angular or in strong close aspect to the Ascendant or Midheaven.

(2) Mercury will frequently be found combined by aspect with Neptune or planets in Pisces. Mercury is the planet of movement. These contacts denote movement on the widest possible scale.

(3) Mercury will often be in aspect with Uranus, Jupiter or Pluto, especially if there is no contact with Neptune.

(4) The revolutional Mercury will often fall on its own place in the radix.

(5) There will frequently be an emphasis on Gemini and Sagittarius, the signs of travel. Sagittarius especially, will occur as the sign rising in the Solar Revolution.

(6) There is also likely to be an emphasis on the ninth house cusp or the Sun may fall in the third or ninth houses of the revolution. The revolutional Ascendant sometimes falls in the natal third or ninth house.

(7) The Moon will frequently be favourably aspected by a benefic. This probably indicates the pleasurable experiences which often result from a long-distance journey or a visit abroad.

(8) A radical configuration indicating travel and generally involving Mercury or the signs Gemini or Sagittarius is likely to be the subject of special emphasis.

(9) Jupiter will often be aspected by Mars and placed near an angle. These planets in combination give an added zest for life which is often reflected in travel and the new experiences encountered.

(10) The Moon will frequently be configured with Uranus, sometimes adversely. Such aspects denote a restless tendency, a desire for novelty, a change in the usual habits and experiences in a new environment, however temporarily. Sometimes the break with the old domestic environment is prolonged, or even permanent.

If the radical Sun is in Gemini, there is a tendency for it to be free from major aspects in the Solar Revolution that covers a period of travel.

Saturn is a planet which encourages the native to stay put and is rarely emphasized at this time unless the need to travel is occasioned by a bereavement or unless an element of duty is involved or a lack of capital and other limiting circumstances combine to accentuate the more uncomfortable aspects of the journey.

Similarly, travel of a hazardous nature through difficult country or travel involving the exploration of little-known territory or the setting up of new standards of performance by land, sea or air, will be indicated by a proportion of inharmonious aspects and a greater prominence of the malefics.

Examples of typical configurations in Solar Revolutions covering the year in which a notable amount of travel took place will be found in the horoscopes listed below. The necessary data for their calculation are given in Appendix 4.

Case No. 19	Nativity No. 14	PNSR (Non-pr.)	No. 14 a
	(Male)	PNSR (Pr.)	No. 14 b
		ANSR (Non-pr.)	No. 14 c
		ANSR (Pr.)	No. 14 d
Case No. 20	Nativity No. 15	PNSR (Non-pr.)	No. 15 a
	(Female)	PNSR (Pr.)	No. 15 b
		ANSR (Non-pr.)	No. 15 c
		ANSR (Pr.)	No. 15 d
Case No. 21	Nativity No. 2	PNSR (Non-pr.)	No. 2 i
	(Male)	PNSR (Pr.)	No. 2 j
		ANSR (Non-pr.)	No. 2 k
		ANSR (Pr.)	No. 2 l
Case No. 22	Nativity No. 16	PNSR (Non-pr.)	No. 16 a
	(Female)	PNSR (Pr.)	No. 16 b
		ANSR (Non-pr.)	No. 16 c
		ANSR (Pr.)	No. 16 d

Financial Fluctuations

Variations in salary, the success or failure of speculations and windfalls of various kinds or the lack of them may make all the difference to the native's comfort and sense of general well-being. For this reason the prominence of the benefics and the nature of the aspects received by them are usually the most important factors in determining the probable financial climate of the period. The revolution covering a year in which the native's financial condition shows a marked improvement will probably contain the following factors:

(1) Radical configurations of a benefic nature will be favourably stimulated and well placed in relation to the revolution.

(2) Jupiter will be well supported by aspects from the major planets, Saturn, Uranus, Neptune and Pluto.

(3) The money signs, Taurus and Scorpio, will often be tenanted by well-aspected planets.

(4) The cusp of the second house or planets in the second or eighth houses will probably be well supported by aspects, especially from Uranus or Pluto.

In the revolution covering a year in which there is a marked deterioration in the native's financial situation the following factors are likely to be present:

(5) Radical afflictions to Jupiter and Venus will be adversely stimulated.

(6) Jupiter is likely to be afflicted, especially by an angular Saturn. This type of affliction will frequently be found in cases of real hardship.

(7) Saturn is likely to be afflicted by Neptune and Pluto. Severe restriction and irritating frustrations as a result of losses are indicated by such contacts, which also suggest that disillusionment and the challenge of poverty may give birth to a determination to begin again on some new line of activity.

(8) The cusp of the second house or planets in the second or eighth houses are likely to be adversely aspected by a malefic planet.

(9) The radical Sun is likely to be afflicted.

(10) The money signs, Taurus and Scorpio, will often be occupied by afflicted malefics.

Examples of typical configurations in Solar Revolutions covering the year in which the native experienced a marked improvement or deterioration in his financial affairs will be found in the horoscopes listed below. The necessary data for their calculation are given in Appendix 4.

Case No. 23	Nativity No. 1	PNSR (Non-pr.)	No. 1 m
(Reduced	(Male)	PNSR (Pr.)	No. 1 n
Income)		ANSR (Non-pr.)	No. 1 o
		ANSR (Pr.)	No. 1 p

Case No. 24	Nativity No. 11	PNSR (Non-pr.)	No. 11 e
(Reduced	(Male)	PNSR (Pr.)	No. 11 f
Income)		ANSR (Non-pr.)	No. 11 g
		ANSR (Pr.)	No. 11 h
Case No. 25	Nativity No. 17	PNSR (Non-pr.)	No. 17 a
(Increased	(Male)	PNSR (Pr.)	No. 17 b
Income)		ANSR (Non-pr.)	No. 17 c
		ANSR (Pr.)	No. 17 d
Case No. 26	Nativity No. 9	PNSR (Non-pr.)	No. 9 i
(Legacy)	(Male)	PNSR (Pr.)	No. 9 j
		ANSR (Non-pr.)	No. 9 k
		ANSR (Pr.)	No. 9 l

Bereavement

Although many of the factors given below will be common to all horoscopes covering the period in which a bereavement was sustained by the native, there will be certain variations in individual cases, depending upon the native's type of attachment to and depth of feeling for the deceased and also upon his mental and emotional reactions to the phenomenon of death itself. In addition any financial repercussions and domestic rearrangements consequent upon the death will naturally vary from case to case and so produce modifications in some of the typical features to be expected.

(1) Pluto, the planet of transformation, elimination and death, is likely to be particularly active at this time and will frequently be found on an angle afflicted by a malefic or, if not angular, afflicting a malefic planet which is.

(2) Mars, Saturn, Uranus or Neptune is also likely to be angular. Often these planets are found in mutual affliction. (It will generally be found that malefic configurations in the nativity fall on the angles of the revolution and afflictions in the revolution similarly fall on the angles of the nativity.)

(3) The Sun will be afflicted by at least one, and often by more malefics.

(4) Venus is likely to be afflicted by malefics and will often be found in adverse aspect with Jupiter. These afflictions are especially indicative of the grief occasioned by the death of a loved one. The adverse aspect of Jupiter here will signify great emotional activity of a sorrowful nature.

(5) There will generally be a special emphasis on the signs Taurus and Scorpio. Scorpio is the sign of death and transmutation and is frequently tenanted by a malefic or involved in a malefic configuration. Alternatively, the sign may be present on one of the angles of the revolution. The opposite sign, Taurus, is also frequently involved.

(6) The cusp of the eighth house or planets in the second or eighth houses are likely to be afflicted. Alternatively the cusp of the radical eighth house may appear on an angle of the revolution, or the degree on the eighth house cusp of the revolution may be that of the radical Ascendant or Descendant.

When the above factors are present it may be possible to determine from which direction the bereavement is likely to come by paying particular attention to planets which are angular and afflicted and to the signs involved in malefic configurations. The following additional factors are often found in special cases:

(7) The death of the father is often shown by Saturn angular and afflicted in the revolution. There is often an afflicted planet in the fourth house and a malefic configuration involving the signs Cancer and Capricorn.

(8) The death of the mother will often be shown by an affliction to an angular Moon in the revolution, together with afflictions to the fourth house and a malefic configuration involving the signs Cancer or Capricorn.

(9) The death of the husband will usually be shown by afflictions to an angular Sun and Mars in the revolution, together with a malefic configuration involving the signs Aries or Libra or planets in the natal seventh house.

(10) The death of the wife will usually be shown by afflictions to an angular Venus in the revolution, together with a malefic configuration involving the signs Aries or Libra or planets in the radical seventh house. The Moon is also likely to be prominent and afflicted.

(11) The death of a son will usually be shown by afflictions to both Mercury and Mars in the revolution, together with afflictions involving the cusp of the fifth house or planets in the fifth or eleventh houses and in the signs Leo and Aquarius. The death of a daughter will usually be shown by the same indications except that Venus will be afflicted instead of Mars.

(12) The death of a brother will usually be shown by afflictions to an angular Mercury in the revolution and by adverse aspects to planets in Gemini or Sagittarius. The cusp of the third house or planets in the third or ninth houses will often be afflicted by a malefic.

Examples of typical configurations in the Solar Revolutions covering the year in which the native suffered a bereavement will be found in the horoscopes referred to below. The necessary data for their calculation are given in Appendix 4.

Case No. 27 (death of wife)	Nativity No. 18 (Male)	PNSR (Non-pr.) PNSR (Pr.) ANSR (Non-pr.) ANSR (Pr.)	No. 18 a No. 18 b No. 18 c No. 18 d
Case No. 28 (death of husband)	Nativity No. 3 (Female)	PNSR (Non-pr.) PNSR (Pr.) ANSR (Non-pr.) ANSR (Pr.)	No. 3 e No. 3 f No. 3 g No. 3 h
Case No. 29 (Death of father and daughter)	Nativity No. 8 (Female)	PNSR (Non-pr.) PNSR (Pr.) ANSR (Non-pr.) ANSR (Pr.)	No. 8 e No. 8 f No. 8 g No. 8 h
Case No. 30 (Death of mother and daughter)	Nativity No. 3 (Female)	PNSR (Non-pr.) PNSR (Pr.) ANSR (Non-pr.) ANSR (Pr.)	No. 3 i No. 3 j No. 3 k No. 3 l
Case No. 31 (Death of brother)	Nativity No. 2 (Male)	PNSR (Non-pr.) PNSR (Pr.) ANSR (Non-pr.) ANSR (Pr.)	No. 2 m No. 2 n No. 2 o No. 2 p

Illness

Several important astrological works have been dedicated solely to the study of medical astrology and a whole volume could be written on the relationship between the various types of configurations present in Solar Revolutions at the time of illness and the various diseases to which they correspond.

A number of basic factors, however, appear as common denominators in nearly all Solar Revolutions covering a period of serious illness:

(1) The presence of an afflicted benefic on an angle. This is a perfect astrological symbol for 'dis-ease'! A clue to the type of disease will often be given by the nature of the afflicting planet, Mars suggesting feverish and inflammatory conditions; Saturn, chill, obstruction or secretion; Uranus, nervous or spasmodic complaints or danger of paralysis; Neptune, wasting away or complaints caused by the abnormal functioning of some bodily organ; Pluto, the flaring up of some deep-seated trouble often due to the accumulation of poisons in the body over a long period.

(2) Saturn will usually be found afflicting an angle. The action of Saturn in affliction is to hamper and restrict the smooth functioning of the various parts of the physical body. Saturn demands perfection and its afflictions denote times of testing. When the physical body is tested and found wanting, illness results. This is nature's way of attempting to eliminate imperfections. The prominence of Saturn can also indicate special dieting or fasting in order to combat the disease.

(3) The Sun is likely to be in aspect to Saturn. Such a contact indicates the probability that the vital forces are below par so that the body is less equipped to ward off disease. It also symbolizes a time of testing with particular reference to the native's individual approach to life. The causes of illness are rarely purely physical. Rather are they to be found in some mental, moral or emotional maladjustment which subtly affects the working of the physical functions, so closely are they interconnected with the rest of man's being. If such a maladjustment is not corrected, sooner or later a crisis must result and this crisis will frequently be reflected in the state of the native's physical health.

(4) Frequently Uranus, Neptune or Pluto will also afflict the Sun. Any of the three outer planets, combined with Saturn and the Sun, often indicate a rather severe illness. Such aspects also suggest a struggle to make adjustments to the inner life.

(5) The Moon will very often be in aspect to Saturn. Such an aspect will represent the sluggish functioning of the various organs of the body and may indicate a less buoyant frame of mind than usual, thus decreasing resistance to disease.

(6) Mars will frequently be afflicted, often by Jupiter or Neptune. Afflictions from Jupiter to Mars suggest exhaustion through reckless dissipation of energy and should be regarded as a warning to the native to take things as easily as possible. Mars–Neptune afflictions indicate the possibility of an insidious sapping of the bodily energies as a result of wrong habits or emotional attitudes.

(7) Jupiter, the major benefic, will very often be afflicted.

(8) A contact between Mercury and Neptune is by no means uncommon. This may denote the possibility of mental worry consequent upon illness or it may indicate that a disturbed mental condition has paved the way for the onset of disease.

(9) Afflictions in the nativity involving Pluto will nearly always be stimulated. A serious illness is nearly always brought about as a natural means of ridding the body of accumulated poisons or of remedying the damage caused by the continual repetition of wrong habits. The eliminative action of Pluto works to produce a healing crisis, whereby long-standing toxic conditions may be forced to manifest themselves openly in a burst of hectic activity rather than being left to work secretly to clog and poison the system.

(10) There will nearly always be an emphasis on the Virgo–Pisces sign polarity, through the connection of these signs with health and disease and there are likely to be afflictions to the cusps of the sixth and twelfth houses.

In addition to the above general indications, there will be groups of planets in mutual affliction according to the particular organ or organs affected by the illness. Briefly, the main parts of the body ruled by the planets are these:

Sun	Heart, spleen, eyes, back.
Moon	Stomach, digestive organs, eyes, bodily fluids.
Mercury	Nerves, lungs, intestines, hands, arms.
Venus	Throat, tonsils, kidneys, internal reproductive system.
Mars	Head, blood, muscular system, excretory organs.
Jupiter	Liver, arterial system, thighs, hips and feet.
Saturn	Joints and bony structure of the body, gall bladder.
Uranus	Higher nervous system and body electricity.
Neptune	Psychic energies
Pluto	Sexual organs and eliminative system.

The signs containing afflicted planets will also provide clues as to the nature of the ailment. The parts of the body ruled by opposite signs often function in such close harmony that an afflicted planet in one sign may well indicate some disturbed condition in the part of the body ruled by the opposite sign. For all practical purposes, therefore, it is a useful plan to group the signs together into their six polarities when considering their anatomical relationships, which are as follows:

Aries–Libra	Head, kidneys, lumbar region.
Taurus–Scorpio	Neck, throat, tonsils, ears, nose, bladder, excretory and reproductive organs.
Gemini–Sagittarius	Lungs, nervous system, hips, thighs, arms, legs.
Cancer–Capricorn	Stomach, pancreas, breasts, womb, elbows, knees, joints, bony framework of the body.
Leo–Aquarius	Heart, dorsal region of the spine, circulation of the blood, forearm, lower leg.
Virgo–Pisces	Abdomen, intestines, spleen, duodenum, hands, feet.

A more detailed list of planetary and sign correspondences will be found in *The Technique of Prediction*.

Examples of typical configurations in Solar Revolutions covering the year in which the native contracted a serious illness will be found in the horoscopes referred to below. The necessary data for their calculation are given in Appendix 4.

Case No. 32	Nativity No. 19	PNSR (Non-pr.)	No. 19 a
(Suspected	(Female)	PNSR (Pr.)	No. 19 b
Polio-		ANSR (Non-pr.)	No. 19 c
myelitis)		ANSR (Pr.)	No. 19 d
Case No. 33	Nativity No. 7	PNSR (Non-pr.)	No. 7 e
(Scarlet	(Female)	PNSR (Pr.)	No. 7 f
Fever)		ANSR (Non-pr.)	No. 7 g
		ANSR (Pr.)	No. 7 h
Case No. 34	Nativity No. 18	PNSR (Non-pr.)	No. 18 e
(Operation:	(Male)	PNSR (Pr.)	No. 18 f
Pleurisy)		ANSR (Non-pr.)	No. 18 g
		ANSR (Pr.)	No. 18 h
Case No. 35	Nativity No. 1	PNSR (Non-pr.)	No. 1 q
(Pneu-	(Male)	PNSR (Pr.)	No. 1 r
monia)		ANSR (Non-pr.)	No. 1 s
		ANSR (Pr.)	No. 1 t

Accidents

The following factors are likely to be present in the Solar Revolutions for the year in which an accident is sustained by the native. Trivial accidents, which cause only passing inconvenience and little physical pain will naturally not be signalled prominently in the Solar Return but accidents of a more serious nature, which cause the native to interrupt or change his normal routine, will be indicated by certain definite patterns, mainly malefic, among the planets on the revolutional day:

(1) A strong radical configuration indicating the possibility of accident will be stimulated.

(2) Mars and Saturn will combine to afflict an angle. These signify the inevitable cuts, bruises and abrasions likely to be sustained in an accident.

(3) The Moon will be combined with Mars and Uranus, usually in mutual affliction. Such aspects are indicative of the shock to the sympathetic nervous system usually resulting from sudden accident. Such aspects tend to coincide with physically painful experiences.

(4) There will usually be mutual afflictions between Mars, Saturn, Uranus and Pluto. Very often all four planets will be combined together in one configuration, with a preponderance of adverse aspects.

(5) There will usually be at least one benefic configuration. As the major indications are predominantly adverse, the protective and preservative influence of such a configuration will be necessary to prevent total disaster. Such an aspect will also denote the medical care and attention bestowed upon the native to assist his recovery.

(6) An afflicted Mercury will often be angular. This probably represents an element of negligence or bad judgement which is usually a factor in accident cases, whether the fault was that of the victim or not. There is also the possibility that some mental 'preconditioning' will render the native accident-prone. Many accidents occur during the course of travel and Mercury will almost always be angular in such cases.

(7) Neptune may be angular or configured with Mercury. Neptune is the planet which can indicate muddle and confusion and is often combined in afflictions when an

accident results from misunderstandings or imperfect perceptions.

(8) A major affliction to Jupiter is likely. Not only does this detract from the power of Jupiter to support and protect the native but it indicates that he may suffer through lack of judgement or through over-confidence that may be prejudicial to his safety.

(9) The Sun is usually afflicted.

(10) The natal Mars, Saturn and Uranus are almost invariably stimulated.

(11) The Moon, Mercury and Uranus are nearly always in mutual configuration. These aspects relate to the shocks likely to be sustained by the general nervous system.

(12) There is frequently a contact between Uranus and Neptune. Such aspects indicate the possibility of some kind of shock to the finer bodies. (Neptune is related to the super-sensory system.) Alternatively the contact may represent some subtle tension in the super-sensory system which eventually has to be worked out on the physical level.

(13) Venus and Neptune are very often linked, usually by adverse aspect. Such aspects symbolize the sympathy and help that the victim of an accident will usually receive.

Examples of typical configurations in Solar Revolutions covering the year in which an accident took place will be found in the horoscopes referred to below. The necessary data for their calculation are given in Appendix 4.

Case No. 36	Nativity No. 20	PNSR (Non-pr.)	No. 20 a
	(Male)	PNSR (Pr.)	No. 20 b
		ANSR (Non-pr.)	No. 20 c
		ANSR (Pr.)	No. 20 d
Case No. 37	Nativity No. 4	PNSR (Non-pr.)	No. 4 e
	(Female)	PNSR (Pr.)	No. 4 f
		ANSR (Non-pr.)	No. 4 g
		ANSR (Pr.)	No. 4 h
Case No. 38	Nativity No. 2	PNSR (Non-pr.)	No. 2 q
	(Male)	PNSR (Pr.)	No. 2 r
		ANSR (Non-pr.)	No. 2 s
		ANSR (Pr.)	No. 2 t

Case No. 39 Nativity No. 16 PNSR (Non-pr.)   No. 16 e
      (Female)   PNSR (Pr.)   No. 16 f
                  ANSR (Non-pr.)   No. 16 g
                  ANSR (Pr.)   No. 16 h

Marriage of Son or Daughter

Such an event will naturally not take place before the native is approaching middle age. Although normal parents desire, above all things, a happy marriage for their offspring, they are not always able to contemplate an event of this nature with unmixed feelings, especially as an element of separation is almost always involved. Sometimes the parents are unable to approve whole-heartedly of their son's or daughter's choice. In such cases a greater or lesser degree of disharmony will be reflected in the revolutional horoscope. However, this type of event is essentially a joyous one, as well as one which opens up new possibilities of development for the family. For these reasons the benefic planets, Venus and Jupiter and the outer planets Uranus, Neptune and Pluto are especially active at this time. The principal factors present in the Solar Revolution covering the year in which the marriage of a son or daughter takes place are as follows:

(1) Jupiter or Venus will often be angular or Venus will be in good aspect to an angular Jupiter or Neptune.

(2) Uranus, Neptune and Pluto will frequently be angular. Uranus signifies the introduction of new blood into the family; Neptune, the fulfilment of hopes and wishes (and also, perhaps, an element of renunciation); Pluto, the official beginning of a new chapter of family history and the promise of a future generation.

(3) The Sun is often angular and well supported by Neptune, or Neptune may be the angular body. These aspects not only show the joyous nature of the event but also the enhanced prestige enjoyed by the parents at such a time.

(4) The Sun is frequently well aspected by Mars and Jupiter or by Mars and Uranus, and by Pluto. One strong adverse aspect to the Sun is usually present also, presumably to signify the emotional stress occasioned by the departure of a son or daughter from the parental home. These aspects may relate also to extra expenditure involved as a result of the wedding.

(5) When a daughter marries, Mars–Uranus contacts will almost invariably be present. In the case of a son marrying, there will be Venus–Uranus aspects instead. Pluto, as well as Uranus will sometimes enter into these configurations. These are the most striking single indications present at this time, signifying in the first case the entry of a new masculine element into the family and in the second, the advent of a new feminine influence.

(6) The marriage of a daughter is usually accompanied by a Venus–Jupiter contact and often by an affliction of Saturn to Venus as an indication that some measure of separation must be expected. The marriage of a son is often accompanied by similar aspects to Mars.

(7) The Moon will frequently be found very close to an angle and very often joined by aspect with Venus, Mars, Jupiter and Uranus. The Venus, Mars, Jupiter configuration is nearly always present, signifying the happy union of the two sexes. The Moon is the luminary connected with domestic affairs and is also related to publicity and to people in the mass. All these sides of the lunar influence are likely to manifest at this time.

(8) There is nearly always a strong stimulus to the natal Jupiter, Part of Fortune and Part of Marriage.

(9) There is very often a special emphasis on Libra, the sign of marriage and Leo, the sign of offspring.

(10) The cusp of the fifth house, the house of children, is likely to be strongly aspected, or planets in the fifth or eleventh houses may be well supported. A Saturnian affliction to the fifth cusp is sometimes present to mark the parting from a son or daughter.

(11) Mercury is frequently in aspect with and often afflicted by Mars and Saturn, sometimes by both. These aspects are probably indicative of the careful preparation and detailed planning beforehand as well as the attendant worries that often accompany the actual function and the problems of adjustment that follow in its wake.

Examples of typical configurations in Solar Revolutions covering the year in which the marriage of a son or daughter took place will be found in the horoscopes referred to below. The necessary data for their calculation are given in Appendix 4.

Case No. 40	Nativity No. 21	PNSR (Non-pr.)	No. 21 a
(Marriage	(Male)	PNSR (Pr.)	No. 21 b
of Son)		ANSR (Non-pr.)	No. 21 c
		ANSR (Pr.)	No. 21 d
Case No. 41	Nativity No. 22	PNSR (Non-pr.)	No. 22 a
(Marriage	(Male)	PNSR (Pr.)	No. 22 b
of		ANSR (Non-pr.)	No. 22 c
Daughter)		ANSR (Pr.)	No. 22 d
Case No. 42	Nativity No. 23	PNSR (Non-pr.)	No. 23 a
(Marriage	(Female)	PNSR (Pr.)	No. 23 b
of Son)		ANSR (Non-pr.)	No. 23 c
		ANSR (Pr.)	No. 23 d
Case No. 43	Nativity No. 24	PNSR (Non-pr.)	No. 24 a
(Marriage	(Female)	PNSR (Pr.)	No. 24 b
of		ANSR (Non-pr.)	No. 24 c
Daughter)		ANSR (Pr.)	No. 24 d

Birth of Grandchildren

The indications for this event do not appear to differ appreciably
from those present in the revolution at the time of parenthood.
In such circumstances, therefore, the age of the native will
probably be a major clue. Examples of typical configurations in
the Solar Revolutions covering the year in which the birth of a
grandchild took place will be found in the horoscopes referred to
below. The necessary data for their calculation are given in
Appendix 4.

Case No. 44	Nativity No. 21	PNSR (Non-pr.)	No. 21 e
(Birth of	(Male)	PNSR (Pr.)	No. 21 f
Grandson)		ANSR (Non-pr.)	No. 21 g
		ANSR (Pr.)	No. 21 h
Case No. 45	Nativity No. 22	PNSR (Non-pr.)	No. 22 e
(Birth of	(Male)	PNSR (Pr.)	No. 22 f
Grand-		ANSR (Non-pr.)	No. 22 g
daughter)		ANSR (Pr.)	No. 22 h
Case No. 46	Nativity No. 25	PNSR (Non-pr.)	No. 25 a
(Birth of	(Female)	PNSR (Pr.)	No. 25 b
Grandson)		ANSR (Non-pr.)	No. 25 c
		ANSR (Pr.)	No. 25 d

Case No. 47	Nativity No. 24	PNSR (Non-pr.)	No. 24 e
(Birth of	(Female)	PNSR (Pr.)	No. 24 f
Grand-		ANSR (Non-pr.)	No. 24 g
daughter)		ANSR (Pr.)	No. 24 h

Divorce

When considering the question of divorce, always assuming that such a possibility is indicated in the nativity, one should bear in mind that the actual events which lead the native to initiate or to become involved in divorce proceedings may considerably ante-date the legal action and the final making absolute of the decree. Therefore the Solar Revolution containing the strongest evidence of the rupture of a marriage partnership may not be the one nearest to the date on which the divorce is finally confirmed.

The principal factors in a Solar Revolution covering the year in which a divorce takes place are as follows:

(1) Strong disruptive natal complexes of planets will be emphasized and in particular the natal Uranus is almost invariably stimulated. An afflicted Uranus in the revolution is often angular or else is itself afflicting another angular planet. Uranus has been called the planet of divorce. Strongly emphasized and afflicted, it shows an inability to work in harmony with others and a strong desire to break free of encumbering bonds, especially when they are seen as an obstacle to new contacts and experiences.

(2) Frequently an afflicted luminary or a malefic afflicting a luminary will be placed on an angle. In addition, a benefic will also be placed on an angle. Such a combination of harmonious and disruptive influences suggests the re-storation of a comparative measure of harmony to the life through the termination of a partnership which has failed.

(3) Pluto or Neptune will often be found on an angle. Pluto is the indicator of new beginnings and is a purgative influence, eliminating and throwing off those elements in the life which would otherwise remain as a source of stagnation and decay. Neptune, paradoxically, represents that which dissolves bonds yet at the same time involves in new entanglements. The native may demand an imposs-ibly high standard of behaviour from his partner when

Neptune is active. If Neptune is heavily afflicted, dis-illusion and diminished prestige may be the result.

(4) There will often be a malefic squaring the Midheaven. This probably indicates the loss of prestige which parties to a divorce may suffer, and also troubles in the domestic sphere.

(5) There will frequently be an affliction involving the natal Ascendant (and therefore the seventh cusp).

(6) Venus will often (but not invariably) be found in adverse aspect to Mars. This is a contact indicative of emotional distress, difficult relationships with the opposite sex and an inability to maintain harmony in dealing with others.

(7) Mercury–Mars and Moon–Pluto afflictions will fre-quently occur, especially the squares. The former contact shows a desire for decisive action, the latter an inflexible emotional attitude (as well as the break-up of domestic conditions). The two sets of contacts combine to produce an uncompromising state of mind that is hardly likely to make sufficient allowance for human frailty!

The above indications will be found to occur irrespective of the sex of the native. Certain additional factors may be anticipated in the Solar Revolution of the husband:

(8) The Sun will nearly always be afflicted, especially by Saturn, Mars and Uranus. These aspects are probably connected with such loss of prestige as is usually suffered by parties to a divorce. They can also refer to the native's apparent inability to carry out the role of husband.

(9) The Moon in the first or seventh house is often opposed by a malefic. This suggests difficulties in relationships with women, especially where legal partnership is involved.

(10) Venus will often be afflicted by Uranus and frequently by Mars or Saturn. These contacts are indicative of emotional distress and sometimes of new attractions that may have given rise to the occasion for divorce.

The following additional factors are likely to be present in the Solar Revolution of the wife:

(11) The Sun will often be found in adverse aspect to Jupiter and in the first or seventh houses, opposed by a malefic.

This suggests difficulties in relationships with the marriage partner. The Sun–Jupiter affliction may signify the various difficulties connected with the bringing of legal action and the likelihood of adverse publicity as a result.

(12) Mars will often be afflicted by Pluto, Uranus or Saturn. These contacts are unhelpful for contacts with the opposite sex and increase the probability of quarrels and separation. They may also indicate the appearance of a new man in the life whose presence breaks up the marriage.

In the case of both sexes it will often be found that

(13) The Moon receives a number of afflictions from the malefics. The main significance of these aspects probably derives from the fact that the Moon is the luminary relating to the domestic life of the native. It also relates to the feelings and general popularity of the party concerned.

At the time of marriage, strong harmonious configurations nearly always predominate. When divorce is threatened, a majority of inharmonious aspects will be present.

Should the husband and wife separate but take no steps to have the partnership legally dissolved, many of the above factors will still be present but there is also likely to be an emphasis on Saturnian contacts to natal planets in Libra or in the seventh house, and adverse aspects of Saturn to the Moon. When a separation takes place temporarily, owing to the pressure of external circumstances, then in the case of a man Venus is usually afflicted by Uranus but well aspected by Saturn or Jupiter. In the case of a woman, Mars is likely to receive the same combination of good and bad aspects.

Examples of typical configurations in Solar Revolutions covering the year in which divorce took place will be found in the horoscopes referred to below. The necessary data for their calculation are given in Appendix 4.

Case No. 48 Nativity No. 10 PNSR (Non-pr.)   No. 10 e
                (Male)   PNSR (Pr.)   No. 10 f
                            ANSR (Non-pr.)   No. 10 g
                            ANSR (Pr.)   No. 10 h

Case No. 49	Nativity No. 26 (Female)	PNSR (Non-pr.) PNSR (Pr.) ANSR (Non-pr.) ANSR (Pr.)	No. 26 a No. 26 b No. 26 c No. 26 d
Case No. 50	Nativity No. 17 (Male)	PNSR (Non-pr.) PNSR (Pr.) ANSR (Non-pr.) ANSR (Pr.)	No. 17 e No. 17 f No. 17 g No. 17 h
Case No. 51	Nativity No. 16 (Female)	PNSR (Non-pr.) PNSR (Pr.) ANSR (Non-pr.) ANSR (Pr.)	No. 16 i No. 16 j No. 16 k No. 16 l

Death

Heavy afflictions predominate at this time, with few relieving good aspects, although Jupiter is sometimes angular as a reminder that death may come as a happy release when the physical body is no longer able to function without causing its owner grave distress. The following factors are worthy of special mention:

(1) The Sun will often be angular and afflicted by several malefics.
(2) The Moon is likely to be afflicted by one or two malefics.
(3) The ruler of the natal Ascendant is likely to be similarly afflicted.
(4) Many of the above contacts are likely to be a repetition of those that occur in the natal horoscope. The exact nature of the natal aspect need not be repeated. It is sufficient for the same planets to be connected by any type of aspect.
(5) The preponderance of inharmonious aspects involving the malefics will generally mean that most of the malefics are combined in affliction among themselves. In particular, Saturn–Pluto and Mars–Pluto afflictions are likely to be present and will sometimes fall on the angles of the nativity.
(6) The eighth cusp will usually be afflicted by a malefic.
(7) There will frequently be afflictions involving the sign of death, Scorpio and the opposite sign Taurus.

Examples of typical configurations in Solar Revolutions covering the year of the native's death will be found in the horoscopes referred to below. The necessary data for their calculation are given in Appendix 4.

Case No. 52	Nativity No. 27 (Male)	PNSR (Non-pr.)	No. 27 a
		PNSR (Pr.)	No. 27 b
		ANSR (Non-pr.)	No. 27 c
		ANSR (Pr.)	No. 27 d
Case No. 53	Nativity No. 28 (Male)	PNSR (Non-pr.)	No. 28 a
		PNSR (Pr.)	No. 28 b
		ANSR (Non-pr.)	No. 28 c
		ANSR (Pr.)	No. 28 d
Case No. 54	Nativity No. 29 (Female)	PNSR (Non-pr.)	No. 29 a
		PNSR (Pr.)	No. 29 b
		ANSR (Non-pr.)	No. 29 c
		ANSR (Pr.)	No. 29 d
Case No. 55	Nativity No. 30 (Female)	PNSR (Non-pr.)	No. 30 a
		PNSR (Pr.)	No. 30 b
		ANSR (Non-pr.)	No. 30 c
		ANSR (Pr.)	No. 30 d

6.
THE SOLAR REVOLUTION —
SOME FURTHER CONSIDERATIONS

So far we have only considered the Solar Revolution from the point of view of forecasting major events. Not all years, however, are marked by important milestones in life's journey, nor are one or two events, however vital a part they may play in the native's destiny, the only happenings of the year. Events of minor importance are always taking place and although their effects may soon be forgotten, it should be possible to account for their occurrence astrologically in terms of the Composite Solar Revolution and its various progressions.

We have seen how major events are foreshadowed by the arrival of important configurations in the revolution itself at conjunctions or oppositions of the progressed Midheaven and Ascendant of the revolutional figure at the same time as configurations of a similar nature in the nativity are also strongly stimulated. Minor events will be shown by the arrival of the daily progressed Midheaven and Ascendant of the revolutional figure at conjunctions and oppositions of planets in the revolutional figure itself and of planets on the directional day itself, at times when there is no great emphasis on any monthly and weekly directions based on the revolution or on any configurations in the nativity that are already given special prominence as a result of falling on any of the revolutional angles.

As in all other cases of forecasting the probable effects of directions, it must be remembered that nothing can come to pass that is not foreshadowed in the nativity. It would also be well to bear in mind that nothing is likely to happen during the year that is not indicated in the Composite Solar Revolution.

As a general indication of the type of event to be expected when various configurations are stimulated by the progressed angles of the revolutional figures, and by transits to revolutional planets, it is a good plan to refer to the example readings given for the same planets in combination when they occur in secondary directions and then make appropriate adjustments to the scale of the events and the scope of their operation. Where, for instance, a Sun–Venus aspect might be indicative of marriage if it occurred at a suitable time by secondary direction, a contact between the two bodies falling upon a progressed angle of the revolution might do no more than signal transitory though happy contacts with the female sex during the day, or a visit to the theatre, or the arrival of some new adornment for the home. If, at the same time, either body were much afflicted, none of these effects would be likely and some emotional distress, resulting from an inability to maintain harmony in a relationship, or a loss of prestige in some direction, would probably be experienced.

To take account of all the possible planetary combinations that could occur in the daily progressions of the Solar Revolution would need a considerable amount of space and even then it would hardly be possible to take into account the variations arising from the condition of each planet in the nativity. For all general purposes it is probably better to give a brief outline of the general effects to be expected when the luminaries and planets fall on the progressed angles of the revolutional figures, taking each singly and leaving the reader to make his own adjustments in the light of the special conditions of the particular case he is considering and bearing in mind the benefic or malefic nature of any aspects to that body at the same time.

The general nature of the day-to-day events which occur when the luminaries and planets fall on the angles of the revolutional figures may be gauged from the following suggestions:

Sun
An accent on matters connected with personal prestige and on dealings with those in authority. Recognition for work done, opportunities for consolidation, stabilization and expansion. An emphasis on personal pride and independence of spirit. Events involving the father.

Moon
An accent on the domestic side of life and on contacts with the female sex. Personal sensitivity likely to be stimulated. Problems requiring the exercise of sympathetic understanding. Contacts with the public and an emphasis on matters relating to personal

popularity. Events involving the mother. Sometimes a journey or a change of environment.

Mercury

An accent on travel and movement and on matters requiring an attention to detail. All types of mental activity are likely to be stimulated, with opportunities for self-expression verbally or in writing. Contacts with relatives, neighbours or the very young. Situations calling for the exercise of adaptability or opportunism. An emphasis on restlessness and nervous energy.

Venus

An accent upon pleasurable activities, romantic interests and artistic pursuits. Situations involving the creation of a harmonious atmosphere. Contacts with the female sex. House decoration. An emphasis on the emotional life. Meetings with friends. Social occasions. Financial gains.

Mars

An accent on drive and initiative. Activities involving hard work and the expenditure of energy, especially in clearing the ground for new undertakings. Situations calling for an appreciation of basic essentials. Contacts with young men and with the male sex in general. Opportunities for the vigorous prosecution of special interests. An emphasis on the passional side of life and on personal courage. Events which encourage the competitive instinct.

Jupiter

An accent on powers of judgement and capacity for growth and expansion. Pleasant social activities. Financial gain. Situations calling for the exercise of confident optimism and benevolence of outlook. Contacts with influential people.

Saturn

An accent on self-reliance and personal integrity. Situations calling for the exercise of practical commonsense and persevering effort. Opportunities for taking responsibility, demonstrating organizing ability and powers of self-discipline. Activities requiring application and concentration. Contacts with older people or those of a serious disposition. Events involving the father. Matters requiring patient handling. A tendency for enterprises to hang fire.

Uranus

An accent on the unexpected, the unconventional and the unusual. Situations calling for the exercise of originality, ingenuity and will-power and sometimes for drastic and decisive personal action. Contacts with unusual people. Meetings with friends of long ago. Opportunities for introducing short-cuts and labour-saving methods. The start of new friendships, new interests. Abrupt changes of course. Experiences involving electrical apparatus. Difficulties in personal relationships. Possibility of sudden flashes of inspiration, sudden flashes of intuitive understanding or clarification of ideas through applied logic.

Neptune

An accent upon the need for emotional satisfaction, through personal contacts or through artistic activities. Situations which arouse the sympathies and charitable instincts and which test the powers of adaptability to other people. Travel and movement, especially near water or by air. Opportunities for quiet reflection or gaining inspiration from scenes of natural beauty or else the fulfilment of some private dream. Sometimes muddled or obscure situations demanding the exercise of clear-sighted perceptivity. Unusually vivid dreams.

Pluto

Stimulation of deep-seated psychological urges in such a way as to produce a crisis, bringing opportunities for resolving problems and clearing up loose ends. Plans mature or new ventures begin. Action is sometimes compelled by the subtle pressure of outside circumstances. Chance meetings which may have far-reaching effects. A change of direction arising from a deeper understanding of already held ideas.

There appears to be some connection between the prominent features of the Solar Revolution and the contacts made during the year. It will often happen that the degrees occupied by the revolutional angles or those tenanted by prominently emphasized planets will be ascending, culminating or occupied by the Sun in the nativities of those with whom important new friendships or associations are formed during the year.

7.

SOME SPECIAL CASES CONSIDERED IN DETAIL

We shall now present some special cases in greater detail so that the student can more easily accustom himself to handling the Composite Solar Revolution and gain a better idea of the various factors to be considered when formulating an interpretation. The examples have been chosen for their special interest and because, in each case, the main event of the year was either the culmination of a series of other activities or events or else brought about by a considerable modification in the native's circumstances and environment.

The first solo crossing of the Atlantic by aeroplane was made by Colonel Charles Lindbergh on 20 May 1927. Positions of the natal and revolutional planets and angles are set out below in tabular form (precessional positions in brackets). The necessary data for the setting up of these and subsequent horoscopes referred to in this chapter are to be found in Appendix 4.

Case No. 56	MC	Asc.	☉	☽	☿	♀	♂	♃	♄	♅	♆	♇
Nativity	20° ♍	3° ♐	14° ♒	25° ♐	2° ♓	1°♈ R	26° ♒	29° ♑	21° ♑	20° ♐	29°♓ R	16° ♓
Postnatal Solar Revolution	13° ♎ (14° ♒)	23° ♐ (7° ♓)	(15° ♒)	13° ♓ (18° ♓)	19° ♒	2° ♓	21° ♈	4° ♓	6° ♐	27° ♓	26°♌ R	14°♋ R
Antenatal Solar Revolution	16° ♌ (16° ♈)	9° ♏ (29° ♋)	(14° ♒)	21° ♎ (16° ♎)	29°♑ R	21° ♑	13° ♐	25° ♐	7° ♓	23°♌ R	2° ♈	22° ♈

We shall first of all expect to find some indication of a long journey. The principal factors involved will thus be Mercury and Neptune (especially as air travel is involved) and a special emphasis on the signs Gemini and Sagittarius and on the third and ninth houses. The following configurations provide suitable indications of the event:

MC a.n. ☍☿ p.n. ♂♅ a.n. ♂♆ p.n.
(MC p.n. ♂☿ p.n. ☍♅ a.n. ☍♆ p.n.)
(Asc. a.n. ☍☿ p.n. ☍♃ r. △♅ p.n. in ✕)
Asc. a.n. ☍♆ a.n. △☿ r.
Asc. p.n. ♂☽, ♅ r. ♂♃ a.n. in ♐
(Asc. p.n. in ✕ ♂♂ a.n. ☍♄ p.n. in ♐)
(MC p.n. ♂☉ r. ♂Cusp 3 r.)
MC a.n. ☍☉ r. ☍Cusp 3 r.
(Cusp 3 p.n. ☍♀ a.n. ✳♂ p.n. ☍♄ r. ✳♇ a.n.)
(Cusp 3 a.n. ☍☽ p.n. □♂ a.n.)

In order to call attention to the presence of planets within about 12° of the angles, the usual wide orbs have been allowed in assessing the conjunctions and oppositions to the Meridians and Horizons of the composite revolution. Neptune is angular in three out of the four revolutional figures and so is Mercury. The radical Mercury is well supported:

☿ r. ♂♀ r. ♂♀ p.n. ♂♃ p.n. ♂♄ a.n. △♆ a.n.

Mercury is in the sign Pisces, a sign frequently emphasized at the time of long journeys, due no doubt to the association of the sign with the idea of the dissolution of boundaries and the widening of horizons. The benefic aspects to the natal Mercury promise a happy and rewarding outcome from travel, while the conjunction with Saturn is a reminder of the hazards and loneliness involved. No event can come to pass that is not promised in the nativity, thus we should expect to find stimulated at this time all those factors in the natal horoscope that indicate fame through long journeys. The radical Sun on the cusp of the third house in trine to Pluto in Gemini and the conjunction of the Moon and Uranus in Sagittarius, as well as Mercury in Pisces square to the radical Ascendant, all indicate a predisposition to travel and a pioneering attitude towards travel that should serve to bring the native into relative prominence. These natal factors are shown to be well emphasized and supported in the lists of 'travel' aspects set out above.

Next we should consider the fact that the native achieved world-wide recognition as a result of his feat. Popularity and fame are largely connected with the prominence of well supported luminaries. In the Composite Solar Revolution the following factors appear to be indicative of the spontaneous acclamation of the success of Colonel Lindbergh's courageous enterprise:

(MC a.n. ☍☽ a.n.⚹☉ r. △♂ a.n⚹ ♇ r.)
Asc. p.n. ☌☽, ♅ r, ☌♃ a.n. △♅ a.n. △♆ p.n.

MC p.n. ☍☽ a.n. △☉ r.⚹♂ a.n. △♇ r.
MC a.n. ☍☉ r.⚹☽ a.n. △♂ a.n.⚹ ♇ r.
(MC p.n. ☌☉ r. △☽ a.n.⚹♂ a.n. △♇ r.)

As a result of the flight there was a considerable improvement in
Lindbergh's financial position, a condition usually denoted by
good aspects between the major planets and Jupiter and by an
appropriate emphasis on planets in Taurus and Scorpio and in the
second and eighth houses. In the Composite Solar Revolution the
following factors may be singled out for special notice:

Asc. p.n. ☌♃ a.n. ☌♅ r. □♅ p.n. △♅ a.n. △♆ p.n.
(Asc. a.n. ☌♃ r. △♅ p.n.)
♃ p.n. ☌♄ a.n.⚹♆ a.n.
♀ a.n. ☌♄ r. △♂ p.n. △♇ a.n. in ♇
Cusp 2 p.n. 28°♉ ☌♃ r.
(Cusp 2 p.n. ☌♋ ☌♆ r. △♀ r.)
(Cusp 2 a.n. 20°♌ ☍☿ ☌♅ a.n. △♅ r.)

The crossing of the Atlantic by air was regarded by many as being
a foolhardly enterprise, especially in such a fragile aircraft as *The
Spirit of St Louis* undoubtedly was, by any standards. The element
of personal risk, the determination to carry out the project in the
face of considerable obstacles, and the necessary foresight and
imagination to plan and go through with such an operation
successfully, together with the possession of the necessary technical knowledge, should all be indicated in the Composite Solar
Revolution for the year. The natal Moon–Uranus conjunction in
Sagittarius suggests considerable foresight and a strong dis-
inclination to be limited by orthodox opinions and concepts. The
conjunction is given force and direction by the sextile from Mars
in the radical third house, the house of travel, while the necessary
imaginative flair is added by the opposition from Neptune in
Gemini, the sign of journeys. The pioneering role that Lindbergh
was to play depended largely upon his response to the stimulus
of this planetary configuration, which promised great things. The
Composite Solar Revolution for 1927 indicated a very special

opportunity for enlarging upon and expanding his response to this configuration through the following combination of aspects:

Asc. p.n. ☌☽, ♅ r. ☌♃ a.n. □♅ p.n. △♅ a.n. △♆ p.n.

Moreover, contacts present in the nativity were repeated:

♂ p.n. □♆ p.n. (stimulated by ♇ a.n. ☌♂ p.n.)
☽ a.n. ✶♅ a.n. ✶♆ p.n.

The radical Saturn–Jupiter conjunction in Capricorn shows a good deal of down-to-earth common sense, which would act to prevent any excess of reckless foolhardiness, much of which would already have been worked off in his earlier barn-storming days. This conjunction is suitably stimulated in the following manner:

(Asc. a.n. ☍☿ a.n. ☍♃ r.)
♀ a.n. △♂ p.n. ☌♄ r. △♇ a.n.

Aspects suggesting the hazardous nature of the flight and the determination needed to carry it through will be those where the malefics are mutually configured, while Saturnian contacts with the Moon and the benefics will indicate the loneliness and boredom of the actual journey. In this connection the following aspects may be noted:

♂ p.n. △♄ r. □♅ a.n. □♆ p.n. ☌♇ a.n. □☿ p.n.
♂ r. ☍♅ a.n. ☍♆ p.n. □♂ p.n., ♇ a.n.
(Asc. p.n. ☍♂ a.n. ☍♄ p.n.)
☽ p.n. □♄ p.n. ☌♄ a.n.
♀ p.n. □♄ p.n. ☌♄ a.n.
☽ a.n. □♀ a.n. □♄ r.

Because of the preponderance of the favourable aspects and the prominence of the benefics, the afflictions noted above merely denoted obstacles that were overcome and not insuperable difficulties and overwhelming disasters. The inflexible determination to succeed and the ultimate triumph are probably best indicated by the angular Sun (in both the precessional and the non-precessional figures) which is in trine to the radical Pluto and is further stimulated by the close sextile of the antenatal Mars.
From the above survey it will be appreciated that the Composite

Solar Revolution reflects faithfully the varied circumstances and the many facets of experience that are likely to be encountered during the year. In the foregoing example we have confined ourselves to the consideration of one main event but it should be remembered that the whole year must largely have been dominated by that one event; firstly in the arduous preparation and campaigning for support and then in coping with the new possibilities opened up as the result of achieving a world-wide reputation overnight.

As a comparison of the way in which the same nativity can furnish the materials of triumph or tragedy, let us now turn the clock on another five years to 1932, when on 1 March there came the news of a tragic occurrence that shocked a nation, the kidnapping of the Lindbergh baby, subsequently found to be murdered. The positions of the planets and angles in the Composite Solar Revolution for the year and in the nativity are set out below (precessional positions in brackets):

Case No. 57	MC	Asc.	☉	☽	☿	♀	♂	♃	♄	♅	♆	♇
Nativity (No. 31)	20° ♍	3° ♐	14° ♒	25° ♐	2° ♓	1°R ♓	26° ♒	29° ♑	21° ♑	20° ♐	29°R ♓	16° ♓
Postnatal Solar (e) Revn (f)	10° ♑ (12° ♓)	20° ♈ (14° ♍)	(15° ♒)	20° ♑ (26° ♑)	29° ♑	20° ♓	13° ♒	18°R ♌	27° ♑	16° ♈	7°R ♍	20°R ♋
Antenatal Solar (g) Revn (h)	22° ♓ (21° ♑)	22° ♍ (8° ♑)	(14° ♒)	5° ♐ (30° ♏)	21° ♑	4° ♑	9° ♓	22°R ♋	16° ♑	28°R ♈	21° ♍	17° ♋

We shall expect to find a strong emphasis upon any radical afflictions together with an accentuation of the planet Pluto in combination with the other malefics, and afflictions involving the Taurus–Scorpio and Leo–Aquarius sign polarities, together with a corresponding accent on the cusps of the fifth and eighth houses. The following aspects bear this out:

MC a.n. ☍ midpoint ☽, ♅ r. ☌ midpoint ♇, ♆ r. □ ♀ p.n.
Asc. p.n. □ ♄ r. □ ♄ a.n. ☌ ♅ p.n. ☌ ♆ a.n. □ ♇ p.n.
(MC p.n. ☌ ♇ r.)
(MC a.n. ☌ ☽ p.n. ☌ ☿ a.n. ☍ ♃ a.n. ☌ ♄ r., p.n. and a.n.
  □ ♆ a.n. ☍ ♇ p.n.)
☉ r. ☌ ♂ p.n. □ ♇ a.n. in ♋ ☍ ♃ p.n. in ♌
Cusp 5 r. 21° ♈ ☌ Asc. p.n. □ ♄ r. etc.

Cusp 5 a.n. 27° ♉ ♂♃ r. ♂♄ p.n. ☍♅ a.n.
(Cusp 5 p.n. 16° ♉ ♂♄ a.n. □♅ p.n. 150° ♇ r.)
(Cusp 5 a.n. 16° ♌ ☍☉ r. ☍♂ p.n. ♂♃ p.n. □♇ a.n.)
Cusp 8 a.n. 20° ♈ □☽ p.n. □☿ a.n. □♃ a.n. □♄ r. ♂♆ a.n. □♇ p.n.

The array of afflictions here is sufficient to account for a bereavement under such terrible circumstances. There are present, however, in the Composite Solar Revolution several benefic configurations, which are noted below:

Asc. p.n. △♃ p.n. △♅ r. △♅ p.n.
Asc. a.n. ♂☽ p.n. ☍♀ p.n. ✶♃ a.n. ☍♇ p.n.
(MC a.n. ✶♀ p.n. ☍♃ a.n. ☍♇ p.n.)
♀ a.n. △♆ p.n.

Viewed in isolation, these aspects do not seem to point to any major catastrophe but the heavy and simultaneous involvement of the majority of angles of the revolutional figures is enough to outweigh the protective influence of the benefics. Nor, indeed, have we included all the afflictions in our preliminary survey, for the antenatal Moon, close to the radical Ascendant, is squared by antenatal Mars and postnatal Neptune, while the precessional postnatal Ascendant is squared by the radical Pluto. In addition we may note that the position of the radical fifth cusp almost exactly coincides with the Ascendant of the non-precessional postnatal figure and the eighth cusp of the non-precessional antenatal figure. As this cusp is squared by Saturn in the nativity and Saturn in the revolutional figure is close to its radical position and afflicted at the same time by the other major planets, there is every reason for regarding such a coincidence as threatening in the extreme. However, the benefic aspects were not without their special significance, for not only did the affair arouse nation-wide sympathy but later on in the same year a second child was born to the Lindberghs. The two configurations which appear to have most bearing upon the fact that a huge wave of popular sympathy was aroused are these:

Asc. p.n. △♃ p.n. in ♌ ♂♅ p.n. ♂♆ a.n.
(MC a.n. ✶♀ p.n. in ♓ ☍♃ a.n. ☍♇ p.n.)

Because the same set of figures has to show several main trends during the year, some bringing happiness and some the reverse, there will often be a mixture of good and bad aspects. The overshadowing tragedy of the year, the memory of which no subsequent joy could possibly efface, is clearly threatened by the mass of afflictions which pick out some of the major stresses in the nativity. There is still sufficient emphasis on the benefic configurations in the revolutional figures, however, to denote the arrival of a second child. To herald such an event we should expect to see an emphasis on Mercury and Uranus, on the polarities of Gemini–Sagittarius and Leo–Aquarius and on the fifth house. We should also expect to find the luminaries configured with the benefics, with both the benefics and the Moon in angular houses. These conditions are fulfilled by the following configurations:

Asc. p.n. ☌♅ p.n. □☿ a.n.
(MC a.n. ☌☿ a.n. ☍♅ a.n.)
(MC p.n. ☌♇ r. in ♊ △♂ p.n. ☉ r. in ♒)
Cusp 5 r. ☌♆ a.n. △♃ p.n. in ♌
Cusp 5 a.n. ☌♃ r.
(Cusp 5 a.n. ☌♃ p.n. △♅ p.n.)
☉ r. ☍♃ p.n. in ♌
☽ p.n. in 10th p.n. ⚹♀ p.n. ☍♃ a.n.
MC a.n. ☍☽ r. □♀ p.n.
Asc. r. ☌☽ a.n. □♀ r.
(MC a.n. ☌☽ p.n. ☍♃ a.n. ☌♃ r.)
Asc. a.n. ☍♀ p.n.

Here, the benefic nature of the aspects is deliberately stressed in order to demonstrate the presence of harmonious factors in the Composite Solar Revolution operating in spite of the malefic configurations interwoven with them.

The long-term effect of the murder of their son was that the Lindberghs eventually sought sanctuary in England, remaining in Europe until war broke out. That the events of 1932 were to pave the way for such a move were shown by the configurations involving the radical planets in Capricorn. Planets in this sign and in the opposite sign, Cancer, have a special relationship with conditions governing the home. The Moon, Mercury and Uranus are all bodies inclining towards restlessness and change and the following aspects involving the radical Jupiter and Saturn in Capricorn are worthy of special notice:

Asc. p.n. □☽ p.n. □☿ a.n. □♃ a.n. ♂♅ p.n. ♂♆ a.n.
□♇ p.n. □♄ r.
(MC a.n. is configured with the same planets)
(☽ p.n. ♂☿ p.n. ♂♄ p.n. ☍♅ a.n. ♂♃ r.)

Within a year of the Lindbergh tragedy, Adolf Hitler became Chancellor of Germany. The details of his nativity and the Composite Solar Revolution for the year of his triumph are given below (precessional positions in brackets):

Case No. 58	MC	Asc.	☉	☽	☿	♀	♂	♃	♄	♅	♆	♇
Nativity	1° ♌	24° ♎	0° ♑	6° ♉	25° ♈	16°♑ R	16° ♈	8° ♉	13° ♌	19°♎ R	1° ♓	4° ♓
Postnatal Solar Revolution	27° ♐ (7° ♌)	23° ♓ (27° ♎)	0° ♑ (1° ♑)	4° ♏ (13° ♏)	14°♈ R	16° ♓	13° ♈	12° ♌	4° ♒	20° ♈	5°♍ R	20° ♋
Antenatal Solar Revolution	4° ♓ (22° ♋)	9° ♋ (16° ♎)	0° ♑ (0° ♑)	3° ♓ (24° ♒)	27°♈ R	16° ♓	17° ♓	18° ♑	28° ♒	11° ♈	27° ♒	24° ♈

As the principal indicators of Hitler's accession to power we should expect to find radical configurations promising success strongly stimulated, the benefics angular in the revolutional figures and the Sun and Mars well supported, together with an accent on the sign Leo, the sign of power and leadership. The following configurations conform to such a pattern:

☉ r. △☽ r., ♃ r. stimulated by ☽ p.n. ☍☉ r. ✳ ☽ r., ♃ r.;
   ♆ p.n. △☉ r. △☽ r., ♃ r.; and ☽ a.n. ✳☉ r. ✳ ☽ r., ♃ r.
Asc. a.n. ☍♃ r.
Asc. p.n. ♂♀ a.n. ✳♃ a.n.
(MC p.n. ♂♃ p.n. in ♌ △♂ p.n., ♅ a.n., ☿ p.n.)
(Asc. p.n. ☍☉ r. △♄ a.n., ♆ a.n.)
(Asc. a.n. ☍♂ p.n. △♀ p.n. ✳ ♃ p.n., ♄ r. in ♌)
♂ r. ♂♀ r. ✳ ♀ a.n. ♂♃ a.n. (☍☽ p.n.)

The popular acclaim which carries political candidates to success in elections is often represented astrologically by Moon–Neptune contacts, suggesting a wave of popular emotion which sweeps the favourite on to victory, irrespective of what might rationally be expected to happen. In the Composite Solar Revolution we find these aspects present:

☽ p.n. ☍ ☉ r. ⚹ ♆ p.n. (but □♄ p.n.)
MC a.n. ☌☽ a.n. in ♓ ☍♆ p.n.
☽ r. ☌♃ r. △♆ p.n.
　　and in addition (☽ p.n. △♀ a.n. ☍♃ a.n.)

The square between the postnatal Moon and Saturn is probably indicative of the loneliness that must assail the chosen leader of a country as he contemplates the tasks and duties that lie before him. Saturn in Leo in the tenth house of the nativity shows ambition and the probability of a rise to power, while the conjunction of the postnatal Jupiter with the radical Saturn, together with the trine from the postnatal Mars and the antenatal Uranus, both in Aries, appears to be the dominant configuration of the year. The Mars–Uranus conjunction in Aries is a reminder of the afflicted radical Mars in the nativity (in square to Saturn, both planets being debilitated) and shows the successful demonstration of force in the pursuit of success and the ruthless manner in which the party prosecuted their campaign under Hitler's leadership. This is shown by the number of Mars–Saturn–Uranus contacts present in the Composite Solar Revolution:

♂ p.n. ☌☿ p.n. ☌♅ p.n., a.n. in ♈ △♄ r. ☍♅ r. △♇ a.n.
(Asc. a.n. ☌♅ r. ⚹♄ r. △♂ a.n.)
(☽ p.n. ☍♂ r. □♄ r.)

The radical Mars–Saturn square is also inflamed by a double conjunction from Jupiter:

♃ p.n. □♂ r. ☌♄ r.
♃ a.n. ☌♂ r. □♄ r.

The totalitarian outlook and the drastic changes of policy characteristic of the new regime are shown spectacularly by the following aspects:

Asc. r. ☍☿ a.n., ♇ a.n.
(MC a.n. □♅ p.n. ☌♇ p.n.)
(Asc. a.n. ☌♅ r. □♇ p.n.)

The plotting, subterfuge and underground manoeuvres preceding the bid for power are shown by the following configuration:

MC a.n. ☌☽ a.n. in ♓ ☐♆ ♇ r. ☍♆ p.n.

Tests of integrity are usually denoted by aspects between Saturn and Neptune, when the Saturnian concept of duty is often disturbed by the nebulous and fanciful schemes of Neptune and ambition is stimulated beyond legitimate grounds by wild dreams of unlimited self-fulfilment. Opportunities are also afforded for ideals (Neptune) to be put into practice (Saturn).

The composite revolution shows the following:

♄ p.n. 150° ♆ p.n. ☐☉ r. ☐☽ p.n. △♆ ♇ r.
♀ a.n. ⚹ ♄ a.n., ♆ a.n.

Hitler's financial position was considerably improved by his election to the Chancellorship. Favourable aspects to Jupiter from the major planets and benefic configurations involving the signs Taurus–Scorpio and the second house cusp are typical indications of increased financial prosperity:

♃ r. ☍Asc. a.n. △♆ p.n.
♃ p.n. ☌♄ r. △♅ a.n.
(☽ p.n. in ♏ △♀ a.n. ☍♃ a.n. in ♑ △♇ p.n.)
Cusp 2 r. 21° ♏ ☍♃ a.n. in ♑ △♇ p.n.
Cusp 2 p.n. 15° ♑ ☌♀,♂ r. ☌♃ a.n. ⚹ ♀ a.n.
(Cusp 2 a.n. 12° ♏ ☌☽ p.n. ☍♀, ♂ r. ☍♃ p.n. ⚹ ♀ a.n.)

As a contrast to the case we have just reviewed, let us now consider astrologically the abdication of Edward VIII, which took place on 11 December 1936. The details of the Composite Solar Revolution and of the nativity are given below:

Case No. 59	MC	Asc.	☉	☽	☿	♀	♂	♃	♄	♅	♆	♇
Nativity	7° ♐	8° ♒	2° ♋	4° ♓	27° ♋	23° ♑	0° ♈	18° ♓	18° ♎	11° ♏ R	14° ♓	10° ♓
Postnatal Solar Revolution	24° ♑ (6° ♍)	24° ♑ (17° ♏)	(3° ♋)	1° ♍ (9° ♍)	10° ♓	0° ♋	28° ♓	18° ♐ R	22° ♓	8° ♑	14° ♍	26° ♋
Antenatal Solar Revolution	14° ♎ (29° ♒)	13° ♐ (3° ♋)	(1° ♋)	18° ♍ (9° ♍)	25° ♓	6° ♌	6° ♍	14° ♏ R	14° ♑	7° ♑	11° ♓ R	1° ♑

The abdication of Edward VIII aroused a great deal of controversy. While it is no part of our purpose to examine the controversial aspects of the case, the student will find useful material in the

Composite Solar Revolution covering the year in question. It is sufficient to remark in passing that, in mundane astrology, the horoscope of a country's ruler, whether or not he possesses real power, reflects in a general way the fortunes of his subjects during the period in which he reigns. The horoscope of Edward VIII, unlike that of his brother George VI, could hardly be regarded as promising victory in war. Also the nativity of George VI, with its elevated Jupiter in Leo, indicated the possibility of a rise to the throne. Had Edward VIII not chosen to abdicate, would his brother still have succeeded him and would Britain have entered World War II having a monarch born with the Sun square Mars, Moon square Pluto and Ascendant square Uranus? Did the stars in their courses already know which choice would be made?

As a result of his romance with Mrs Simpson, whose two previous marriages had both ended in divorce, Edward VIII was faced with a problem of renunciation. It was made clear to the King by the Church and Government that their interpretation of the Constitution was such that he could not remain as monarch except by giving up all thought of marriage to Mrs Simpson. He had either to relinquish his position as monarch or the prospect of marriage to the one he loved. We shall therefore expect to find a strong Neptunian accentuation in the Composite Solar Revolution to indicate the element of renunciation. In the nativity we find:

MC □ ☽ ✕ ☍ ♆, ♇

In the revolutions the following configurations are present:

Asc. a.n. ☍ ♆ r. □ ♆ p.n. and a.n.
(MC p.n. ☌ ☽ p.n. and a.n. ☌ ♆ p.n.)
(MC a.n. ☌ ☽ r. ☌ ♆ a.n. in ✕)
☿ p.n. □ ♆ p.n.
☽ a.n. ☍ ♆ a.n.

Romance is often shown by contacts between Venus and Mars, Uranus and Pluto. Here we find:

Asc. r. ☍ ♀ a.n. □ ♅ p.n. and a.n. □ ♅ r. □ ♇ a.n.
Asc. p.n. ☌ ♀ r. ✶ ♇ p.n.
(Asc. a.n. ☌ ♀ p.n. ☌ ♂ p.n. □ ♂ r. ✶ ♇ a.n.)

The Venus–Uranus squares are extremely significant. The radical Uranus squares the seventh cusp from the inflexible sign Scorpio, indicating great difficulties in personal relationships and partnerships at some time. By its motion before and after birth, Uranus had arrived at the opposition of its own place, squaring the radical Ascendant and the postnatal Venus in the royal sign Leo. Venus is the planet of harmony. There could therefore be little hope of maintaining harmony during the year, though it should be noted that the Venus–Uranus contact did not break up a romance or have any direct relationship to divorce, except for the fact that his prospective marriage partner had been involved in two previous divorces, a situation which was at the heart of the controversy over the proposed marriage. With Venus so afflicted there could be little hope of maintaining harmony during the year, whatever course the King decided to choose. Harmony in official relationships would have been achieved only at the expense of harmony in personal relationships and vice versa. There is every indication of an abnormal situation developing. In the event, the King opted for romance and found himself as a result virtually exiled from his family, his friends and his country.

The clash between constitutional issues, orthodox religious opinion and the desire for some measure of freedom in personal self-expression, we should expect to see represented by afflictions to and between Saturn, Jupiter and Uranus, while the subtle compulsion of mass opinion, often mobilized with devastating effect by zealous crusaders, will have Pluto as its planetary counterpart. The following configurations show the turmoil brought about by these various conflicting elements:

Asc. a.n. ♂♃ p.n. □♄ p.n. □♆ p.n. ☍♇ r.
(Asc. p.n. ♂♃ a.n. ☍♄ a.n. ♂♅ r.)
Asc. a.n. □☽ a.n. ♂♃ r. □♆ p.n.
☿ a.n. ♂♂ p.n. □♄ p.n.

The angular Jupiter, as well as showing the prominent part played by religious leaders in shaping the decisions of the year, is an index of personal happiness. The natal Jupiter is in trine to Saturn in Libra, the sign of marriage, but is involved with Neptune and Pluto in the dual sign Gemini and close to an opposition of the radical Midheaven. A prominent and afflicted Jupiter in the revolutional figures would not therefore deny happiness but would make it very difficult to hold on to. The afflicted Jupiter is also a reminder that as a result of the abdication the Duke of Windsor was less well off financially. In such circumstances we should also expect to find afflictions involving the signs Taurus and Scorpio and the cusp of the second house. These configurations conform to such expectations:

Asc. r. ☍♀ a.n. □♅ p.n. and a.n. in ♑
(Asc. a.n. ☌♃ a.n. ☌♅ r. in ♏ ☍♄ a.n. in ♑)
Cusp 2 p.n. 18° ♓ ☌♃ r. ☍♃ p.n. □☽ a.n. □♄ p.n.
   □♆ p.n.
(Cusp 2 p.n. 18° ♐ ☍♃ r. ☌♃ p.n. □☽ a.n. □♄ p.n.
   □♆ p.n.)
(Cusp 2 a.n. 19°♋ □♄ r.)

In spite of the attitude of Church and State dignitaries, the Duke remained firm in his resolve to marry Mrs Simpson. Determination and fixity of purpose are frequently shown by Mercury–Mars and Moon–Pluto contacts. In the nativity we find:

☽ in the first house □♇
☿△♂

In the Composite Solar Revolution we find:

☽ p.n. △♇ a.n.
(☽ p.n. and a.n. □♇ r.)
☿ p.n. □♂ a.n.
☿ a.n. ☌♂ p.n.

and in addition

☽ r. ☍♂ a.n. △♅ a.n. (☍MC p.n.)
☽ p.n. ✳ ♂ r. ✳ ♂ p.n.
(☽ p.n. and a.n. ☌♂ a.n.)
☿ r. ☌♇ p.n. ☍MC p.n.
☿ p.n. ☌♇ r. ☍MC r.

Such aspects as these offer little hope of compromise, nor was it possible for any acceptable compromise to be found and so the drastic step was taken. The radical Sun–Moon trine involving the sign Pisces suggests self-fulfilment through renunciation. That this was the time for the crucial test is indicated by the following eloquent configuration:

(Asc. a.n. ☌ ☉ r. ☌ ♀ p.n. ☌ ♂ p.n. ⚹ ♇ a.n. △ ☽ r.)

The antenatal Pluto stands midway between the radical trine of
the luminaries, while the Sun is placed on the antenatal Ascendant, conjoined with Mars and Venus in the postnatal figure. That
the affair was ultimately to attract world-wide attention could
only be expected from the angular position of the Sun in Cancer
and its natal trine to the first house Moon. The various Moon–
Neptune contacts indicate popular sympathy for the King in his
most crucial dilemma.

The fifth house is traditionally related to love affairs but also
appears to have much to do with the amount of power and
influence wielded by the native. It is therefore an important house
in the horoscopes of all high dignitaries. In the case under review
we may note the following:

Cusp 5 r. 25° ♓ ☌ ☿ a.n. ☌ ♂ p.n. □ ♄ p.n.
Cusp 5 p.n. 17° ♌ ☽ ♃ r. ⚹ ♄ r.
Cusp 5 a.n. 9° ♑ □ ♀ a.n. ☌ ♅ p.n. and a.n. ☍ ♅ r.
(Cusp 5 a.n. 2° ♎ ☍ ♂ r. □ ☉ r.)

The prevailing atmosphere here is decidedly stormy and in
keeping with the actual trend of events.

A constitutional crisis (Capricorn) and the planning of marriage (Libra) were the keynotes of the year. These two signs
occupied respectively the Midheaven of the non-precessional
postnatal and antenatal figures:

MC p.n. in ♑ ☍ ☿ r. ☍ ♇ p.n.
MC a.n. in ♎ ☌ ♄ r. △ ♃ r.

In the first case the angular Pluto heralded the close of one
chapter and the start of a new one; in the second the angular
Saturn indicated the consolidation of a partnership which was to
bring great personal happiness (trine Jupiter).

When dealing with the Composite Solar Revolution it is
necessary in every case to assess carefully the potentialities of the
nativity. When this has been done the revolutionary figures should
be inspected to determine which parts of the nativity will be
activated, either by the angles of the revolution falling on the
places of the radical planets or by close aspects being thrown by
the revolutional planets to the radical planets and angles. It

should also be observed whether the main emphasis of the stimulus is likely to be benefic or malefic.

The revolutional figures may then be assessed in terms of their own component parts, special attention being paid to angular configurations and to the nature of the angular planets. Then the various groups of event configurations given in the previous chapter may be consulted in order to gain a more exact idea of the possibilities contained in the revolutional figures. Constant practice in the handling of the Composite Solar Revolution along these lines should soon enable students to gauge their probable significance with confidence and accuracy.

8.
THE PART OF FORTUNE

Although various authors have dealt with the subject of the Part of Fortune in their several ways, astrological opinion is by no means unanimous as to whether the point has any significance or, if it has, what that significance may be. There appears to be a good deal of value in the point as applied to nativities, where the planets in closest aspect to Fortuna, according to their nature and the signs they are placed in, nearly always play a dominant role in the nativity, having a connection with both the native's character and destiny.

The reason for the special importance of Fortuna will become more apparent when we consider the symbology of the factors involved. The longitudinal arc between the Ascendant and Fortuna is the same as that between the radical Sun and Moon, so that Fortuna is where the Moon would be if the Sun were placed exactly on the Ascendant. The exact alignment of the Sun and Ascendant symbolize the light of the Inner Being shining out through the physical vehicle, the two becoming as one. Fortuna therefore represents where the natal Moon would be if such an ideal state of affairs existed, or in other words, the kind of adjustment to be made to the radical Moon in order to bring about this 'ideal' conjunction. The Moon represents our habits and instincts, relating to the kind of responses that come automatically to us, so that the Part of Fortune by its sign and aspects shows how we should seek to adjust our habits and responses in order to speed our evolution. Convenient examples are furnished by the horoscopes used in the previous chapter.

In the case of Colonel Lindbergh, Fortuna is in 14° Libra in trine to the Sun on the cusp of the third house in 14° Aquarius and also in trine to Pluto in 16° Gemini. Lindbergh the aviator is well shown by this grand trine in air and the fame achieved as a result of his long-distance flights across the Atlantic and to the orient is aptly symbolized by the presence of the Sun on the third cusp. Pluto is also in the sign of travel. Anne Morrow Lindbergh, his wife, was also an aviator and accompanied him on his flight to the Far East. Fortuna is in Libra, the marriage sign, in trine to the seventh house Pluto. Libra and the seventh house are also connected with politics and Lindbergh's interest in Nazi Germany had some repercussions upon his popularity at the outbreak of World War II. The totalitarian nature of the planet Pluto has led to its being regarded as the planet of Fascism. The Sun in Aquarius is in the sign polarity connected with children and the tragic death of the Lindbergh baby is a reminder that the grand trine was not always regarded as favourable by the ancients. It seems more probable that the favourable or unfavourable effects of the grand trine are not inherent in the angular distances themselves but derive from the fact that the bodies related by the grand trine tend to act according to their own natures. As the so-called malefic planets outnumber the benefics the chances are always that the three or more planets forming a grand trine will contain a preponderance of malefics which, acting in concert, will tend to produce more difficulties than blessings. If two points of the triangle are occupied by malefics, a benefic standing at the third point will be midway between the two malefics, a position of some difficulty! In the example we have been considering, the Part of Fortune stands at the midpoint of the Sun and Pluto. Although the radical trine between the two bodies produced its quota of strikingly favourable results, the Sun–Pluto combination is not without its more destructive side, producing situations which challenge a man to find within himself a hidden reservoir of power and sustenance that will carry him through his darkest hours.

In the case of Adolf Hitler, the Part of Fortune is at the extreme end of Gemini, in sextile to the Sun and in semi-sextile to Neptune. Such aspects as the semi-sextile, usually regarded as minor, are none the less important when close to exactitude. In addition, the Sun, Neptune, Fortuna and the Midheaven are separated from each other by almost equal 30-degree arcs, a pattern not without significance! Hitler became obsessed with the idea of regenerating Germany (Neptune and Pluto, the planets of obsession stand together in the eighth house, the house of regeneration). He first made his name as a propagandist, orator and writer (*Mein Kampf*), a reflection of the Geminian position of Fortuna and became a political leader (Fortuna sextile Sun in the seventh house) and later dictator of Germany, finally falling a prey to his megalomania (Neptune stands midway between Fortuna and the Sun, ruling his tenth house).

Our third example is the Duke of Windsor in whose horoscope the Part of Fortune is in 9° Libra in trine to Pluto in 10° Gemini. Pluto is in quincunx to Uranus and conjoins Neptune opposing the Midheaven. Pluto in Gemini suggests the compulsion to make a choice and the opposition of Pluto to the Midheaven the disastrous results of that choice, so far as his public 'career' was concerned. Fortuna in the marriage sign Libra, placed in the testing eighth house, indicates in this case the exceptionally important repercussions which his decision to marry Mrs Simpson was to have on the whole course of his life. Pluto in the sign of travel in the fourth house promises a great deal of moving about and considerable difficulty in establishing permanent roots. Such was indeed the pattern of the Duke's life after his abdication.

As the Part of Fortune in the nativity is a point of special significance there is reason for believing that the Part of Fortune in the Solar Revolution may also provide valuable evidence as to which planet or planets are likely to exert a dominant influence during the year. Tests have shown this to be the case provided Fortuna is calculated according to a certain formula. It is customary to calculate the Part of Fortune by using the formula:

$$\text{Longitude of Ascendant} + \text{Longitude of Moon} - \text{Longitude of Sun} = \text{Longitude of Part of Fortune}$$

When this formula is applied to the Solar Revolution it will be evident that the longitude of the Sun will be the same as in the nativity (or very nearly so in the case of figures calculated with an allowance for precession). This factor therefore, may be regarded as a constant in the calculation of the radical and the revolutional Part of Fortune, the two variable factors being the longitudes of the Moon and the Ascendant. If, as an experiment we introduce another constant for calculating the revolutional Part of Fortune, retaining as well as the longitude of the radical Sun, the longitude of the radical Moon or alternatively, the longitude of the radical Ascendant, we shall arrive at the following:

$$\text{Longitude of Ascendant rad.} + \text{Longitude of Moon rev.} - \text{Longitude of Sun rad.} = \text{Longitude of Part of Fortune rev.}$$

Longitude of Ascendant rev. + Longitude of Moon rad.
– Longitude of Sun rad. = Longitude of Part of Fortune rev.

If we employ the first formula, it will be equivalent to moving the radical Part of Fortune by the amount of arc between the longitudes of the radical and the revolutional Moon. In the case of the second formula, it is as if we were to move the radical Part of Fortune by the amount of arc between the longitudes of the radical and revolutional Ascendants. The sign position of and planetary aspects to the Part of Fortune thus derived will often furnish valuable pointers to the general trend of events during the year. Although it is difficult to formulate a comprehensive set of rules for the interpretation of aspects to the revolutional Part of Fortune, it can be stated as a general principle that a marked preponderance of favourable aspects to the several Parts of Fortune derived from the Composite Solar Revolution will be a strong indication that the year will be one in which pleasant and profitable events are likely to occur, while a corresponding emphasis on adverse aspects will mark a period of catastrophe and loss. Although it is possible to derive no less than eight subsidiary Parts of Fortune for the year by applying the suggested formulas to both the postnatal and antenatal precessional and non-precessional figures, it is highly significant that there will always be a large measure of agreement between the nature of the aspects thrown to all eight points.

Because it is possible to derive eight such points, a problem arises as to how these points should be named in order to differentiate one from the other. As the difference in position between the radical and revolutional Part of Fortune depends in the one case on the difference in position between the radical and revolutional Ascendant and in the other on the difference between the radical and revolutional Moon, it is proposed to distinguish between the two types of Fortuna by placing the letters (AD) and (LD) after each to denote in the first case that the position was derived by taking into account Ascensional Difference and in the second, Lunar Difference. It will thus be possible to distinguish between the various points as follows:

Revolutional PF (Precessional) p.n. (AD)
Revolutional PF (Precessional) p.n. (LD)
Revolutional PF (Precessional) a.n. (AD)
Revolutional PF (Precessional) a.n. (LD)

Revolutional PF (Non-Precessional) p.n. (AD)
Revolutional PF (Non-Precessional) p.n. (LD)
Revolutional PF (Non-Precessional) a.n. (AD)
Revolutional PF (Non-Precessional) a.n. (LD)

In order to demonstrate the usefulness of these points we will examine the effect of placing them in the horoscopes reviewed in the previous chapter.

In the case of the Composite Solar Revolution covering the year in which Colonel Lindbergh made his record-breaking solo flight across the Atlantic the following results are obtained:

Precessional figures
   PF p.n. (AD) 18° ♈ △♅ ♐ r. ✶ ♇ ♓ r.
   PF p.n. (LD) 6° ♉ ✶ ♃ p.n., ♄ a.n. in ♓
   PF a.n. (AD) 11° ♊ △☉ ♒ r. ☍♂ ♐ a.n.
   PF a.n. (LD) 5° ♌ △♄ ♐ p.n.

Here there is a pronounced emphasis on the signs of travel, Gemini and Sagittarius, and the aspects, although strenuous, are favourable. The radical third house Sun is also stimulated.

Non-precessional figures
   PF p.n. (AD) 4° ♍ △☿ ♓ r., ♀ ♓ p.n. ♃ ♓ ☍♆ ♇ a.n.
   PF p.n. (LD) 1° ♉ ☽☿ ♓, ♀♓ r. ✶ ♀ ♓ p.n. △♆ a.n.
   PF a.n. (AD) 20° ♍ ♂MC r. □♅ ♐ r. △♄ ♇ r.
   PF a.n. (LD) 9° ♌ No close aspects

Here the emphasis is on a well-aspected Mercury in Pisces, which together with Neptune is an indicator of long-distance travel. Apart from the stimulus to the radical Uranus–Midheaven square, all the aspects are favourable.

Applying the same series of points to the Composite Solar Revolutions for the year in which the Lindbergh baby was kidnapped and murdered, we get the following results:

Precessional figures
   PF p.n. (AD) 25° ♋ ☍☽ p.n., ♄ p.n. in ♇ ♂♅ ♋ a.n.
   PF p.n. (LD) 14° ♏ □☉ r., ♂ p.n. in ♒ ☍♇ ♇ a.n.
   PF a.n. (AD) 19° ♓ ☍MC r. □♅ ♐ r. □♇ ♓ r. ♂♀ p.n.
             △♃ ♋ a.n. △♇ ♋ p.n.
   PF a.n. (LD) 18° ♍ ♂MC r. □♅ ♐ r. □♇ ♓ r. ♂♀ p.n.
             △♄ ♇ a.n. △♇ ♇ a.n.

Here there is no mistaking the strongly malefic trend of the configurations linked with the several Parts of Fortune. An afflicted Moon, in the sign polarity related to parenthood, afflictions to the radical Sun in Aquarius in the third house, which appears to have a connection with young children (and Aquarius is part of the sign polarity relating to offspring) from Mars and Pluto, the latter planet opposed to Fortuna in Scorpio, the sign of death, and the Venus–Uranus–Pluto afflictions are all ominous portents. The presence of some benefic aspects among the overwhelming preponderance of afflictions probably accounts for the fact that during the same year a second baby was born.

Non-precessional figures
   PF p.n. (AD) 1° ♓ ♂☿ ♀ r. 45° ♄ ♑ a.n. 45° ♅ ♈ p.n.
   PF p.n. (LD) 9° ♏ Δ♂ ♓ a.n. ✶ ♆ ♍ a.n.
   PF a.n. (AD) 4° ♌ ♂ Cusp 5° p.n. Δ☽ ♐ a.n. 135° ♅ ♐ r.
   PF a.n. (LD) 24° ♍ □☽ ♐ r. 150° ♂ ♒ r. ♂Asc. a.n.

Although the main trend here is predominantly adverse, the afflictions are not quite so striking as in the case of the pre-cessional figures. The postnatal (LD) Fortuna is in trine to the antenatal Mars and in sextile to the antenatal Neptune. This only serves to stimulate the opposition between the two revolutional planets. Similarly, the trine between the antenatal Moon and the antenatal (AD) Fortuna has no benefic significance, for the luminary is squared by both Mars and Neptune. Aspects from the Part of Fortune only serve to emphasize the nature of the planetary configurations already present in the horoscope.

In the Composite Solar Revolution for the year of Hitler's dramatic rise to power, the various Parts of Fortune pick out the following configurations:

Precessional figures
   PF p.n. (AD) 3° ♋ Δ☽ p.n. and a.n. ✶ ♆ p.n.
   PF p.n. (LD) 7° ♈ Δ☽ ♃ r in ♑
   PF a.n. (AD) 22° ♓ Δ♅ ♎ r. ✶ ♅ ♈ p.n.
   PF a.n. (LD) 18° ♋ Δ♀ ♓ a.n. ✶ ♃ ♈ a.n. ♂♇ p.n.
         □♅ ♎ r.

These contacts emphasize a well-aspected Moon, essential for matters where personal popularity is a deciding factor and place a focus upon the radical Uranus in the political sign, Libra.

Non-precessional figures
    PF p.n. (AD) 30° ♑ □⊙ ♄ r. △♆ ♓ r.
    PF p.n. (LD) 27° ♈ ♂☿ r. and a.n. ♂♇ a.n. △MC p.n. ⚹ ♄,
        ♆ ♒ a.n.
    PF a.n. (AD) 15° ♓ ⚹ ♀, ♂ ♅ r. ♂♀ a.n. □♀ p.n., ♂ a.n.
        in ♓
    PF a.n. (LD) 27° ♌ △MC p.n. △☿ ♈ a.n. ☍♄.,
        ♆ ♒ a.n.

The radical Sun–Neptune–Fortuna contact is repeated and a strong emphasis placed upon a well-supported Mercury in Aries.

The final example is taken from the Composite Solar Revolution for the Duke of Windsor, cast for the year of his abdication from the throne. The positions and aspects of the various Parts of Fortune are as follows:

Precessional figures
    PF p.n. (AD) 19° ♋ □♄ ≏ r.
    PF p.n. (LD) 16° ♈ ☍♄ ≏ r. ⚹ ♃, ♆ ♓ r.
    PF a.n. (AD) 5° ♓ ♂☽ r. △⊙ ♋ r.
    PF a.n. (LD) 15° ♈ ☍♄ ≏ r. ⚹ ♃, ♆ ♓ r.

Here, the emphasis upon the radical Saturn in the marriage sign Libra is remarkable and, together with the stimulus to the radical Neptune and to the Moon in Pisces, both connected with renunciation, is typical of the event.

Non-precessional figures
    PF p.n. (AD) 25° ♑ ♂MC p.n. △♀ ♅ r. ☍♇ ♋ p.n.
    PF p.n. (LD) 7° ♈ △♀ ♌ a.n. 150°♂ ♍ a.n. 30° ♅ ♅ a.n.
    PF a.n. (AD) 15° ♌ △♃ ♐ p.n. ⚹ ♆ ♓ r.
    PF a.n. (LD) 24° ♈ □MC p.n. in ♑ □♇ ♋ p.n.

The idea of a constitutional crisis is well portrayed by the Midheaven–Pluto opposition picked out by the Part of Fortune, occurring in the signs Cancer–Capricorn. The revolutional Venus–Uranus square is also emphasized and the radical Venus stimulated as an indication of the romantic interest that entered the Duke's life at this time.

The foregoing examples are sufficient to call attention to the usefulness of the Part of Fortune in the Composite Solar Revolution, when the point is determined by using only one variable factor. Fortuna may therefore be regarded as a valuable auxiliary in facilitating the interpretation of Solar Revolutions.

To a lesser degree the radical Part of Fortune is likely to be stimulated by the revolutional planets at the time of important happenings. When Colonel Lindbergh flew the Atlantic, the Part of Fortune in his nativity received these aspects:

PF r. 14° ♎ ☌MC p.n. ⚹ ♂ a.n. □♇ p.n.
PF r. (☍MC a.n. ☌☽ a.n.)

When it is remembered that Fortuna in the radix formed a grand trine with the Sun and Pluto, the Sun being in the third house and Pluto in Gemini, the importance of these stimuli becomes obvious.

At the time of the kidnapping, the same Part of Fortune was configured thus:

PF r. △♂ p.n. □♄ a.n. ☍♅ p.n.

Three malefics in combination act to bring out the least desirable effects of the radical Fortuna–Sun–Pluto grand trine. The first event, with Mars aspecting the configuration from Sagittarius emphasized the Gemini–Sagittarius connection with travel. The second event, with Mars in Aquarius on the radical Sun, worked out in terms of children signified by the Leo–Aquarius polarity.

When Adolf Hitler came to power, we find the radical Part of Fortune receiving these aspects:

PF r. 30° ♊ ☍MC p.n. ⚹ ☿ a.n. △♄ ♆ a.n.

Fortuna is once again angular and, although not spectacularly supported as one might expect from the nature of the event, the aspects are all helpful and indicative of the undertaking of extra responsibility.

Fortuna in the Duke of Windsor's horoscope was configured at the time of his abdication in the following manner:

PF r. 10° ♎ ☌MC a.n. △☿ p.n. 150° ♆ a.n.

Mercury is in square to Neptune, both aspecting an angular Fortuna in Libra, the sign of marriage.

PART III:
THE MINOR FIGURES IN DETAIL

9.

THE TIMING OF EVENTS

The usual method of estimating when events foreshadowed by the Solar Revolution are likely to take place is to calculate a Lunar Revolution for each lunar month during the year covered by the solar figure. The Lunar Revolution which most nearly reproduces the planetary conditions present in the Solar Revolution is then selected and the month covered by this lunar figure is considered to be the most likely period for the precipitation of major events.

It is also valid to construct a series of monthly solar figures based on the moment of the Sun's arrival each month at successive distances of 30° from its place in the Solar Revolution. These figures may be regarded as the equivalent of mundane maps cast for the entry of the Sun each month into each succeeding zodiacal sign.

I have devised what I consider to be a simpler way of finding out when events shown by the Solar Revolution will come to pass. Each day's motion of the planets, both before and after the revolutional date, is taken to represent, in turn, a month, a week and a day. Once the Solar Revolution has been set up it is thus possible to find, merely from an inspection of the Ephemeris, the month in which major events are likely to be precipitated. Such directions based on the Revolution must be considered not only in relation to the figure itself but also in relation to radical planets and angles.

The important contacts, therefore, will be those formed within twelve days immediately preceding or following the birthday anniversary and it is for this reason that planets removed some twelve or fifteen degrees on either side from the angles are considered powerful, for the Midheaven of the figure may be progressed, as in the case of the various major and minor series of secondary directions, by the amount of the Sun's progress in the zodiac measured from the birthday anniversary to the directional day under consideration; thus a planet within twelve degrees of the Midheaven will be in conjunction with the progressed Midheaven at some time during the year. When the position of the progressed Midheaven has been calculated, the corresponding Oblique Ascendant may be extracted from the appropriate tables of houses for the place where the native was living at the time when the Solar Return occurred. It should be observed that the signs Pisces and Aries are signs of short ascension in the Northern Hemisphere, so that when these signs rise, thirty degrees are passing over the Ascendant, while only twelve degrees are passing over the Midheaven. Conversely, Virgo and Libra are signs of long ascension in the Northern Hemisphere and only cover an arc of nine degrees when rising while twelve degrees pass over the Midheaven. For this reason it may be advisable to consider planets 'angular' over a wider area measured in both directions from the horizon when Pisces or Aries is on the revolutional Ascendant than when Virgo or Libra is rising. This position will be reversed in the Southern Hemisphere, where Pisces and Aries are signs of long ascension, while Virgo and Libra are signs of short ascension.

Aspects formed within the fifty-two days immediately following and preceding the birthday anniversary (the day of the Solar Return) will represent the influences in force during the successive weeks of the year. Once the day-for-a-month directions have been calculated and a special emphasis has been observed to fall on one particular month as a result of the directions then in force, corroborative evidence may then be sought in the weekly directions covering the same period with the further object of narrowing down the climax to one particular week.

When this has been done, the 'day-for-a-day' directions may be consulted in order to confirm the trends already noted and also to provide evidence as to the particular day on which the anticipated event is likely to occur. If at any stage during these investigations one series of progressions fails to confirm the indications given by the previous stage in the process it would be advisable to reconsider the available evidence and, if necessary, modify the original interpretation or select another period as the most crucial one in relation to the subject under investigation.

A system which is astrologically sound and which has been found by experience to be of practical value should be capable of application, with suitable modifications, to any type of horoscope. It follows, therefore, that Monthly Lunar Returns may also be progressed, using the same measure of a day's motion of the planets, both before and after the day of the Return, to represent the passage of a week or a day. In this manner the crucial week and the most important days during the month covered by the figure should easily be identified. As the Midheaven of the Lunar Revolution will not move more than about 4° either way as a result of the weekly progressions it would appear that planets should be appreciably nearer the angles in this type of figure (as compared with the Solar Revolution) for the effect to be strongly marked during the month.

When handling directions based on any type of revolutional figure the same basic principles apply to these as to the various major and minor measures set forth in *The Technique of Prediction*. They are as follows:

1. One single unit of time — the true solar day — can be equated to a month, a week or a day. These three types of direction are not to be regarded separately but, taken together, they form a completely integrated whole.
2. Progressions are equally valid whether measured forward or backward in time from the day of the Solar or Lunar Return.
3. The Midheaven of the Solar or Lunar Revolution moves at a rate equal to the speed of the Sun's progress through the zodiac on the days immediately following and prior to the day of the Return.
4. The angles of the revolutional figure, both progressed and radical, are the most sensitive points and their position is of paramount importance in determining both the timing of events and their nature.

When estimating the effects of the various series of minor directions, it is important to observe whether there are any contacts between converse and progressed positions, especially if the progressed and converse angles are involved. It is also necessary to bear in mind that strong directions forming in the daily series will only herald important events if there are aspects in the revolution itself promising such events and if suitable monthly or weekly directions have also formed in such a way as to be precipitated by these daily progressions.

It is a moot point whether a Solar Revolution can be regarded as beginning its period of influence on the day when it falls due. Some figures seem to act precipitately and it may well be that the revolutional day stands, in fact, at the middle of the period to which it is related. Certainly there are well defined cases where the revolution seems to have worked strongly during the two or three weeks prior to the date for which it was cast. Our lives are not divided neatly into watertight compartments from the point of view of the time-factor and we do not experience a dramatic change of outlook each time our birthday comes round. Any changes are almost always gradual, one day's experience merging into the next, one year's experience merging into the next, so that when an important event antedates the revolutional figure by a few weeks, this later figure must naturally show the probable trend of the native's psychological and physical reactions to such a recent event as well as to any modifications or changes in his environment that may follow upon it. These indications will often be suggestive of the event itself and will therefore appear to indicate the event. It is this factor which makes it difficult to assert categorically that the twelve months following the birthday anniversary is ruled exclusively by one Solar Return. Just as in a relay race one runner overlaps another in order to make the baton change, so there is probably a transitional period when one revolutional figure takes over from the other. The earlier figure may gradually diminish in power as the new figure gets ready to take over, with the power of the succeeding figure becoming ever more dominant as the take-over period approaches.

In assessing the significance of directions it is necessary to take into account the general character of those directions, viewed as a whole. Each separate direction is therefore important in that it forms a part of the total picture. Some directions are, however, more important than others and it is desirable to differentiate between the various types of directions in terms of strength in order to determine in which quarter the principal emphasis lies. The most powerful directions are those which involve the angles or planets in the nativity. Next in order of strength are those involving the angles and planets in the revolutional figures themselves. Last in order come aspects formed between the progressed angles and planets and other progressed planets. In this connection it cannot be emphasized too strongly that there is no essential difference in strength or quality between postnatal and antenatal figures or between progressed and converse directions. A contact between a conversely directed antenatal planet and a progressed postnatal planet or angle is not essentially more or less powerful than a similar contact between a progressed postnatal angle and a progressed postnatal planet or between a converse antenatal angle and a converse antenatal planet. More important is the nature of the aspect by which the two (or more) factors are combined.

The most significant directions are those in which a planet is either in conjunction with or in opposition to the Midheaven or the Ascendant (whether radical revolutional or progressed). Whether the effect will be favourable or unfavourable will largely depend upon aspects from other planets received by the angular planet, trines and sextiles producing favourable situations, squares and unrelieved oppositions introducing stresses and difficulties. A preponderance of malefic planets, however well combined by aspect, will tend to indicate trouble ahead. Particular attention should be paid to the radical relationship between the planets in the nativity itself. Unfavourable aspects arising by progression between planets favourably configured at birth are less troublesome on that account, while favourable progressions formed between planets unfavourably linked at birth are not so likely to indicate benefit.

Progressions involving angles are the most powerful, then those involving solar aspects. Next in order of importance come aspects involving planets that fall on or near the angles of the Composite Solar Revolution. It almost goes without saying that no aspect forming by progression should be regarded as operative until it is within a degree of completion.

In order to demonstrate the application and usefulness of the several directional measures proposed let us now examine, in some detail, the progressions measuring to Ann Harding's marriage that are based on the Postnatal and Antenatal Solar Revolutions used as examples for calculation earlier. The positions of the planets and angles in these figures are set out below in tabular form, with the positions of the angles and luminaries in the precessional figures placed in brackets.

	MC	Asc.	☉	☽	☿	♀	♂	♃	♄	♅	♆	♇
Nativity	27° ♍	14° ♐	14° ♌	6° ♎	10° ♌	15° ♋	12° ♋	12° R ♒	23° R ♑	17° R ♐	2° ♋	19° ♊
Postnatal Solar Revolution	23° ♋ (5° ♐)	19° ♎ (16° ♒)	14° ♌ (14° ♌)	4° ♌ (8° ♌)	14° R ♌	17° ♋	3° ♉	23° R ♒	19° ♏	29° R ♓	24° ♌	15° ♋
Antenatal Solar Revolution	17° ♐ (7° ♌)	5° ♓ (1° ♏)	14° ♌ (14° ♌)	3° ♐ (29° ♏)	10° ♍	14° ♋	28° ♌	0° R ♒	2° R ♈	28° ♌	9° ♉	26° ♉

As a first step we may tabulate the main angular and inter-planetary configurations, remembering to allow a generous orb in the case of the former to cover the movement of the revolutional Midheaven and Ascendant during the year. Configurations involving positions in the precessional figures are placed in brackets. The principal aspect groupings are these:

MC p.n. ♂♀ r., p.n. and a.n. ☍♄ r. △♄ p.n. ♂♇ p.n.
MC a.n. ♂♅ r. ☍♇ r.
Asc. p.n. in ♎△♇ r.
(MC p.n. ♂☽ a.n. □♂ a.n., ♅ a.n. ☍♇ a.n.)
(MC a.n. ♂☉ r. ☍♃ r. ☍♃ a.n.)
(Asc. p.n. ☍☉ r., ☽ p.n. ♂♃ r.)
(Asc. a.n. ☍♂ p.n. △♆ r.)
♅ p.n. ♂MC r.
☽ p.n. □♂ p.n. ☍♃ a.n. △♄ a.n. □♆ a.n.
☽ a.n. ✶♃ a.n. △♄ a.n.
♀ a.n. ♂♀., ♂ r. ♂♇ p.n.

The angular configurations, particularly those in the precessional figures, are typical of the event, with suitable emphasis on the Sun, Jupiter, Mars and Venus. We shall expect to find these configurations as the principal points stimulated by the directions in the monthly, weekly and daily series measuring to the event, which took place 75 days after the day of the Postnatal Revolution. This period is 2½ months and the directional days in the day-for-a-month series will therefore fall 2½ days before and after the days of the revolution, that is, on 5 and 9 August 1926, and on 4 and 8 August 1878. The Midheaven of each revolutional figure will move by the exact amount of the Sun's progress in the 2½ days and the corresponding Ascendants may then be calculated for Chicago. These are the principal monthly directions in force:

MC p.n. p. ✶♇ p.n.
MC a.n. p. ☍♇ r.
MC a.n. con. △☉ r.
Asc. p.n. con. △♅ r.
Asc. a.n. p. ✶♆ a.n.
(MC a.n. p. ♂☽ p.n. □♆ a.n.)
(Asc. p.n. p. △♇ r.)
(Asc. p.n. con. ☍☉ p.n. con. and a.n. con. ♂♃ r.)
(Asc. a.n. p. △♆ r.)

(Asc. a.n. con. in ♎ ✶ ♂, ♅ a.n.)
♀ p.n. con. ♂ ♇ p.n.
♀ p.n. p. △♄ p.n. □Asc. p.n. in ♎
♂ p.n. p. □☽ p.n.

Most of these directions either by their intrinsic nature, or because of the radical significance of the planets concerned, suitably represent the nature of the event and several represent the completion of aspects within orbs in the parent figures. It should be noted that the progressed Sun will always form the same aspects to the natal planets at the same time every year and thus the Sun opposition Jupiter in the radix will always reach completion in the second month of the year beginning on 7 August. This aspect falling due at a time when other aspects indicative of marriage were also forming produced an added stimulus to their influence.

Marriage took place eleven weeks after the day of the Solar Revolution. The weekly directional days will therefore fall 11 days before and after the revolutional days, that is, on 18 August and 27 July 1926, and on 17 August and 26 July 1878. The principal aspects in the weekly series of directions are these:

MC p.n. p. ♂☉ p.n. con. ♂☽ p.n. □♂ p.n. △♄ a.n.
MC p.n. con. ♂♀, ♂ r. ♂♀ a.n.
MC a.n. p. △♂ a.n. △♂ p.n. con.
Asc. p.n. p. in ♎ ✶ ♂ a.n.
Asc. p.n. con. in ♎ △♃ r.
Asc. a.n. con. ✶ ♅ r.
(MC p.n. p. ♂♅ r.)
(MC a.n. p. △♅ r.)
(MC a.n. con. ♂♀ a.n. p. ✶ ♇ a.n.)
(Asc. p.n. p. ☍♂ a.n. p.)
(Asc. p.n. con. ♂♃ a.n.)
(Asc. a.n. p. □☿ p.n. p. ☍♂ p.n. p. ☍♆ a.n.)
(Asc. a.n. con. in ♎ △♃ p.n.)
(☉ p.n. con. and a.n. con. △MC p.n. △♄ a.n.)
☉ p.n. p. ☍♃ p.n. con. ♂♆ p.n.
☿ p.n. con. ♂♂ a.n. con. ☍♃ p.n. p.
♀ p.n. p. ☍♃ a.n.
♀ p.n. con. ✶ ♂ p.n.
(♀ a.n. con. △ Asc. a.n.)
♂ a.n. p. ☍Asc. a.n.

This impressive list of directions, all of which are within a degree of exactitude, contains very few which do not at once appear to be in character with the event. Many of the directions formed represent the completion or reinforcement of configurations present in the revolutional figures, or else act as a stimulus to the monthly directions already formed by throwing a direct aspect to one or more factors in the monthly series.

The last part of our survey is concerned with the daily series of directions. The marriage took place on 21 October 1926, 75 days after the day of the Postnatal Solar Revolution. The directional days will therefore fall on this day and on its antenatal counterpart, 23 May 1878 and on 24 May 1926, and 20 October 1878. These are the principal directions formed:

MC p.n. p. ☌☽ r. in ♎ △♃ a.n. con.
MC p.n. con. ☌☿ a.n. con. ✶ ♂ r. and a.n. con.
MC a.n. p. ☍♂ ♅ a.n.
Asc. p.n. p. △☉ r. ☌Asc. r.
Asc. a.n. p. △♃ p.n. ✶ ♆ p.n.
Asc. a.n. con. △☉ r. ☌Asc. r.
(MC a.n. p. ☌♀ p.n. p. ☍♀ p.n. con. △♇ r.)
(MC a.n. con. ☍♄ p.n. p. ☌♇ a.n.)
(Asc. p.n. p. ✶ ☉ r.)
(Asc. a.n. p. △♆ p.n.)
☉ p.n. con. ☍☽ a.n. ✶ ♄ a.n.
☿ p.n. p. △♀ p.n.
♀ p.n. p. ☌Asc. p.n. ☍♀ p.n. con. △♇ r.
♀ a.n. con. △ MC a.n., ♅ r.
(♀, ♂ a.n. p. in ♎ △ Asc. p.n.)
♂ p.n. p. ✶ ♀ r., ♇ p.n.
♂ p.n. con. □Asc. r. △♀ r., ♇ p.n.
♃ p.n. con. ☌♆ p.n. p.
(♃ a.n. con. ☍MC a.n.)
♄ a.n. p. ☍MC r.

Once again we are confronted by an impressive list of aspects, most of which are eminently suitable to the event. A special feature of these directions is the coincidence of the postnatal progressed Ascendant with the antenatal converse Ascendant on the degree of the radical Ascendant and in trine to the radical Sun. Such an interchange as this can take place but rarely and must be expected to occur at times of highly important events.

Another point worthy of special notice is the arrival of the daily postnatal progressed Venus at the conjunction of the postnatal revolutional Ascendant at the same time as the postnatal converse Venus reaches the opposition of the Ascendant. The radical seventh house Pluto is also involved in this configuration.

The combined testimony of the main configurations here, together with the monthly and weekly directions and the impingement upon the relevant factors in the nativity constitutes a most favourable argument in support of the methods used. As a further demonstration of the way in which the nativity and the revolutional figures are linked together at this time and of the manner in which the monthly, weekly and daily directions all combine to act as stimulators to each other and to the natal and revolutional positions of the planets, a schedule is set out on page 120, indicating the interplay of some of the main factors involved:

Nativity	Solar Revolution	Monthly Series	Weekly Series	Daily Series
Asc. 14° ♐		MC a.n. con. 15° ♐		Asc. p.n. p. 15° ♐ Asc. a.n. con. 14° ♐ ♂ p.n. con. 15° ♓ (Asc. p.n. p. 14° ♊)
☉ 14° ♌	(Asc. p.n. 16° ♒)			
♃ 12° ♒		(Asc. p.n. con. 12° ♒) ☉ p.n. 12° ♌ ☉ a.n. 12° ♌	Asc. p.n. con. 11° ♎	
♅ 17° ♐	MC a.n. 17° ♐	Asc. p.n. con. 18° ♎ ☉ p.n. and a.n. p. 16° ♌	Asc. a.n. con. 17° ♒ (MC a.n. p. 17° ♌) (MC p.n. p. 16° ♐	(MC p.n. p. 16° ♒) ♀ a.n. p. 16° ♎ ♀ a.n. con. 17° ♈ ♂ a.n. p. 16° ♎ ♃ p.n. p. 17° ♒
♇ r. 19° ♊	Asc. p.n. 19° ♎	MC a.n. p. 19° ♐ ♀ p.n. p. 20° ♋ (Asc. p.n. p. 19° ♒)		(MC a.n. p. 19° ♎) ♀ p.n. p. 19° ♎ ♀ p.n. con. 19° ♈
♀ r. 15° ♋	♇ p.n. 15° ♋	♀ p.n. con. 14° ♋		♂ p.n. p. 15° ♉ p.n. con. 15° ♓
♂ r. 12° ♋		♀ a.n. con. 11° ♋	MC p.n. con. 13° ♋	MC p.n. con. 11° ♉ ☿ a.n. con. 12° ♉

10.

THE PROGRESSED SOLAR REVOLUTION

The ordinary Solar Revolution is cast for the annual return of the Sun to the place it held at birth. The importance of such a return must be self-evident in view of the dominant position of the Sun in every nativity. It is less easy to appreciate why the yearly return of the Sun to its progressed position should also yield highly significant results, yet earlier writers have been able to demonstrate that a figure based on such a return does give a very adequate indication of the events of the following year. Earlier experiments with Solar Revolutions have led me to believe that there might be some definite and easily recognizable link between secondary directions and Solar Revolutions, particularly in regard to the planets of the progressed nativity and the angles of the revolutional figures. Further investigations have suggested that it is better to consider the two systems separately rather than attempt to integrate the two to any extent.

Two points of contact between the two systems may be mentioned in passing. I have already observed, in my previous work on secondary directions, that transits, or day-for-a-day directions falling on the birthday, are especially important. These daily directions, falling due on the birthday, will also form part of the Solar Revolution for the year and it may well be that the special significance is derived from this connection. Secondly, the progressed day-for-a-day directions, measuring to the actual day of any event, are the common property of any directional system to which they are applied. The planetary positions on 21 October 1926, when Ann Harding married, form the daily directions for the yearly Solar Revolution as well as for the Secondary Progressions and, as we shall see later, for all the other types of yearly and monthly figures based on Solar and Lunar Returns to sensitive points in the nativity. Similarly, the planetary positions on 23 May

1878, the corresponding day before birth, fulfil the function of daily directions to all the converse or antenatal solar and lunar figures based on the periodical return of the luminaries to sensitive points in the nativity as well as being the converse series of daily directions of the secondary directions.

Let us now survey the Progressed and Converse Solar Revolutions, calculated in Chapter 1, for the year of Ann Harding's marriage. The precessional revolutions are calculated for 12.48 a.m. on 1 September 1926, and for 5.41 p.m. on 13 July 1878. Here are the positions of the angles and planets for these dates, together with the natal positions, set out in tabular form for easy reference. The precessional angles and lunar positions are in brackets.

	MC	Asc.	☉	☽	☿	♀	♂	♃	♄	♅	♆	♇
Nativity	27°♍	14°♐	14°♌	7°♎	10°♌	15°♋	12°♋	12°♒R	23°♉R	17°♐R	2°♋	19°♓
Progressed Solar Revolution	15°♌ (24°♐)	7°♏ (18°♓)	7°♍	25°♓ (29°♓)	21°♌	16°♌	14°♑	20°♒R	20°♏	28°♓R	25°♌	15°♋
Converse Solar Revolution	28°♏ (17°♋)	5°♒ (14°♒)	21°♋	17°♑ (12°♑)	2°♌	15°♓	13°♌	3°♒R	3°♈	27°♌	9°♑	26°♑

These are the main configurations:

MC p. ♂☉ r. ♂♀ p. □♂ p. ♂♂ con. ☍♃ r. and p. □♄ p. △♅ r.

MC con. △♅ p. □♅ con. □♆ p. ☍♇ con.

Asc. p. ☍♂ p., ♆ con. ✶ ☉ p.

Asc. con. ☍☿ con. ♂♃ con. ✶ ♄ con.

(MC p. ☍☽ p. ♂♅ r. □♇ r.)

(MC con. ♂☉ con. ☍☽ con. ♂♀, ♂ r. ♂♇ p.)

(Asc. p. □♀ con. □♅ r. □♇ r.)

(Asc. con. ✶ ☉ r. △♀ con. ✶ ♂ con. △♃ r.)

♀ con. ☍Asc. r., ♅ r. ♂♇ r.

♅ p. ☍MC r.

☽ p. ♂♇ r.

Most of these directions are completely in character with the nature of the event and the conjunction of the Midheaven of the Progressed Solar Revolution with the radical Sun, the revolutional Venus and the Converse Solar Revolutional Mars is an ideal significator of the event.

The next step is to examine the progressions formed in the monthly, weekly and daily series based on the Composite Progressed Horoscope. The wedding took place on 21 October 1926, 51 days after the day of the Progressed Solar Revolution. This is 1.7 months, so that the monthly directional days will fall 1.7 days before and after the revolutional days. In order to avoid confusion, the Progressed Solar Revolution planets and angles will be referred to as 'postnatal' (p.n.) and the Converse Revolutional planets and angles will be designated 'antenatal' (a.n.). These are the monthly directions measuring to the time of the event:

MC p.n. p. ☌☿ p.n. con. ☌♀ p.n. △♅ r.
MC p.n. con. ☌☉ r. ☌♀ p.n. con. ☌♂ a.n. p. □♂ p.n.
MC a.n. con. ☍♇ a.n.
Asc. p.n. p. ⚹ ☉ p.n. p. ☌♆ a.n.
Asc. a.n. con. ☍☿ a.n. ☌♃ a.n. ⚹ ♄ a.n.
(MC a.n. p. ☍☉ a.n. con.)
(MC a.n. con. ☌♀ r.)
(Asc. p.n. p. △☉ a.n.)
(Asc. p.n. con. △♀ r. □♀ a.n.)
(Asc. a.n. p. ⚹ ♀ p.n.)
(Asc. a.n. con. ⚹ ♂ a.n.)
☉ a.n. p. ☍♄ r.
♀ p.n. p. ⚹ ♇ r.
♀ a.n. p. ☍♅ r. ☌♇ r.
♀ a.n. con. ⚹ ♂ a.n.
♂ a.n. con. ☍♃ r.

Because of the relatively slight motion of the progressed planets and angles, many of the aspects formed by progressions were within fairly close orbs in the revolutions and some have already been noted as basic configurations. Such an emphasis upon aspects already close to completion in the radix figures will generally mark the time when important developments are due. Nearly all the above progressed aspects are immediately recognizable as being in character with the nature of the event. The special emphasis upon Solar, Venusian and Martian directions is most appropriate.

The event took place just after 7 weeks after the day of the Progressed Solar Revolution and the weekly directional days will therefore fall 7 days before and after the days of the revolutional figures. These are the principal directions in the weekly series:

MC p.n. con. ♂♀ p.n. con. ♂♂ a.n. con.
MC a.n. con. △☉ a.n.
Asc. p.n. p. △♂ r. □♂ a.n.
Asc. a.n. p. ☍☉ r. ☍♀ p.n. △♀ a.n.
(MC p.n. p. △☉ p.n. con.)
(MC p.n. con. △♀ p.n. ♂♅ r.)
(Asc. p.n. p. ♂♄ a.n.)
(Asc. a.n. p. in ♎ △♃ p.n.)
☉ a.n. p. △ MC a.n. △♅ p.n.
(♀ a.n. p. ☍MC p.n. ⚹ ♆ p.n.)
☉ p.n. p. △♂ p.n.
☉ a.n. con. ♂♀ r.
☿ p.n. con. ☍♃ r.
☿ a.n. p. ♂♀ p.n.
♀ p.n. p. ♂♆ p.n.
♂ p.n. p. □♀ p.n.
♂ a.n. p. △♅ r.

These numerous directions are nearly all in character with the nature of the event and several of them stimulate basic configurations already noted, while others stimulate sensitive points in the monthly directions.

The daily series fall due 51 days before and after the revolutional days and the following are the principal progressed aspects formed:

MC p.n. p. ♂☽ r. in ♎
MC p.n. con. △☉ p.n. p. in ♎ △♃ p.n. con. ⚹ ♅ a.n.
MC a.n. p. ☍☽ a.n. ⚹ ☿ p.n. p. □♂ p.n. con.
Asc. p.n. p. ♂Asc. r. △☉ r. ☍♀ a.n. ☍♀ p.n. con.
Asc. p.n. con. ♂MC r. △♃ a.n. p.
Asc. a.n. con. △♀ p.n. △♀ p.n. con. △♀ a.n. p. △♂ p.n. con.
　⚹ ♃ p.n. p. ♂♅ r.
(MC p.n. p. ☍☉ r., ♂ a.n. ☍☿ p.n. con. □♂ p.n.)
(MC a.n. p. ☍☉ p.n.)
(MC a.n. con. □♅ a.n.)
(Asc. p.n. con. △♆ a.n.)
(☉ p.n. con. △♄ p.n. con. △ Asc. p.n.)
♀ p.n. p. △♃ p.n. △♇ r.
♀ a.n. p. ♂MC p.n. △♅ r.
♂ p.n. p. □♀ p.n.
♂ a.n. p. □♀ a.n.

The general character of these numerous aspects is in accordance with the nature of the event and the directions involving the angles of the non-precessional figure are especially worthy of note. The daily progressed Ascendant of the postnatal figure has arrived at the position of the radical Ascendant and receives a double aspect from Venus, while the daily converse Ascendant of the same figure has arrived at the conjunction of the radical Midheaven and is aspected by Jupiter. Many of the aspects listed above stimulate either the basic configurations or the monthly or weekly directions already formed.

The interplay of some of the more important directions in the monthly, weekly and daily series with key points in the nativity and in the revolutional figures themselves is best illustrated in tabular form. The schedule given below provides a striking demonstration of the way in which a special emphasis is built up on these key points.

Nativity	Solar Revolution	Monthly Series	Weekly Series	Daily Series
☉ 14° ♌	♀ p.n. 16° ♌ MC p.n. 15° ♌ (Asc. a.n. 14° ♎) ♂ a.n. 13° ♌	MC p.n. con. 14° ♌ ♂ a.n. 14° ♌ ♀ p.n. con. 14° ♌	Asc. a.n. p. 15° ♒ ♂ a.n. p. 15° ♌	(MC p.n. p. 14° ♒) ☿ p.n. con. 15° ♌ ♀ a.n. p. 16° ♌
Asc. 14° ♐	(Asc. a.n. 14° ♎) ♀ a.n. 15° ♓			Asc. p.n. p. 14° ♐ ♀ p.n. con. 15° ♓
♅ 17° ♐ R	♀ p.n. 16° ♌	MC p.n. p. 17° ♌ ♀ a.n. p. 17° ♓	(MC p.n. con. 17° ♐) ♂ a.n. p. 17° ♌	Asc. a.n. con. 16° ♐ ♀ a.n. p. 16° ♌ ♀ a.n. con. 16° ♈ ♂ p.n. con. 17° ♈ ♃ p.n. p. 17° ♒
♇ 19° ♓	♃ p.n. 20° ♒ R	♀ p.n. p. 18° ♌	(Asc. a.n. p. 20° ♎)	♀ p.n. p. 19° ♎

The various factors in the first two cross-sections may be regarded as interchangeable as the Sun in the nativity is in close trine to the Ascendant. Radical Mars and Venus, although figuring in a few of the directions, are not strongly emphasized and it is interesting to note that the secondary progressed Venus is in 14° Leo, the secondary converse Venus is in 17° Gemini and the secondary converse Mars in 26° Gemini. These Venusian positions are stimulated by the various factors noted in cross-sections 1 and 3, while the Midheaven of the precessional postnatal figure is close to the opposition of the secondary converse Mars. From the theoretical point of view it is not surprising to find that these progressed positions are thrown into prominence, because the revolutional horoscopes are based on the position of the pro- gressed Sun and it would appear that the positions of the planets on that same directional day would also be linked sympathetically with the revolutional figures.

Having established that satisfactory indications of forthcoming events are present in the Secondary Progressed Solar Revolutional and its antenatal counterpart we can now turn our attention to another aspect of the matter. Because there is no essential dif- ference in nature between time measured backwards and time measured forwards from the time of birth, it should also be possible to obtain suitable indications from a figure cast for the Sun's annual return *before* birth to the position of the Secondary Progressed Sun *after* birth and similarly for a figure cast for the Sun's annual return *after* birth to the position of the Secondary Converse Sun (*before* birth). As before, these figures may be calculated with an allowance for precession, the appropriate increment being *deducted* from the position of the Secondary Progressed Sun as the return takes place *before* birth and the same increment being *added* to the position of the Secondary Converse Sun as the day of return is *after* birth.

These two figures may be regarded as complementary.

The Antenatal Progressed and Postnatal Converse Solar Revolutions measuring to Ann Harding's 24th birthday fall on 30 August 1878, at 10.46 p.m. GMT and on 14 July 1926, at 4.38 p.m. GMT, in the case of the non-precessional figure, and on 30 August 1878, at 5.22 p.m. GMT and on 15 July 1926 at 1.03 a.m. GMT in the case of the precessional figures. The positions of the planets and angles in these figures are set out below in tabular form for easy reference (precessional positions in brackets).

	MC	Asc.	☉	☽	☿	♀	♂	♃	♄	♅	♆	♇
Postnatal Converse Solar Revolution	3° ♋ (12° ♏)	2° ♎ (17° ♑)	21° ♋ (21° ♋)	13° ♍ (17° ♍)	17° ♌	18° ♓	19° ♈	26°♒ R	19°♏ R	29°♓ X	23° ♌	14° ♋
Antenatal Progressed Solar Revolution	25° ♏ (29° ♌)	1° ♒ (17° ♏)	7° ♍ (7° ♍)	15° ♎ (11° ♎)	25°♍ R	12° ♌	13° ♍	28° ♑	1°R ♈	0° ♍	9°R ♑	26° ♑

These are the principal configurations:

MC p.n. □♄ a.n. ♂♆ r.
MC a.n. □♃ p.n. ☍♇ a.n.
Asc. p.n. ♂☽ r. ☍♄ a.n. ☍♅ p.n. □♆ r.
Asc. a.n. ♂♃ a.n.
(MC p.n. △♀, ♂ r., ♇ p.n. ☍♆ a.n.)
(MC a.n. ♂♅ a.n.)
(Asc. p.n. ☍♀, ♂ r., ♇ p.n.)
(Asc. a.n. △♀ r., ♇ p.n. ♂♄ p.n.)
♅ p.n. ☍MC r., ☿ a.n. ✶ ♇ a.n.
☉ p.n. □♂ p.n. ♂♇ p.n.
☽ p.n. ♂♂ a.n. ✶ ♀ r., ♇ p.n.
☽ a.n. △♀ p.n. ✶ ☉ r. ✶ ♅ r. △♇ r.
♀ a.n. ♂☉ r. ☍♃ r.
♂ p.n. △♅ r. ✶ ♇ r.

The majority of these configurations are in keeping with the nature of the event and, as a group, these aspects stand up well by comparison with similar groups of aspects produced by other types of revolutional figure.

Now we may turn to the monthly directions, which fall due three and a half days before and after the revolutional days. These are the principal aspects formed:

MC p.n. con. ✶ ♅ a.n.
MC a.n. p. ✶ ♃ a.n. △♅ p.n.
MC a.n. con. △☉ p.n.
Asc. p.n. p. ♂☽ r. in ♎
Asc. a.n. con. ♂♃ a.n. △♇ a.n.
(MC p.n. p. △♀ r.)
(MC p.n. con. ☍♆ a.n.)
(Asc. p.n. p. ☍☉ p.n. □♂ p.n.)

(Asc. p.n. con. ☍midpoint ♀, ♂ r. △♂ p.n. ☍ p.n.)
(Asc. a.n. p. △☉ p.n.)
(Asc. a.n. con. △♀ p.n.)
☉ a.n. p. △♆ a.n.
(☉ p.n. con. ⚹☽ p.n.)
♀ p.n. con. ☍Asc. r. ⚹ ☉ r. △☽ a.n. in ♎
♂ p.n. p.□☉ p.n.
♂ p.n. con. ⚹ ♀ p.n. △♅ r.
♂ a.n. p. ⚹ ♀ r.

This large group of aspects are all in conformity with the nature of the event and several represent the completion of aspects already within orbs in the list of significant configurations already noted. The marriage took place 14 weeks after the day of the postnatal revolution, so that the directional days will fall 14 days on either side of the two revolutional days. These are the principal directions in the weekly series:

MC p.n. p. ☌♀ r.
MC p.n. con. ☌♇ r.
MC a.n. con. △♂ r.
Asc. p.n. p. in ♎ ⚹ ♀ r. △♃ r.
Asc. p.n. con. ☌☉, ♂ a.n. p. ⚹ ☉ p.n.
Asc. a.n. con. ☍♀ r.
(MC p.n. p. △♀ a.n. con. ☍♇ a.n.)
(MC p.n. con. ⚹ ♀ a.n. p. ☍♂ p.n. p.)
(MC a.n. p. ☌♂ a.n.)
(MC a.n. con. ☌☉ r.)
(Asc. p.n. con. ☍♆ r.)
(Asc. a.n. p. ⚹ ♃ a.n.)
♀ a.n. con. △ MC a.n. ⚹ ♇ a.n.
(♀ a.n. p. ☌MC a.n. ☌♅ a.n.)
☉ a.n. con. ☌♆ p.n.
♀ p.n. con. △ Asc. p.n. in ♎ △ Asc. a.n.
(♂ p.n. con. ☍☽ a.n. in ♎)

Once again, an extremely impressive collection of progressed aspects is forthcoming, well in accordance with the nature of the event. Several of these directions either aspect sensitive points in the radical figures, the nativity or in the monthly series of directions already listed above.

The daily directions fall due 99 days before and after the

revolutional days, on 6 April and 21 October 1926, and on 23 May and 7 December 1878. The principal directions formed are as follows:

MC p.n. con. ✶ ♃ a.n. ☌ ♅ p.n.
MC a.n. con. △ ♂ p.n. ☍ ♃ p.n. con.
Asc. p.n. p. △ ☿ p.n. ☍ ♀ p.n. ☌ ♀ a.n. p. △ ♀ a.n. con.
 ✶ ♃ p.n. p. ☌ ♅ r.
Asc. p.n. con. △ ♂ a.n. p.
Asc. a.n. con. ☍ ☿ a.n. con. △ ♂ r. △ ♂ a.n. con.
(MC p.n. p. △ ♀ p.n. △ ♀ p.n. p. in ♎ ✶ ♀ a.n. con. ✶ ♂ p.n.
 ☌ ♃ p.n. p. ✶ ♅ r. △ ♇ r.)
(MC a.n. p. ☍ ♃ a.n. con.)
(MC a.n. p. □ ⊙ a.n. ✶ ♃ a.n. con.)
(MC a.n. con. ☍ ♄ p.n. con. ☌ ♇ a.n. p.)
(Asc. p.n. p. ✶ ⊙ r. ☍ ⊙ a.n. p., ♀ a.n. p.)
(Asc. p.n. con. ✶ ♅ a.n.)
(Asc. a.n. p. ☌ ⊙ a.n. p., ♀ a.n. p.)
(Asc. a.n. con. ☌ ♅ a.n.)
⊙ a.n. con. △ Asc. p.n. △ Asc. a.n.
♄ a.n. p., ♅ a.n. p. ☍ MC r. ✶ ♇ a.n.
(☿ p.n. p. ☌ Asc. a.n.)
(♂ a.n. p. ☌ Asc. a.n.)
⊙ p.n. p. in ♎ △ ♃ p.n. □ ♃ a.n.
⊙ p.n. con. ☍ ☽ a.n. in ♎ □ ♀ r., ♇ p.n. p.
♀ p.n. con. ☍ ♅ a.n.
♂ p.n. p. ✶ ♀ r.
(♂ p.n. con. △ ☽ a.n. in ♎)
♆ a.n. p. △ ⊙ a.n.

These numerous aspects are nearly all in conformity with the nature of the event and several of them fall on sensitive points of the main configurations in the basic figures already noted or in the monthly or weekly series of directions.

There is little doubt, on the basis of the above evidence, that these are valid figures which produce good results when directed. Such testimony shows that it is hardly justifiable to draw a distinction between postnatal and antenatal positions in terms of strength and general significance, as some astrologers have sought to do in the past. Rather does it suggest that we should attempt to gain a better understanding of the real nature and meaning of time in order to obtain the maximum benefit from the great variety of astrological methods available. It will also be evident from the foregoing study that the position of the progressed Sun is a sensitive point in space, and that this very sensitivity may produce a link between postnatal and antenatal figures cast for a return to the same solar longitude even allowing for the fact that the two revolutional days will not fall due exactly the same number of days before and after birth.

11.

THE ANNUAL NEW MOON

The moment of the annual return of the Sun to the exact position it held in the nativity forms the basis for the calculation of the yearly Solar Revolution. Similarly, the moment of the Sun's annual return to the exact position of the other bodies in the nativity should, it seems to me, provide a valid basis for the calculation of other yearly figures that will have a bearing upon the events and experiences of the period. Because the Sun and Moon are always regarded in astrology as being complementary to each other, it is probable that the horoscope cast for the exact time of the Sun's return each year to the place of the radical Moon will produce a particularly significant figure in relation to the trend of events during the following twelve months. It will be remembered that in mundane astrology the monthly conjunction of the luminaries is often used as a basis for prognostication. The annual conjunction of the Sun with the Moon's place in the nativity may be regarded as a kind of personal 'lunation' and it seems logical to call such a figure an 'Annual New Moon'.

Only in a small minority of cases will the radical Moon be found so close to the radical Sun as to render almost identical the period of time covered by the Annual New Moon horoscope and the Solar Revolution. The existence of these two types of horoscope will normally enable the astrologer to take a 'second bearing' on the main influences in force over a given period and, when they are spaced reasonably far apart in time, to assess more easily the period of the year when a climax is likely to be reached in any one field of activity.

As in the case of Solar Revolutions, the time of the Sun's annual return may be computed for the Sun's conjunction with the radical position of the Moon, or with an allowance for the deviation from this position caused by the precessional movement of the equinoctial point. When making such an allowance for precession, care must be taken to calculate the native's exact age at the time of the Sun's return to the radical Moon, so that the precessional movement appropriate for the fractional part of the year may be added to the increment for the number of whole years that the native is old.

In just the same way that it is valid to calculate postnatal and antenatal Solar Revolutions it is also permissible to erect postnatal and antenatal Annual New Moon horoscopes. There is, however, one important difference. Except in rare cases, when the Moon is within a degree of the Sun at birth, the Annual New Moon will not fall on the same day as the Solar Revolution. This means, in effect, that the postnatal Annual New Moon will not measure to exactly the same age as the antenatal Annual New Moon. For instance, if the postnatal Annual New Moon falls 31 days after the native's birthday, we shall find when we count backwards in time that the antenatal Annual New Moon will fall 31 days before we reach the birthday. This exact correspondence in the number of days will not always occur, owing to the elliptical orbit of the earth around the Sun, which causes the Sun's apparent motion to vary in speed at different times of the year. It has already been demonstrated that the postnatal and antenatal Solar Revolutions are complementary figures that should be considered in conjunction with each other. The problem now arises as to whether the two Annual New Moon figures, falling at different intervals of time measured from the birthday, should be regarded as complementary or whether each figure should be considered in relation to the planetary positions on the two corresponding days before and after birth that measure exactly to the age of the native at the time of the two Annual New Moons. There must obviously be a sympathetic link between the day before birth corresponding to the day of the postnatal Annual New Moon and between the day after birth corresponding to the antenatal Annual New Moon.

This problem of differences in timing between the postnatal and antenatal 'halves' of the various types of Solar and Lunar Revolutions described in this volume led me to experiment with a synthetic figure constructed on the basis of the planetary positions on the day before birth exactly corresponding to the revolutional day after birth and similarly with the day after birth corresponding to the revolutional day before birth. By calculating the difference between the longitude of the Midheaven of the

Annual New Moon figure and the longitude of the natal Midheaven and measuring off an equal number of degrees and
minutes on the opposite side of the radical Midheaven it is
possible to arrive artificially at a Midheaven degree for the synthetic figure. The appropriate Ascendant can then be extracted
from the tables of houses used for the determination of the
Ascendant of the revolutional figure. Each postnatal Annual New
Moon will therefore have its antenatal Equivalent, each antenatal
Annual New Moon its postnatal Equivalent. My experience has
led me to regard the postnatal and antenatal Equivalents as the
valid complement and counterpart of the revolutional figure with
which it is equated. Readers will be able to judge the efficacy of
these figures for themselves from the various examples given in
this and subsequent chapters.

Before giving an example of the calculation of the Annual New
Moon figure it is necessary to draw attention to the fact that the
position of the Moon at birth requires to be calculated with rather
more accuracy than that usually allowed by the data given in the
Ephemeris unless on the day in question there is very little
variation in the speed of the Moon. Owing to a number of variable
factors the Moon's speed is never constant but is alternately
subject to acceleration or deceleration over a period of about 14
days. Because of this it is sometimes not possible to achieve
sufficient accuracy of calculation if only the average daily speed
of the Moon is used. A good deal will depend on the time of day
at which birth took place, for if this occurs within an hour or two
of noon or midnight it may not be necessary to take account of
lunar acceleration or deceleration. Much will depend, however,
upon the actual amount of lunar acceleration or deceleration
during the day. In extreme cases the daily variation of the Moon's
speed may be as much as 29', or some 14' in twelve hours. Under
such circumstances, if birth occurred near 6.00 a.m. or 6.00 p.m.
there would be a variation of some 7' between the Moon's speed
at that time and the average speed calculated for noon or
midnight. The Sun travels about 60' per day so that a difference
of 7' between the Moon's speed at that time in terms of solar
motion would represent nearly three hours. Such a discrepancy
would destroy much of the value of a figure which derives its major
significance from the condition of those planets that are angular
in it. Such a discrepancy in terms of lunar motion, which we shall
have to consider later on in the case of certain lunar revolutions,
would entail a difference of some 14 minutes or more in time and

a variation of 3 to 4 degrees on the Midheaven.

In order to estimate the true speed of the Moon at any moment it is necessary to make a number of simple calculations, each of which is designed to give a fairly close approximation of the Moon's hourly speed at a given point in time. By calculating the number of degrees, minutes and seconds of arc between the noon and midnight positions of the Moon on the same day we can arrive at a theoretical figure for the speed of the Moon at 6.00 p.m. (in terms of 12 hours' motion). By calculating the amount of arc between the Moon's position at midnight (the later midnight of the previous calculation) and the following noon we can find the theoretical speed of the Moon at 6.00 a.m. on the following day. We may regard the average of these two speeds (for 6.00 p.m. and 6.00 a.m.) as the theoretical speed at midnight. If it is required to find the speed of the Moon at some intermediate point in time, we can halve the sum of the theoretical speeds obtained for 6.00 p.m. and midnight to find the theoretical speed at 9.00 p.m. By halving the sum of the theoretical speeds at 6.00 p.m. and 9.00 p.m. we shall arrive at the theoretical speed for 7.30 p.m. To adjust the theoretical average speed over shorter periods of time it is often sufficient to calculate the amount of acceleration or deceleration over an hour and to make a proportional adjustment to the theoretical speed already calculated for the time nearest to that actually required.

The exact calculation of the lunar position for the years prior to 1898 is rendered a little more complicated by the fact that Raphael's Ephemerides for these years do not give the Moon's position to seconds of longitude, neither do they record the Moon's position at midnight. In order to compensate to some extent for this lack of precise information it is necessary to apply the same general principle as before, calculating the average lunar speed for periods in advance of and subsequent to the period during which the return takes place, extending the operation to include the twenty-four hours on either side of the day of the return or the nativity.

Let us suppose that we want to find the exact position of the Moon in our example horoscope, the nativity of Ann Harding, born 7 August 1902, at 9.09.35 p.m. GMT. An inspection of the Ephemeris shows that at noon GMT on this date the Moon's position was 1°31'23" ♎, and at midnight 8°03'20" ♎. Our problem now is to find to what extent the Moon's motion varied during this twelve-hour period. In order to do this it is first necessary to calculate the speed of the Moon during the twelve-hour period in which the birth actually took place and also during the twelve hours immediately preceding and immediately following that period. By calculating the Moon's average speed between noon and the preceding midnight and for the period between noon and the succeeding midnight and finding the mean of the two averages, a theoretical lunar speed for noon may be found. A similar operation may then be conducted to determine the theoretical speed at midnight and then, by a process of adjustment, the theoretical mean speed for any time of day may be calculated with sufficient accuracy for all practical purposes. In the special case we are considering, the necessary calculations are made as follows:

Position of Moon at midday, 7 August 1902	$1°31'23''$ ♎
Position of Moon at midnight, 6/7 August 1902	$24°52'55''$ ♍
Moon's progress in twelve hours (A)	$6°38'28''$
Position of Moon at midnight, 7/8 August 1902	$8°03'20''$ ♎
Position of Moon at noon, 7 August 1902	$1°31'23''$ ♎
Moon's progress in twelve hours (B)	$6°31'57''$
Position of Moon at noon, 8 August 1902	$14°29'05''$ ♎
Position of Moon at midnight, 7/8 August 1902	$8°03'20''$ ♎
Moon's progress in twelve hours (C)	$6°25'45''$

Then $\dfrac{A + B}{2}$ = Theoretical mean motion at noon, 7 August 1902

$$6°38'28'' \text{ (A)}$$
$$6°31'57'' \text{ (B)}$$
$$13°10'25''$$
$$\div 2 \qquad 6°35'12'' \text{ (D)}$$

And $\dfrac{B + C}{2}$ = Theoretical mean motion at midnight, 7/8 August 1902

$$6°31'57'' \text{ (B)}$$
$$6°25'45'' \text{ (C)}$$
$$12°57'42''$$
$$\div 2 \qquad 6°28'51'' \text{ (E)}$$

Also $\dfrac{D + E}{2}$ = Theoretical Mean motion at 6.00 p.m., 7 August 1902

$$6°35'12'' \text{ (D)}$$
$$6°28'51'' \text{ (E)}$$
$$13°04'03''$$
$$\div 2 \qquad 6°32'01'' \text{ (F)}$$

And $\underline{E + F}$ = Theoretical mean motion at
  2   9.00 p.m., 7 August 1902   6°28′51″ (E)
                                                    6°32′01″ (F)
                                                   13°00′52″
                                        ÷ 2   6°30′26″(G)

In order to adjust the theoretical mean speed at 9.00 p.m. to the speed at the required time, approximately ten minutes later, proceed as follows:

From the Moon's theoretical speed at 9.00 p.m.	6°30′26″(G)
Subtract the Moon's theoretical speed at midnight	6°28′51″ (E)
Deceleration in three hours	0°01′35″
Deceleration in ten minutes (divide by 18)	0°00′05″
From the Moon's theoretical speed at 9.00 p.m.	6°30′26″(G)
Subtract deceleration in 10 minutes	0°00′05″
Moon's theoretical speed at 9.10 p.m.	6°30′21″

On the basis of this theoretical speed (in terms of twelve hours' motion) we can now calculate the Moon's position at 9.09.35 p.m. GMT in the usual way:

Moon's motion in 6 hours (divide 12 hours' motion by 2)	3°15′10″
Moon's motion in 3 hours (divide 12 hours' motion by 4)	1°37′55″
Motion in 9 hours	4°52′45″
Motion in 9 minutes (divide 9 hours' motion by 60)	0°04′53″
Motion in 30 seconds (divide 9 minutes' motion by 18)	0°00′16″
Motion in 5 seconds (divide 30 seconds' motion by 6)	0°00′03″
Motion in 9 hours 9 minutes 35 seconds	4°57′57″
Add position of Moon at noon	1°31′23″ ♎
Moon's position at birth	6°29′20″ ♎

Using this position as our basis of reference we may now calculate the Solar Returns to this point in the same way as we should calculate a normal Solar Return to its own place. The Ephemeris states that the Sun passes over this degree on 30 September 1926. We may now proceed as follows:

From the position of the Sun at noon,
   30 September 1926   6°33'46" ♎︎
Subtract the position of the radical Moon   6°29'21" ♎︎

   Difference   0°04'25"

Sun's daily motion on 30 September 1926   0°58'59"
Divide by 12 (motion in 2 hours)   0°04'55"
Subtract 12 minutes motion   0°00'30"

1 hour 48 minutes motion   0°04'25"

Subtract 1 hour 48 minutes from noon = time of Annual New
Moon ....10.12 a.m. GMT

Calculate equivalent Sidereal Time at Chicago:
From Sidereal Time at noon, 30 September 1926   12 33 54
Subtract   1 48 00
Also subtract time allowance for difference in
   longitude between Greenwich and Chicago   5 50 36
Also subtract allowance for conversion to Sidereal
   Time   0 01 16

   Sidereal Time at Chicago   4 54 02

This Sidereal Time gives a Midheaven of 14° Gemini and an
Ascendant at Chicago of 17° Virgo.

In order to calculate the antenatal equivalent of this Annual New
Moon figure, the following procedure is recommended:

Day of Annual New Moon   30 September 1926
Number of years and days after birth   24 years (6 leap) 54 days
Equivalent number of days and years before
   birth   24 years (5 leap) 55 days
Day of antenatal equivalent   13 June 1878

Calculate the longitudinal difference between the
   Midheaven at birth   27° ♍︎
And the Midheaven of the Annual New Moon   14° ♓︎

                                       103°

Add 103° to longitude of radical Midheaven   10° ♑︎
The corresponding Ascendant at Chicago is   18° ♈︎

To find the GMT of the Antenatal Equivalent
Subtract from the Sidereal Time at noon,
   13 June 1878   5 24 10
Sidereal Time of Antenatal Equivalent   18 40 00

                                     10 44 10
Subtract correction for GMT   00 01 48
Number of hours before noon, local time   10 42 22

Subtract time correction for difference in longitude between Chicago and Greenwich	5 50 36
Amount of time before noon, GMT	4 51 56
GMT of Antenatal Equivalent	7.08.14 a.m.

The antenatal Annual New Moon which falls on 29 September 1878, at 7.02 p.m. GMT may be calculated in the same manner. The corresponding postnatal equivalent falls on 14 June 1926, at 10.17 p.m. GMT.

In order to calculate the precessional New Moon figures it is necessary to take into account the native's exact age at the time the Sun returns to the radical lunar position. On 30 September 1926, Ann Harding was 24 years and 54 days old. The increment for 24 years is given in Appendix 1 as 20′06″ and the increment for 54 days may be calculated on the basis of twice the increment for 27 days = 4″ × 2 = 8″. The total increment to be added to the Moon's radical position (6°29′21″ ♎) will therefore be 20′14″, giving an adjusted lunar position of 6°49′35″ ♎. The horoscope for the Sun's arrival at this exact point can then be calculated in the usual way. This figure is cast for 6.26 p.m. GMT. The complementary antenatal Equivalent can then be calculated by the same procedure as before, and falls due at 10.51 p.m. GMT on 12 June 1878.

When calculating the antenatal precessional Annual New Moon, remember that it is necessary to recalculate the native's age in terms of the date after birth represented by the day of the antenatal New Moon, in other words, the day of the postnatal equivalent, which falls on 14 June 1926, 54 days short of Ann Harding's 24th birthday. It is therefore necessary to subtract the precessional increment for 54 days, already noted from the increment for 24 years. The adjusted increment should then be subtracted from the position of the radical Moon to give the exact point of return for the solar figure. This is 6°09′23″ ♎. The Sun returns to this point on 29 September 1878, at 10.55 a.m. GMT. The postnatal equivalent falls on 15 June 1926, at 6.24 a.m. GMT.

Our next task is to satisfy ourselves that the indications contained in these horoscopes are appropriate to the event of marriage. The event configurations given in Chapter 5 will be found to apply equally well to this type of figure. Each New Moon horoscope should be considered in conjunction with its complementary equivalent figure and the two figures should also be related to the nativity. For convenience of reference, the positions of the planets and angles in the postnatal New Moon, its corresponding antenatal equivalent and the nativity are set out below in tabular form. The positions of the angles and the luminaries in the precessional figures are in brackets.

	MC	Asc.	☉	☽	☿	♀	♂	♃	♄	♅	♆	♇
Nativity	27° ♍	14° ♐	14° ♌	6° ♎	10° ♌	15° ♋	12° ♋	12°$_R$ ♒	23°$_R$ ♑	17° ♐	2° ♋	19° ♓
Postnatal Annual New Moon	14° ♓ (18° ♎)	17° ♍ (25° ♐)	6° ♎ (6° ♎)	25° ♋ (29° ♋)	14° ♎	23° ♍	19°$_R$ ♓	17°$_R$ ♒	23° ♏	27°$_R$ ♓	26° ♌	16° ♋
Antenatal Equivalent	9° ♉ (5° ♍)	7° ♈ (22° ♏)	22° ♓ (21° ♓)	0° ♐ (25° ♏)	1° ♓	10° ♑	24° ♋	6° ♎	2° ♈	26° ♌	9° ♑	25° ♑

The principal configurations are as follows:

MC p.n. ☍ Asc. r. ☍ ♅ r.
MC a.n. ☍ ♂ r. △ ♀., ♆ a.n.
Asc. p.n. □ ♅ r. □ ♇ r.
(Asc. a.n. ⚹ ♀ p.n. ☌ ♄ p.n.)
♅ p.n. ☌ MC r.
☉ p.n. in ♎ △ ♃ a.n.
☉ a.n. △ ♃ p.n. ☌ ♇ r.
☽ p.n. ⚹ ♀ p.n. ☌ ♂ a.n. ☍ ♄ r. △ ♄ p.n. △ ♅ p.n.

The main trend of these directions is to accentuate the emphasis on Venus, Mars, Uranus and Pluto, while the luminaries are suitably configured with the benefics.

The next step is to scrutinize the directions in force at the time of marriage, which took place on 21 October 1926, 21 days after the day of the postnatal Annual New Moon. As less than a month elapsed between the day of the New Moon and the day of the event, there is no point in examining the day-for-a-month series of directions, as only aspects within about a degree and a half of exactitude in the radix could form directions in the time. The day-for-a-week directions will fall due three days before and after the day of the New Moon figures. The principal aspects are these (those involving the angles of the precessional figures are in brackets):

♀ p.n. p. ☌ MC r. ☍ ♅ p.n.
MC p.n. p. △ ♃ p.n. ☍ ♅ r.

MC a.n. p. ☍ ♂ r.
Asc. p.n. p. ☌♀ p.n. con. △♂ p.n.
Asc. p.n. con. △♀ a.n. p.
Asc. a.n. con. ✶ ♃ r.
(MC p.n. con. in ♎ □♀ r.)
(Asc. p.n. con. ☍☉ a.n.)
(Asc. a.n. p. ✶ ♀ p.n. △♂ a.n. ☌♄ p.n.)
(☉ a.n. p. ☍Asc. p.n.)
☉ a.n. con. ☌♇ r.
♀ a.n. con. □♃ a.n.

These numerous directions are mostly typical of the event and in several cases represent the completion of aspects within fairly close orbs in the radical New Moon figures. Our final operation is to compile a list of the day-for-a-day directions measuring to the event. These directions are represented by the aspects formed by the planetary positions 21 days before and after the days of the two New Moon figures. As usual, the Midheaven of each figure is moved backward or forward according to the amount of arc travelled by the Sun between the directional day and the actual day on which the return or its equivalent took place and the appropriate Oblique Ascendant extracted from the Chicago tables of houses. Here are the daily progressions (precessional positions in brackets):

MC p.n. con. ✶ ☽ p.n. ✶ ♂ a.n. ☌♇ a.n.
MC a.n. con. △♀ a.n. con. ☍♇ r.
Asc. a.n. p. ☌♂ p.n.
Asc. a.n. con. ✶ ♀, ♆ a.n.
(♀ p.n. p. ☌MC p.n. △♇ r.)
(MC p.n. p. ☍♀, ♆ a.n.)
(MC p.n. con. ☍♅ p.n.)
(Asc. p.n. p. ☌ midpoint ♀, ♂ r.)
(Asc. a.n. p. ✶ ☉ p.n., ☽ r. in ♎ ✶ ♃ a.n. △♂ a.n. p.)
♀ a.n. con. ☌Asc. a.n. △♅ r.
☉ p.n. con. △♂ p.n. con.
☉☿ a.n. p. ☌♂ r.
☉ p.n. con. ✶ ☉ p.n. in ♎ ☌♅ a.n. p.
♀ a.n. p. △♃ a.n. p.
♂ p.n. p. ✶ ♇ p.n.

Of this impressive list of fifteen directions it cannot be said that any do not conform to the nature of the event and together they form an overwhelming testimony to the usefulness of the New Moon figure as a basis for prognostication, and convincing evidence of the validity of the day-for-a-day measure and its method of application in these horoscopes. In addition several of the daily progressions fall on significant planets in the weekly series of progressions, acting as stimulators.

So far, we have studied only half the picture, for we have not yet taken into consideration the antenatal Yearly New Moon and its counterpart, the postnatal Equivalent. For easy reference the positions of the planets and angles in these two figures are set out below in tabular form (precessional positions in brackets).

	MC	Asc.	☉	☽	☿	♀	♂	♃	♄	♅	♆	♇
Antenatal Yearly New Moon	27° ♎ (24° ♓)	2° ♑ (25° ♍)	6° ♎ (6° ♎)	21° ♏ (16° ♏)	19° ♍	19° ♍	2° ♎	27° ♑	29°ᵣ ♓	29°ᵣ ♓	2° ♍	9°ᵣ ♑	26° ♑
Postnatal Equivalent	26° ♌ (29° ♐)	15° ♏ (29° ♓)	23° ♓ (23° ♓)	14° ♌ (18° ♌)	5° ♋	3° ♑	30° ♓	27° ♒	20° ♏	29° ♓	22° ♌	13° ♋

These are the principal configurations:

    MC r. ☍ ♂ p.n. △ ♃ a.n. ☍ ♄ a.n. ☍ ♅ p.n.
    MC p.n. ⚹ ☉ p.n. ☍ ♃ p.n. ☌ ♆ p.n.
    MC a.n. □ ♃ a.n. □ ♃ p.n.
    (MC a.n. ☌ ☉ p.n. △ ♃ p.n.)
    (Asc. p.n. ☌ ♂ p.n. ☌ ♄ a.n. ☌ ♅ p.n.)
    (Asc. a.n. ☌ ♀ a.n. △ ♃ a.n. △ ♇ a.n.)
    (☉ p.n. ⚹ ☽ p.n. ☌ ♂ a.n. in ♎)
    ☽ p.n. ☌ ☉ r. □ ♀ p.n.
    ☽ a.n. ⚹ ♀ a.n. ☍ ♇ a.n.
    ♀ p.n. ⚹ ♀, ♂ r., ♇ p.n.
    ♅ a.n. ⚹ ♆ r.

Apart from the blending of the antenatal Saturn with the postnatal Mars–Uranus conjunction, most of the configurations are fairly typical of the event and are slightly more numerous than those furnished by the postnatal New Moon and its antenatal equivalent. The next step is to examine the progressions based on these figures. Marriage occurred 129 days after the day of the postnatal Equivalent. This represents a period of just over four months and the day-for-a-month directions will therefore fall four

days before and after the days of the New Moon figures. The
principal directions formed are these:

MC p.n. con. ✶ ☉ p.n. ♂ ♆ p.n.
MC a.n. con. in ♎ △☉ p.n.
Asc. p.n. p. ☍ ♀ p.n. p.
Asc. p.n. con. △ ♂ r.
Asc. a.n. con. ☐ ♂, ♅ p.n. ☐ ♄ a.n.
(♀ a.n. p. ☐MC a.n.)
(Asc. p.n. p. ☍ ☉ a.n., ☽ r. in ♎)
(Asc. a.n. p. ☍ ♄ a.n. p.)
☉ p.n. p. ✶ MC p.n. △ ♃ p.n.
☉ p.n. con. ♂ ♇ r.
☉ a.n. con. ♂ ♂ a.n. in ♎
♀ p.n. con. ♂ ♆ a.n.
♀ a.n. con. ✶ ♇ p.n.
♂ p.n. p. ☍ ♂ a.n. in ♎
♂ p.n. con. ☍MC r.
♂ a.n. con. ☍ ♂, ♅ p.n. ☍ ♄ a.n. con.

Once again, apart from the rather strenuous intermingling of
Saturn with the Mars–Uranus conjunction, the remaining
aspects are quite typical of the event and many represent the
completion of configurations already noted as being within orbs
in the combined New Moon figures. We may now take our
investigations a stage further and consider the weekly series of
directions. Marriage took place some eighteen weeks after the day
of the postnatal equivalent and thus the directional days will fall
eighteen days before and after the days of the New Moon figures.
The day-for-a-week directions are these:

MC p.n. p. △ ♀ p.n.
MC a.n. p. △ ♀ r.
Asc. a.n. p. △☉ a.n. con. △ ☿, ♀ a.n.
Asc. a.n. con. △ ♂ p.n. con. ♂ ♅ r.
♀ a.n. con. ♂MC p.n. ☍ ♃ p.n.
(MC a.n. p. ♂ ♂ r.)
(☉ a.n. p. in ♎ △MC a.n.)
(Asc. p. con. ♂ ♃ p.n.)
(Asc. a.n. p. ♂ ♀ a.n. p. in ♎ ☍ ♂ p.n. p. △ ♃ r.)
♀ p.n. con. ✶ ☉ p.n. △ ♆ p.n.
♂ a.n. p. in ♎ ✶ ☉ r.

These directions all suitably reflect the nature of the event and several of them act as stimulators to the monthly directions already in force, through the same planetary position or angular degree being involved.

The picture is finally completed by the daily directions, which fall 129 days before and after the days of the New Moon figures. By a strange coincidence the directional day turns out to be the same day of the year, whether measured backwards from the day of the postnatal equivalent or forwards from the day of the Annual New Moon. In the first case the required day is 5 February 1926; in the second, 5 February 1879. Such a coincidence in timing may well be the explanation for the fact that important events in the lives of some people have a tendency to happen on a particular day of the year, especially as it often seems that such recurrences are not explicable in terms of any planetary positions in the nativity. In the present example the daily directions formed are listed below:

MC p.n. con. ☍♀ p.n. p. in ♎ ⚹ ♀ p.n. con. ⚹ ♇ r.
Asc. p.n. p. ⚹ ☉ a.n. con. ☍♂ a.n. in ♎
Asc. a.n. p. ☍☉, ♃ a.n. p. ☍☉ p.n. con.
☉ p.n. p. ☌MC a.n. in ♎(MC p.n. con. ⚹ ☉ p.n. ☌♆ p.n.)
(Asc. p.n. p. ☌☉ r. □♀ p.n.)
(Asc. p.n. con. △♂ r.)
♀ a.n. con. △♅ r.
♂ p.n. p. ☍Asc. p.n. △♀ r.
♂ p.n. con. □ MC r. ⚹ ☉ p.n. p. ⚹ ♃ p.n.
♃ p.n. con. △☉ a.n., ☽ r. in ♎
♅ p.n. con. □☉ p.n.

The general trend of these directions is eminently well suited to the event and the sum total of the monthly, weekly and daily directions built up from the antenatal New Moon and its postnatal Equivalent is equally as impressive as the various groups of directions derived from the postnatal Annual New Moon and its complementary horoscope.

Whether the precessional figures are to be preferred to the horoscopes cast without such an adjustment must be a matter for the individual judgement of the reader. In my opinion, no marked superiority is shown by either series. Sometimes one system appears to register slightly better results, sometimes the other.

12.
THE ANNUAL
SUNRISE HOROSCOPE

Astrologers have always regarded the Sun, Moon and Ascendant as the three key factors in the horoscope. It has already been demonstrated in previous chapters that the Sun's yearly return to its own position and to the position of the radical Moon can be used to construct a figure from which prognostications for the ensuing twelve months can be made. Because of the obvious effectiveness of these two classes of solar return, it seemed logical to me to experiment with yet another class of solar return, that of the Sun to the Ascendant of the birth figure.

The importance of the Sun–Ascendant conjunction has always been recognized by astrologers, some of whom prefer to set up a Sunrise Horoscope when the time of birth is not known. Occultists have always regarded the time of sunrise and sunset as possessing a special potency, so that a horoscope cast for the exact moment of the Sun's return each year to the position of the Ascendant at birth must symbolize in a very special way the spiritual and environmental climate for the next twelve months.

The Annual Sunrise Horoscope may, as in the case of the types of Solar Revolution already discussed, be calculated with or without an allowance for precession, and also for the annual return of the Sun each year *before* birth to the Ascending degree. Except in rare instances, the revolutional day before birth will not coincide with the revolutional day after birth, so that, as in the case of the Annual New Moon, it will be necessary to calculate an antenatal equivalent for each postnatal return, and a postnatal equivalent for each antenatal return. The event configurations in these figures may be assessed in the usual way and the timing of events judged by applying the usual monthly, weekly and daily progressions to each figure.

Let us now examine the Annual Sunrise Horoscope for the year in which Ann Harding married. The position of the radical Ascendant, as determined by the position of the Moon at Epoch (which occurred on 10 December 1901) is 14°40′56″ Sagittarius. The wedding took place on 21 October 1926. The previous return of the Sun to the degree held by the Ascendant in the nativity therefore took place on 7 December 1925. The moment of the Sun's return to this position should be calculated in the usual way and the corresponding antenatal equivalent may be constructed, also in accordance with normal practice. The postnatal Annual Sunrise horoscope falls due at 7.22 a.m. GMT, and its antenatal equivalent, occurring on 6 April 1879, is cast for 9.55 a.m. The precessional postnatal Annual Sunrise horoscope falls due at 1.32 p.m. GMT on the same day as the non-precessional figure, and the corresponding antenatal equivalent also falls on the same day before birth as the non-precessional figure but at 2.14 a.m. GMT. For easy reference the positions of the planets and angles in these figures are set out below in tabular form, the precessional places being in brackets.

	MC	Asc.	☉	☽	☿	♀	♂	♃	♄	♅	♆	♇
Nativity	27° ♍	14° ♐	14° ♌	6° ♎	10° ♌	15° ♋	12° ♋	12°♒ R	23°♉ R	17°♐ R	2° ♋	19° ♓
Postnatal Sunrise Horoscope	7° ♋ (6° ♏)	6° ♎ (10° ♉)	14° ♐ (15° ♐)	1° ♍ (5° ♍)	24°♉ R	1° ♒	16° ♏	23° ♉	20° ♏	21° ♓	24°♌ R	14° ♋
Antenatal Equivalent	16° ♐ (17° ♌)	4° ♓ (9° ♏)	16° ♈ (16° ♈)	9° ♎ (3° ♎)	1° ♑	15° ♑	13° ♒	2° ♓	7° ♈	0° ♍	8° ♑	25° ♑

Here are the principal configurations:

MC a.n. ☍ ☉ p.n. ⚹ ♂ a.n. ♂ ♅ r. ☍ ♇ r.
Asc. p.n. ♂ ☽ r. and a.n. in ♎ ☍ ♄ a.n.
Asc. a.n. ☍ ☽ p.n. ♂ ♃ a.n. ☍ ♅ a.n. △ ♆ r.
(MC p.n. ☍ midpoint ☿, ♀ a.n. ☍ ♆ a.n.)
(MC a.n. ♂ ☉ r. □ ♀ a.n. ☍ ♂ a.n. □ ♂ p.n. ☍ ♃ r.)
(Asc. p.n. ☍ ♀, ♂ r. ☍ ♇ p.n.)
(Asc. a.n. ☍ midpoint ☿, ♀ a.n. ☍ ♆ a.n.)
☉ a.n. ☍ ☽ a.n. ⚹ ♂ a.n. ⚹ ♃ r. △ ♅ r. ⚹ ♇ r.
(☽ a.n. △ ♀ p.n.)
♀ a.n. ⚹ ♂ r.
♂ p.n. △ ♀ r. △ ♇ p.n.
♃ p.n. ♂ ♄ r. ⚹ ♄ p.n. ⚹ ♅ p.n. △ ♇ a.n.

We shall now examine the directions measuring to the time of marriage, which occurred 318 days after the day of the Annual Sunrise figure. This period represents between ten and eleven months and so the monthly directions will fall due between ten and eleven days before and after the day of the Sunrise horoscope and its equivalent. The principal aspects formed in the monthly series are these:

MC a.n. con. ✶ ☽ r. ✶ ♃ a.n. con. △ ♄ a.n.
Asc. p.n. p. ☍ ☉ a.n.
Asc. p.n. con. △ ♀ a.n. p.
Asc. a.n. p. □ ☿ p.n. ✶ ♃ p.n. ✶ ♄ r.
Asc. a.n. con. ✶ ☉ a.n. ✶ ♅ r.
☉ a.n. con. ☍ Asc. p.n. and ☽ r. in ≏ ✶ ♂ a.n. con. ♂ ♄ a.n.
♃ a.n. p. ♂ Asc. a.n.
(MC p.n. con. in ≏ ☍ ☉ a.n. p.)
(MC a.n. con. ✶ ☽ r. ☍ ♃ a.n. con. △ ♄ a.n.)
(Asc. p.n. p. ♂ ♀ p.n. con. ✶ ♂ p.n. p. ♂ ♃ p.n. con.
  ✶ ♅ p.n.)
(Asc. p.n. con. △ ☿ a.n. △ ♅ a.n.)
(Asc. a.n. p. ♂ ♂ p.n. ☍ ♀ a.n.)
(Asc. a.n. con. ☍ ☿ a.n. □ ♀ p.n. ✶ ♅ a.n.)
(♂ p.n. con. ♂ Asc. a.n.)
☉ p.n. p. △ ♆ p.n.
☉ p.n. con. □ Asc. a.n.
(☉ a.n. con. ✶ ☽ a.n. in ≏)
♀ a.n. con. ✶ ♃ a.n.

None of the above aspects is more than a degree short of completion and the great majority are immediately recognizable as being consistent with the event of marriage. Several of the directions mark the completion of aspects already within orbs that have been noted under the basic configurations already listed. We have now to examine the weekly directions in force to see whether the trends already noted are repeated in this series. About 45 weeks elapsed from the time of the postnatal Sunrise horoscope before marriage took place, so that the directional days in the day-for-a-week series fall 45 days before and after the day on which the Sunrise figure and its equivalent fall due, that is, on 20 February and 21 May 1879, and on 21 January 1926, and 23 October 1925. The following directions are then in force:

MC p.n. p. △ ☿ p.n. △ ♆ p.n.

MC a.n. p. ♂☉ p.n. p. ♂♀ p.n.
MC a.n. con. □☉ p.n. p. ♀ p.n.
Asc. p.n. p. □☉ r. ♂♂ a.n. △♀, ♂ r. △♇ p.n.
Asc. a.n. p. △♃ p.n. △♄ r.
♀ p.n. con. ♂☉ p.n., Asc. r. △☉ r.
♂ p.n. p. ♂MC a.n. △☉ a.n. ♂♅ r.
(MC a.n. con. △♃ a.n. ♂♆ r.)
(Asc. p.n. p. △♀ r. ♂♂ a.n. p. △♂ p.n.)
(Asc. a.n. p. ✶ ♃ r. △♄ a.n. p.)
(Asc. a.n. con. in ≏ △♀ p.n.)
(♀ a.n. p. △ Asc. a.n.)
(♂ a.n. con. ♂Asc. p.n. ✶ ♃ a.n. p. △♆ a.n. p.)
☉ a.n. p. □♅ a.n.
☉ a.n. con. ☍♅ a.n.
♀ a.n. con. △♄ p.n. □♇ r.
♂ p.n. con. in ≏ ☍☉ a.n.
♂ a.n. p. □♅ r.
♃ p.n. con. △♀ a.n. ☍♀ r.
(♃ p.n. p. △☽ a.n. in ≏)
♄ p.n. con. ☍♀ a.n. △♇ p.n.

Even allowing for the fact that over a wider span of time the movement of Jupiter and the major planets enables them to form aspects with the revolutional planets, the number of strong close aspects formed by progression is suitably impressive and very few of the directions can be regarded as out of character with the event. Our final operation is now to examine the daily directions in force on 21 October 1926. The corresponding dates are 23 January 1925, 18 February 1880, and 23 May 1878, the latter two being the directional days based on the antenatal equivalent figure. Here are the principal directions:

MC p.n. p. ☍♄ p.n.
MC p.n. con. ♂♅ a.n. con.
MC a.n. con. △☉ a.n. con. ♂♀ p.n. △♂ a.n. p.
Asc. p.n. p. ✶ ☉ p.n. p. ♂♆ p.n. p.
Asc. p.n. con. ☍♀ a.n. △♀ r., ♇ p.n. ☍♂ p.n. p.
Asc. a.n. con. ♂♇ a.n.
♃ a.n. con. △ Asc. p.n.
(MC p.n. p. ☍♃ a.n. p. □♇ r.)
(MC p.n. con. ♂☿ p.n. △♆ p.n.)
(Asc. p.n. p. ✶ ♀ p.n.)

(Asc. p.n. con. ♂ ♃ a.n. p. □ ♇ r.)
(Asc. a.n. con. ✶ ♂ a.n. △ ☉ r. ✶ ♃ r.)
(♀ a.n. con. △ MC a.n. ✶ ♃ p.n. p. △ ♅ r.)
(♀ p.n. con. ☍ ♂ a.n. con. ♂ Asc. p.n.)
♀ p.n. p. △ ♇ r.
♀ a.n. p. ♂ ♃ p.n. ♂ ♄ r.
♂ p.n. con. △ ♆ p.n. con.
♃ p.n. con. ☍ MC p.n.
(♃ p.n. p. ☍ MC a.n.)
(☉ p.n. con. △ ☽ a.n. in ♎)

Here again the aspects are numerous and, for the most part, typical of the event. A number of them involve the same degrees already stimulated by the monthly and weekly directions and act to precipitate their effects.

Our study of the Annual Sunrise figure is not yet complete for we have yet to consider the antenatal Annual Sunrise horoscope and its postnatal counterpart. It will be remembered that the date before birth in the day-for-a-day series of directions corresponding to 21 October 1926, the marriage day, is 23 May 1878. The nearest return of the Sun before this date to the degree of the radical Ascendant is on 6 December 1878, the conjunction being exact at 9.21 p.m. GMT. The return calculated with an allowance for precession occurs some hours earlier, at 1.32 p.m. GMT. The corresponding postnatal Equivalent falls on 7 April 1926 at 7.55 p.m. in the case of the non-precessional figure and some hours later, at 3.45 a.m. GMT on the following day, in the case of the precessional figure. For easy reference, the positions of the planets and angles in these figures and in the nativity are set out below in tabular form, the precessional positions being placed in brackets.

	MC	Asc.	☉	☽	☿	♀	♂	♃	♄	♅	♆	♇
Nativity	27° ♍	14° ♐	14° ♌	6° ♎	10° ♌	15° ♋	12° ♋	12°$_R$ ♒	23°$_R$ ♉	17°$_R$ ♐	2° ♋	19° ♓
Antenatal Sunrise Horoscope	5° ♒ (11° ♎)	29° ♑ (19° ♐)	14° ♐ (14° ♐)	11° ♑ (7° ♑)	5° ♉	15° ♐	18° ♏	5° ♒	26° ♓	4° ♍	7°$_R$ ♑	25°$_R$ ♑
Postnatal Equivalent	18° ♑ (12° ♍)	25° ♌ (27° ♏)	17° ♈ (17° ♈)	13° ♒ (17° ♒)	4°$_R$ ♈	1° ♓	11° ♒	20° ♒	25° ♏	26° ♓	22°$_R$ ♌	12° ♋

These are the principal configurations:

MC p.n. ☍ ♂ a.n. ♂ ♇ a.n.

MC a.n. △☽ r. ☌♃ a.n. □♆ a.n.
Asc. a.n. ☌♇ a.n.
Asc. p.n. □♄ p.n. ☌♆ p.n. □♇ a.n.
(MC a.n. △♂ p.n. △♃ r.)
(Asc. a.n. ☌☉ a.n. ☌♀ a.n. ✶♃ p.n. ☌♅ r. ☍♇ r.)
(Asc. a.n. ☌♄ p.n. △♄ a.n. △♅ p.n. ☍♇ a.n.)
☉ a.n. ✶☽ p.n. ✶♂ p.n. △♃ r.
☉ p.n. ✶♃ p.n. △♆ p.n.
(☉ p.n. ✶☽ p.n. △♅ r. ✶♇ r.)
☽ a.n. ✶♂ r. ✶♇ p.n.
(☽ a.n. □♃ a.n. ☌♆ a.n.)
♀ p.n. ☍♅ a.n. △♆ r.

With the exception of the T-square between Saturn, Uranus and Pluto, the configurations listed above are all appropriate to the nature of the event.

We may now turn our attention to the directions in force at the time of Ann Harding's marriage, which occurred 197 days after the day of the postnatal Equivalent. This period is about 6½ months and therefore the directional days in the day-for-a-month series will fall 6½ days before and after the days of the Sunrise figures. The principal directions are these:

MC p.n. p. ☍♄ p.n. ☌♇ a.n.
MC p.n. con. ☌☽ a.n. ✶♂ r. □♂ p.n. □♃ r. ✶♇ p.n.
MC a.n. p. ☌♂ p.n. ☌♃ r.
Asc. p.n. p. ☍♀ p.n.
Asc. p.n. con. ☍♃ p.n.
Asc. a.n. p. ☍☉ a.n. con. ☍♀ a.n. con. △♃ a.n. p.
  △☽ r.
Asc. a.n. con. □♃ p.n.
(MC p.n. p. □♇ r.)
(MC p.n. con. ☍♀ p.n. p.)
(MC a.n. p. ☍☉ p.n. △☽ p.n. ✶♅ r.)
(MC a.n. con. ☍☿ p.n.)
(Asc. p.n. con. ☌♂ a.n. p. ✶♄ r. □♆ p.n.)
(Asc. a.n. con. ☌☉ a.n. △☉ r.)
☉ p.n. p. △♀ a.n. p. △♆ p.n.
☉ a.n. p. ✶♃ p.n.
♀ p.n. con. ☍ Asc. a.n.
♂ p.n. con. ☌MC a.n. △☽ r. ☌♃ a.n.
♂ a.n. con. △♇ p.n.

These directions are equally as effective and numerous as those based on the postnatal Sunrise horoscope and its complementary figure. Twenty-eight weeks elapsed between the time of the postnatal equivalent and the marriage. The weekly directional days are therefore 5 May and 10 March 1926, 3 January 1879, and 8 November 1878. These are the weekly directions in force:

MC p.n. p. ☍♀ a.n.
MC p.n. con. ✶♃ p.n.
MC a.n. p. ☍♅ a.n.
MC a.n. con. △♆ a.n.
Asc. p.n. p. ☍☉ p.n. con ✶♂ a.n. □♅ r. □♇ r.
Asc. p.n. con. ☍♃ a.n.
Asc. a.n. con. ✶☽ p.n. △☉ r.
♀ p.n. p. ♂♅ p.n. p. ✶ Asc. a.n.
(MC p.n. p. in ♎ △♂ p.n. △♃ a.n. p.)
(MC p.n. con. ♂☉ r. △☉, ♀ a.n.)
(MC a.n. p. ♂♀ a.n. con.)
(MC a.n. con. △☉ a.n. p. ✶♂ r., ♇ p.n.)
(Asc. p.n. p. △☉ p.n. ✶☽ p.n. ♂♅ r. ☍♇ r.)
(Asc. p.n. con. ☍♆ a.n.)
(Asc. a.n. p. ☍♀, ♂ r.)
☉ a.n. con. △♀ r.
☿ p.n. con. △☽ r. △♂ a.n. p.
♀ p.n. con. ♂☽ p.n. ♂♂ p.n. ♂♃ r.
♃ p.n. con. ✶ Asc. r., ☉ a.n. ☍☉ r.

A fair proportion of these aspects either stimulate the main configurations present in the Sunrise figures or the monthly directions already noted above. The long sequence of favourable directions all falling due simultaneously is typical of the arrival of such a happy event.

The last part of our survey concerns the daily directions in force at the time of the marriage, which took place 197 days after the day of the postnatal equivalent. The directional days are therefore the marriage day itself, 21 October 1926, 22 September 1925, 21 June 1879, and 23 May 1878. The principal directions in the daily series are as follows:

MC p.n. con. △♀ p.n. ✶♅ a.n. p.
MC a.n. p. ☍♃ p.n.
MC a.n. con. ☍♄ △♅ p.n. con.

Asc. p.n. p. ♂♃ a.n. con.

Asc. a.n. p. ☍☽ a.n. ☍☿ a.n. con. △♂ r. □♂ p.n.
  △♂ a.n. con. ♂♄ p.n. con. ☍♆ a.n. p.

Asc. a.n. con. ♂♀ p.n. p. in ♎ △⚷ r.

(MC p.n. p. ♂♅ p.n. con.)

(MC a.n. p. ☍☉ p.n. p. in ♎ △♆ p.n. p.)

(MC a.n. con. ☍☉ p.n. con. □☉ a.n. p.)

(Asc. p.n. p. ♂♀ r. ⚹ ♂ p.n. p. ♂♇ p.n. p.)

(Asc. p.n. con. △♃ a.n. ♂♇ r.)

(Asc. a.n. p. △♂ a.n. p.)

☿ a.n. p. ♂♆ r.

♀ a.n. p. ♂☉ r. ☍☽ p.n.

♂ p.n. con. ⚹ ♄ p.n. ☍♄ a.n. ☍♅ p.n. △♇ a.n.

♄ p.n. p. □ Asc. p.n. ☍♇ a.n.

♄ a.n. p. △ Asc. r. △☉ r. △☉, ♀ a.n.

♅ a.n. con. ♂Asc. p.n. □♇ a.n. □♄ p.n.

(♀ p.n. p. ⚹ Asc. a.n. △♇ r.)

(♀ p.n. con. ☍☽, ♆ a.n.)

(♀ a.n. con. ♂☉ p.n. ⚹ ☽ p.n.)

(♃ p.n. p. ⚹ ☉ p.n. ♂☽ p.n. ⚹ ♅ r.)

(♃ p.n. con. ☍♂ r. ☍♇ p.n. △ MC p.n.)

(♃ a.n. p. ☍MC p.n. △♂ r., ♇ p.n.)

This massive array of aspects contains very few which appear to be out of character with the main event and many which fall on degrees already stimulated by the monthly and weekly directions. Together with the various series of directions derived from the postnatal Annual Sunrise horoscope and its complementary antenatal equivalent, they form a convincing argument in favour of the Annual Sunrise figure. It will be remembered that this figure is derived from the exact position of the radical Ascendant, as derived from the Prenatal Epoch. In the past some astrologers have not seen fit to accept the theory of the Prenatal Epoch. If they wish to discount the evidence of the above example, they will have to postulate that a suitable rising degree was obtained only by a most fortuitous coincidence, for the dovetailing of the radical and progressed planets and angles in such a way as to produce an exceptionally large number of suitable progressions could hardly occur otherwise. The only alternative is that the Epochal theory is a valid one!

13.
THE LUNAR REVOLUTION

The Lunar Revolution is a figure cast for the return of the Moon each month to the exact place that it held in the nativity. Those events that are foreshadowed by the Solar Revolution for the year are most likely to come to pass during the period of that Lunar Revolution which most nearly reproduces the planetary configurations and angular stresses of the solar figure. An inspection of the Ephemeris may help to single out the most significant Lunar Revolutions of the year but only when the exact moment of the return is calculated will the angular planets, which play such a large part in determining the major emphasis of the period, become apparent.

While not denying the effectiveness of the Lunar Return as a method of narrowing down the timing of events, I believe that equally effective results may be obtained with less labour by applying the monthly, weekly and daily series of directions to the main Solar Revolution. For the sake of completeness, however, and in order to allow the reader to judge for himself, instructions for the calculation of the Lunar Return are given below, together with typical examples of this kind of figure.

In order to calculate the time of the Lunar Return accurately it is necessary to know the position of the radical Moon to the nearest second of arc. Instructions for calculating the position of the radical Moon, making an allowance for the amount of acceleration or deceleration during the day, were given in Chapter 11. It is also necessary to make allowances for the lunar acceleration or deceleration on the day of the Lunar Revolution, as otherwise the correct angles of the Lunar figure will not be obtained.

As in the case of Solar Revolutions, both postnatal and antenatal figures may be calculated. Except in rare cases, the day of the postnatal Lunar Revolution will not measure exactly in time to the day of the antenatal Lunar Revolution, so that the complementary figure to the postnatal Revolution will be its antenatal equivalent, and to the antenatal Revolution its postnatal equivalent. Revolutions may be calculated with or without an allowance for precession, each type, of course, being matched with its appropriate solar counterpart.

As an example, let us calculate the Lunar Revolution covering the period of Ann Harding's marriage, which took place on 21 October 1926. The Lunar Revolution immediately preceding this fell on 6 October 1926. Here is the method of calculation:

(1) Estimate the time on 6 October 1926 when the Moon will return to its radical position.

From the Moon's position at noon on 6 October 1926	7°45′37″ ♎
Subtract the Moon's position at birth	6°29′21″ ♎
Difference	1° 16′ 16″

Distance travelled by the Moon in 12 hours preceding noon, 6 October 1926	6°00′04″

Average speed of Moon = 30′ per hour (approx.)

Time needed to cover 1°16′16″   2h 32m (approx.)
2h 32m before noon = 9.28 a.m.

(2) Calculate theoretical speed of the Moon at 9.30 a.m.

Position of Moon at midnight, 5/6 October 1926	1° 45′ 33″ ♎
Position of Moon at noon, 5 October 1926	25°46′59″ ♍
Moon's progress in 12 hours	5°58′34″(A)
Position of Moon at noon on 6 October 1926	7°45′37″ ♎
Position of Moon at midnight, 5/6 October 1926	1° 45′33″ ♎
Moon's progress in 12 hours	6°00′04″(B)
Position of Moon at midnight 6/7 October 1926	13°47′18″ ♎
Position of Moon at noon, 6 October 1926	7°45′37″ ♎
Moon's progress in 12 hours	6°01′41″ (C)

Then $\dfrac{A + B}{2}$ = Theoretical mean motion at midnight
          5/6 October 1926

	5°58′34″
	6°00′04″
	11° 58′38″
÷ 2 =	5°59′19″(D)

And $\dfrac{B + C}{2}$ = Theoretical mean motion at noon

	6 October 1926	6° 00′ 04″
		6° 01′ 41″
		12° 01′ 45″
	÷ 2 =	6° 00′ 52″ (E)

Also $\dfrac{D + E}{2}$ = Theoretical mean motion at 6.00 a.m.

	6 October 1926	5° 59′ 19″
		6° 00′ 52″
		12° 00′ 11″
	÷ 2 =	6° 00′ 05″ (F)

And $\dfrac{E + F}{2}$ = Theoretical mean motion at 9.00 a.m.

	6 October 1926	6° 00′ 52″
		6° 00′ 05″
		12° 00′ 57″
	÷ 2 =	6° 00′ 28″ (G)

To adjust rate of Moon's progress at 9.00 a.m. to rate at 9.30 a.m.

Subtract from the theoretical mean motion at noon (E)	6° 00′ 52″
The theoretical mean motion at 9 a.m. (G)	6° 00′ 28″
Increase of theoretical mean motion in 3 hours	0° 00′ 24″
Increase of theoretical mean motion in 28 minutes	0° 00′ 04″
Add rate of Moon's progress at 9.00 a.m.	6° 00′ 28″
Moon's theoretical motion at 9.28 a.m.	6° 00′ 32″

(3) Using this rate of progress, calculate the time required for the Moon to travel 1°16′16″.

Moon's theoretical mean motion in 12 hours	6° 00′ 32″
Divide by 6 = 2 hours' motion	1° 00′ 05″
Divide 2 hours' motion by 4 = 30 minutes' motion	0° 15′ 01″
Divide 2 hours' motion by 60 = 2 minutes' motion	0° 01′ 00″
Divide 2 minutes' motion by 6 = 20 seconds' motion	0° 00′ 10″
Motion in 2 hours 32 minutes 20 seconds	1° 16′ 16″

Time of Moon's return to radical position, 2 hours 32 minutes 20 seconds, before noon = 9.27.40 a.m.

(4) Calculate equivalent Sidereal Time at Chicago (87° W 39′)

From Sidereal Time at noon, 6 October 1926	12 57 33	
Subtract amount of time before noon when Moon returns to natal position	2 32 20	
Also subtract allowance for longitude of Chicago	5 51 00	
And subtract correction for Sidereal Time	0 01 23	
Sidereal Time at Chicago	4 32 50	

This Sidereal Time gives a Midheaven of 10° Gemini and an Ascendant at Chicago of 13° Virgo.

The antenatal equivalent for the same period is calculated as follows:

(1) Find the day on which the equivalent figure falls due:

Day of postnatal Lunar Return	6 October 1926
Number of years and days after birth	24 years (6 leap) 60 days
Equivalent number of years and days before birth	24 years (5 leap) 61 days
Day of antenatal Lunar Return Equivalent = 7 June 1878	

(2) Calculate Midheaven of antenatal lunar return equivalent:

Find longitudinal distance between MC of postnatal Lunar Return	10° ♓
And natal MC	27° ♍
	107°
Add 107° to longitude of natal MC	14° ♑
Extract appropriate Ascendant from Chicago Table of Houses	26 ♈

(3) Find GMT of antenatal lunar return equivalent:

From Sidereal Time at noon, 7 June 1878	5 03 00
Subtract Sidereal Time of antenatal Lunar Return Equivalent	19 00 50
	10 02 10
Subtract correction for GMT	00 01 40
	10 00 30
Subtract allowance for difference in longitude between Greenwich and Chicago (87° W 39′)	5 50 36
Amount of time before noon GMT	4 09 54
GMT of Lunar Return Equivalent	7.50 a.m.

The antenatal Lunar Return covering the month in which the marriage occurred is calculated as follows:

Date of marriage   21 October 1926
Number of years and days after birth   24 years (6 leap) 75 days
Equivalent number of years and days
    before birth   24 years (5 leap) 76 days
                                                    = 23 May 1878
Nearest day preceding this date (in converse motion) when the
Moon passes over the degree of the radical Moon 9 June 1878

(1) Estimate the time on 9 June 1878 when the
    Moon will return to its radical position:
        From the position of the Moon at birth   6° 29′ 21″ ♎
        Subtract Moon's position at noon,
            9 June 1878   6° 11′ 00″ ♎

            Longitudinal difference   0° 18′ 21″

        Moon's daily progress   14° 16′ 00″
        Progress in 24 minutes   0° 14′ 16″
        Progress in 6 minutes   0° 03′ 35″
        Progress in 1 minute   0° 00′ 36″

            Progress in 31 minutes   0° 18′ 27″

            Time of return (approx.)   12.31 p.m.

(2) Calculate theoretical mean speed of Moon at 12.31 p.m.
        From the Moon's longitude at noon on
            8 June 1878   21° 58′ 00″ ♍
        Subtract the Moon's longitude at noon on
            7 June 1878   7° 50′ 00″ ♍

        Theoretical speed at midnight 7/8 June
            1878   14° 08′ 00″ (A)

        From the Moon's longitude at noon on
            9 June 1878   6° 11′ 00″ ♎
        Subtract the Moon's longitude at noon on
            8 June 1878   21° 58′ 00″ ♍

        Theoretical speed at midnight
            8/9 June 1878   14° 13′ 00″ (B)

        From the Moon's longitude at noon on
            10 June 1878   20° 27′ 00″ ♎
        Subtract the Moon's longitude at noon on
            9 June 1878   6° 11′ 00″ ♎

        Theoretical speed at midnight
            9/10 June 1878   14° 16′ 00″ (C)

        From the Moon's longitude at noon on
            11 June 1878   4° 45′ 00″ ♏
        Subtract the Moon's longitude at noon on
            10 June 1878   20° 27′ 00″ ♎

Theoretical speed at midnight
    10/11 June 1878   14° 18′ 00″(D)

Then average of A + B = theoretical speed at noon
    8 June 1878   14° 10′ 30″(E)

Average of B + C = theoretical speed at noon
    9 June 1878   14° 14′ 30″(F)

Average of C + D = theoretical speed at noon
    10 June 1878   14° 17′ 00″(G)

Also average of E + F = theoretical speed at midnight
    8/9 June 1878   14° 12′ 30″(H)

Average of F + G = theoretical speed at midnight
    9/10 June 1878   14° 15′ 45″(I)

Then average of H + I = theoretical speed at noon
    9 June 1878   14° 14′ 07″(J)

And average of I + J = theoretical speed at 6.00 p.m.
    9 June 1878   14° 14′ 56″(K)

Average of J + K = theoretical speed at 3.00 p.m.
    9 June 1878   14° 14′ 32″

Adjust rate of progress for 12.32 p.m.

From theoretical speed at 3.00 p.m.	14° 14′ 32″
Subtract theoretical speed at noon	14° 14′ 07″
Increase of speed in 3 hours	0° 00′ 25″
Increase of speed in 30 minutes	0° 00′ 04″
Add 4″ to theoretical speed at noon	14° 14′ 11″

(3) Using this rate of progress, calculate the time
    required for the Moon to travel 18′ 21″.

Moon's progress in 24 hours	14° 14′ 11″
Moon's progress in 24 minutes	0° 14′ 14″
Moon's progress in 8 minutes	0° 4′ 45″
Moon's progress in 32 minutes	0° 18′ 59″
Subtract Moon's progress in 1 minute	0° 00′ 36″
Moon's progress in 31 minutes	0° 18′ 23″

Time of Moon's return to 6° 29′ 21″ ♎ = 12.31 p.m.

(4) Calculate equivalent Sidereal Time at Chicago.

To Sidereal Time at noon on 9 June 1878	5	10	53
Add amount of time that after noon the			
Moon returns to its radical position	0	31	00
Also add correction for Sidereal Time	0	00	05
	5	41	58
Subtract allowance for longitude of Chicago	5	50	36
Also subtract correction for Sidereal Time	0	01	17

Sidereal Time of antenatal Lunar Return   23 50 05

This Sidereal Time gives a Midheaven of 27° Pisces
and an Ascendant at Chicago of 17° Cancer.

The postnatal equivalent for the same period is calculated as follows:

(1) Find the day on which the equivalent figure falls due.
    Day of antenatal Lunar Return   9 June 1878
    Number of years and days before
    birth   24 years (5 leap) 59 days
    Equivalent number of days and years
    after birth   24 years (6 leap) 58 days
    Day of postnatal equivalent   4 October 1926

(2) Calculate Midheaven of postnatal Lunar Return Equivalent
    Find longitudinal distance between radical MC   27° ♍
    And MC of the antenatal Lunar Return   27° ♓
                                                        ─────
                                                        180°
    Subtract 180° from longitude of radical MC   27° ♓
    The corresponding Ascendant at Chicago is   17° ♋

(3) Find GMT of postnatal Lunar Return Equivalent
    From Sidereal Time of postnatal Lunar Return
    Equivalent   23 48 00
    Subtract Sidereal Time at noon,
    4 October 1926   12 49 40
                                       ─────────
                                       10 58 20
    Subtract correction for GMT   0 01 50
                                       ─────────
                                       10 57 30
    Add allowance for difference in longitude
    between Greenwich and Chicago
    (87° W 39′)   5 50 36
    Amount of time after noon, GMT   16 48 06
        = 4.48 a.m. (5 October 1926)

If it is required to calculate the postnatal Lunar Return for the same
period, making an allowance for precession, the following procedure is
recommended:

(1) Calculate amount of precessional increment to
    be added to longitude of natal Moon.
    Date of postnatal Lunar Return   6 October 1926
    Number of years and days after birth   24 years 60 days
    To longitude of Moon at birth   6° 29′ 21″ ♎

Add precessional increment for 24 years   0° 20′ 06″
Also add precessional increment for 60 days
  (2 months)   0° 00′ 08″
                 6° 49′ 35″ ≏

(2) Estimate the time of the Moon's return to this position.
     From the Moon's position at noon,
       6 October 1926   7° 45′ 37″ ≏
     Subtract longitude of radical Moon +
       precessional increment   6° 49′ 35″ ≏
     Difference   0° 56′ 02″

     Estimate time needed for the Moon to travel
       0°56′02″, taking Moon's average speed as
       30′ per hour (see calculations for postnatal
       Lunar Return without precession   1 hour 52 minutes
     1 hour 52 minbutes before noon = 10.08 a.m.

(3) Find theoretical speed of the Moon at 10.08 a.m.
     (using previous calculations for postnatal lunar
     return without precession (see page 153).
       To the Moon's theoretical speed at 9.00 a.m.   6° 00′ 28″
       Add the Moon's theoretical speed at noon   6° 00′ 52″
                 12° 01′ 20″

       Divide by 2 to give theoretical speed at
         10.30 a.m.   6° 00′ 40″
       To find the rate of progress for 10.08 a.m.
       Subtract from theoretical speed at 10.30 a.m.   6° 00′ 40″
       Theoretical speed at 9.00 a.m.   6° 00′ 28″

         Increase of speed in 90 minutes   0° 00′ 12″

         Increase of speed in 22 minutes = 3″
           (approx.)
       From the theoretical speed at 10.30 a.m.   6° 00′ 40″
       Subtract 22 minutes' increase   0° 00′ 03″

       Theoretical speed at 10.08 a.m.   6° 00′ 37″

(4) Using this theoretical speed, calculate the time
     required for the Moon to travel 0°56′02″.
       Moon's progress in 12 hours   6° 00′ 37″
       Divide by 12 (1 hour's progress)   0° 30′ 03″
       Divide 1 hour's progress by 2 (30 minutes'
         progress)   0° 15′ 01″
       Divide 30 minutes progress by ⅔ (20
         minutes' progress)   0° 10′ 00″

Divide 20 minutes progress by 10 (2 minutes'
        progress)   0° 01' 00"
1 hour 52 minutes progress   0° 56' 04"
1 hour 52 minutes before noon = 10.08 a.m. GMT

(5) Calculate the equivalent Sidereal Time at Chicago.
        From Sidereal Time at noon on
        6 October 1926   12 57 33
    Subtract amount of time before noon that the
        Moon returns to its radical position
        (+ precession)   1 52 00
                                                     11 05 33
    Subtract allowance for difference in longitude
        between Greenwich and Chicago
        (87° W 39')   5 50 36
    Also subtract combined correction for GMT   0 01 17
                                                      5 13 40

This Sidereal Time gives a Midheaven of 19° Gemini and
an Ascendant at Chicago of 20° Virgo.

The corresponding antenatal equivalent is calculated as follows:

(1) Find the day on which the equivalent figure falls due.
    This was 7 June 1878 (see previous calculation for figure
    without precession, page 155)

(2) Calculate Midheaven of antenatal equivalent.
        Find longitudinal difference between MC of
            postnatal figure   19° ♓
        And natal MC   27° ♍
                                                      98°
        Add 98° to longitude of radical MC   5° ♑
        The corresponding Ascendant at Chicago is   9° ♈

(3) Find GMT of antenatal equivalent.
        From Sidereal Time of antenatal equivalent   0 33 04
        Subtract Sidereal Time at noon, 7 June 1878 17 04 30
                                                      7 28 34
        Subtract correction for GMT   0 01 15
                                                      7 27 19
    Add allowance for difference in longitude
        between Greenwich and Chicago meridians   5 50 36
                                                     13 17 55

GMT of antenatal equivalent = 1.17.55 a.m.
on 8 June 1878

It will be observed that the result of the calculation based on the
Moon's adjusted (theoretical) speed at 10.08 a.m. does not differ
from the original estimate made on the basis of the Moon's speed
calculated without such an adjustment. This is due, in this case,
to the relatively slight variation in the Moon's speed over the
required period of time. The various examples are expressly given
to illustrate the method of estimating the Moon's speed at any
given time of day but the student should note that it is not always
necessary to embark upon such detailed calculations unless the
difference between the lunar speeds varies considerably from day
to day, nor is it necessary to make complicated adjustments to the
apparent speed of the Moon when the time of the return is within
an hour, more or less, of noon or midnight (when the midnight
positions are available).

If it is required to calculate the antenatal Lunar Return for the
same period, making an allowance for precession, the following
procedure is recommended:

(1) Calculate the amount of precessional increment to be
subtracted from the longitude of the natal Moon.

Day of antenatal Lunar Return	9 June 1878
Number of years and days before birth	24 years 59 days
Extract from tables in Appendix appropriate precessional increments	
24 years	0° 20′ 06″
59 days (say 2 months)	0° 00′ 08″
	0° 20′ 14″
Then from the Moon's position at birth	6° 29′ 21″ ≏
Subtract precessional increment	0° 20′ 14″
Adjusted longitude of Moon	6° 09′ 07″ ≏

(2) Estimate the time of the Moon's return to this position.

From the position of the Moon at noon on 9 June 1878	6° 11′ 00″ ≏
Subtract adjusted position of natal Moon	6° 09′ 07″ ≏
Longitudinal difference	0° 01′ 53″

The Moon will take approximately three minutes to cover
this distance.

(3) Calculate time required for the Moon to travel 1′ 53″, using

previously calculated speed of Moon (14°14′07″) (see pages 156-7).

Moon's motion in 24 minutes	0° 14′ 14″
Divide by 8 = motion in 3 minutes	0° 1′ 47″

This figure is 6″ short of the required progress
The Moon will cover 7″ in 12 seconds
Time of return is 3 minutes 11 seconds before
 noon = 11.56.49 a.m.

(4) Calculate equivalent Sidereal Time at Chicago.

From Sidereal Time at noon on 9 June 1878	5	10	53
Subtract amount of time before noon that the			
Moon arrives at adjusted radical position	0	3	12
	5	07	41
Subtract allowance for difference in longitude			
between Chicago and Greenwich meridians	5	50	36
Also subtract correction for Sidereal Time	0	1	17
	23	15	48

This Sidereal Time gives a Midheaven of 18° Pisces and an Ascendant at Chicago of 10° Cancer.

The corresponding postnatal equivalent is calculated as follows:

(1) Find the day on which the equivalent figure falls due.
 This was 4 October 1926 (see previous
  calculation on page 158 for figure without
  precession)

(2) Calculate Midheaven of postnatal equivalent.

Find difference in longitude between natal MC	27° ♍
And MC of antenatal figure	18° ♓
	171°
Subtract 171° from the longitude of natal MC	6° ♈
The corresponding Ascendant at Chicago is	24° ♋

(3) Find GMT of postnatal equivalent

From Sidereal Time of postnatal equivalent	0	22	02
Subtract Sidereal Time at noon on			
4 October 1926	12	49	40
	11	32	22
Subtract correction for GMT	0	01	55
Local Time at Chicago	11	30	27 p.m.
Add allowance for difference in longitude			
between Chicago and Greenwich meridians	5	50	36
	17	21	53

GMT of postnatal equivalent = 5.21.53 a.m.
on 5 October 1926

In order to facilitate a scrutiny of the various configurations
formed in these lunar returns, the positions of the angles and
planets of each, together with the positions of the natal angles and
planets are set forth below in tabular form. The angles of the
figures cast with an allowance for precession are given in brackets.
Because there is only about half an hour's difference in the timing
of the precessional and non-precessional figures, no adjustment
has been made to the position of the planets given for the time
of the non-precessional figures.

First we shall consider the postnatal Lunar Revolution together
with its antenatal equivalent.

	MC	Asc.	☉	☽	☿	♀	♂	♃	♄	♅	♆	♇
Nativity	27° ♍	14° ♐	14° ♌	6° ♎	10° ♌	15° ♋	12° ♋	12°ᴿ ♒	23°ᴿ ♉	17°ᴿ ♐	2° ♋	19° ♓
Postnatal Lunar Revolution	9° ♓ (19° ♓)	12° ♍ (20° ♍)	12° ♎	6° ♎	24° ♎	0° ♎	19°ᴿ ♑	17°ᴿ ♒	23° ♏	26°ᴿ ♓	26° ♌	16° ♋
Antenatal Lunar Equivalent	14° ♉ (5° ♉)	26° ♈ (9° ♈)	17° ♓	5° ♍	23° ♑	4° ♑	20° ♋	7°ᴿ ♒	1°ᴿ ♈	26° ♌	8° ♑	25° ♑

The principal configurations are listed below:

MC a.n. ☍♀, ♂ r. ☍♇ p.n.
Asc. a.n. △♅ a.n. △♆ p.n.
(MC p.n. ♂☉ a.n. △♃ p.n. ♂♇ r.)
(Asc. a.n. ☍midpoint ☉, ☽ p.n. in ♎ ✶ ♃ r.)
☽ r. and p.n. ♂♀ p.n. △♃ a.n.
(Asc. p.n. △♂ p.n. ✶ ♂ a.n.)
☉ p.n. ☐♂ r.
☉ a.n. ☍♅ r.
☽ a.n. △♀ a.n.

Because the Lunar Revolution is a sub-division of the major Solar
Revolution it is also important to consider aspects between the
principal factors in the Composite Lunar Revolution and the main
factors in the Composite Solar Revolution. The following additional configurations give added testimony to the importance of
this period:

Monthly MC a.n. e. ☍ Yearly ♀ a.n.
Monthly Asc. a.n. e. △ Yearly ♂ a.n., ♅ a.n.
Monthly ☉ a.n. ☍ Yearly MC a.n.
Monthly ♀ a.n. (☍ Yearly Asc. a.n.) ☌ Yearly ♂ p.n.
Monthly ♂ p.n. ⚹ Yearly ♀ p.n. ☍ Yearly ♄ p.n.
Monthly ♂ a.n. ☌ Yearly ♀ p.n. □ Yearly ♄ p.n.
Monthly ♃ a.n. (☌MC a.n.)

Most of the configurations listed in Chapter 5 as being typical of marriage will be found to be present in the Lunar Revolutions taken in conjunction with the nativity and also emphasized in the contacts between the monthly and yearly positions listed above.

Now let us examine the directions in the Lunar horoscopes measuring to the time of marriage, which took place on 21 October 1926, fifteen days after the day of the postnatal Lunar Return. The weekly directions will therefore be represented by the planetary positions two days before and after the days on which the lunar figures fall due. Here are the aspects for that event:

MC a.n. p. ☍♀ r.
Asc. a.n. p. ☌♀ a.n. con.
MC a.n. con. ☍♂ r.
(MC p.n. con. ☌☉ a.n. △♃ p.n. ☍♅ r.)
(Asc. p.n. con. △♂ p.n.)
(Asc. a.n. p. ☍☉ p.n. in ♎ ⚹ ♃ r.)
(Asc. a.n. con. ☍♀ p.n. p. in ♎)
☉ a.n. p. ☌♇ r.
♀ a.n. p. △☽ a.n.

Only those aspects within about a degree of exactitude are included in this list and no aspects formed by progression should be considered unless they conform to this requirement.

In addition the following aspect occurs:

Monthly ♀ a.n. con. (☍ Yearly Asc. a.n.)

We may now turn our attention to the daily series of progressions formed by the planets fifteen days before and after the day of the lunar figures. The significant aspects in this series are listed below:

Asc. p.n. p. ☍♅ p.n. p.
MC p.n. con. ☍♄ p.n. p.

MC a.n. p. ☍ ♂ a.n. p.
Asc. a.n. p. ☌ ♀ a.n. p.
Asc. a.n. con. ☌ ♅ p.n. con.
♀ p.n. con. ☌ Asc. p.n.
(MC a.n. con. ☍ ♇ r.)
(MC a.n. p. △ ♂ p.n.)
(Asc. a.n. p. ☌ ♀ a.n.)
♀ a.n. p. ⚹ ♂ a.n. (⚹ Asc. p.n.)
☉ p.n. con. ☍ ♅ p.n. con.
♀ a.n. con. △ ♅ r.

Also the following aspects are formed:

Monthly ☉ a.n. con. ☍ Yearly ☽ a.n. ⚹ Yearly ♄ a.n.
Monthly ♀ p.n. p. ☌ Yearly Asc. p.n. in ♎

Of this impressive list of directions, the most significant are probably those formed by the progressed angles of the antenatal figure, which simultaneously form contacts with Venus and Mars. The basic configurations in the postnatal lunar return and its antenatal equivalent, together with the weekly and daily progressions of these horoscopes, give most adequate indications of impending marriage. But so far we have examined only one side of the picture. There is also the antenatal lunar return for the same period, together with its postnatal equivalent. For easy reference the positions of the planets and angles in these two figures are set out below in tabular form.

	MC	Asc.	☉	☽	☿	♀	♂	♃	♄	♅	♆	♇
Antenatal Lunar Revolution	27° ♓ (18° ♓)	17° ♋ (10° ♋)	18° ♓	6° ♎	25° ♑	6° ♑	21° ♋	6° ♒ R	1° ♈	26° ♌	8° ♑	16° ♋
Postnatal Equivalent	27° ♓ (6° ♈)	17° ♋ (24° ♋)	11° ♎	22° ♍	22° ♎	29° ♍	19° ♐ R	17° ♒ R	23° ♏	27° ♓ R	26° ♌	25° ♑

Once again we should first take stock of the main configurations present in these figures and the connection which they have with the principal factors in the nativity. They are as follows:

MC a.n. and p.n. ☍ ♀ p.n. ☌ ♅ p.n. ☍ MC r.
Asc. p.n. ☌ ♀ r. ☌ ♂ a.n. ☌ ♇ p.n.
Asc. a.n. ☌ ♀ r. ☌ ♂ a.n. ☌ ♇ p.n.

(MC p.n. ☍ ☉ p.n. ☍ ☽ r. and a.n. in ♎)
(Asc. p.n. ☌ ☌ a.n. Δ ♄ p.n. Δ ♅ p.n.)
(Asc. a.n. ☌ ☌ r.)
☉ p.n. Δ ♃ r.
☉ a.n. Δ ♃ p.n. ☍ ♅ r. ☌ ♇ r.
☽ a.n. Δ ♃ a.n.
☽ p.n. ☌ ♀ p.n. ☍ ♅ p.n. Δ ♇ a.n.
♀ a.n. ☐ ♃ a.n. ☌ ♆ a.n.

In addition we have also to consider the following aspects:

Monthly Asc. p.n. and a.n. ☌ Yearly ♀ p.n. Δ Yearly
  ♄ p.n.
Monthly ☉ p.n. in ♎ (Δ Yearly Asc. p.n.)
Monthly ☉ a.n. ☍ Yearly MC a.n.
Monthly ☿ in ♎ Δ Yearly ♃ p.n.
Monthly ♀ p.n. ☍ Yearly ♅ p.n.
Monthly ♂ a.n. ☌ Yearly MC p.n.
Monthly ♃ p.n. (☌ Yearly Asc. p.n.)

Now let us examine the directions in this pair of lunar horoscopes measuring to the time of marriage, which took place on 21 October 1926, 16 days after the day of the postnatal equivalent figure. The weekly directions will therefore be represented by the planetary positions two days before and after the days on which the lunar figures fall due. Here are the aspects measuring to the event:

MC p.n.p. ☍ ♀ p.n.
♀ p.n. con. ☍ MC p.n. and a.n.
Asc. p.n. and a.n. con. ☌ ♀ r.
(Asc. p.n. con. ☌ ☌ a.n.p. ☍ ♄ r.)
(Asc. a.n. p. ☌ ☌ r.)
☉ a.n. con. Δ ♃ p.n. ☍ ♅ r.
♀ a.n.p. ☌ ♆ a.n.

Also the following aspects involving the main Solar Revolution:

Monthly MC p.n. and a.n. ☌ Yearly ♅ p.n.
Monthly ☉ a.n. con. ☍ Yearly MC a.n.
Monthly ♀ p.n. p. in ♎ ☍ Yearly ♄ a.n.
Monthly ♀ a.n. con. ☌ Yearly ♂ p.n.
Monthly ♂ a.n. p. ☌ Yearly MC p.n.

Our last task is to examine the daily series of progressions, formed by the planets 16 days before and after the day of the lunar figures and by the movement of the Midheaven at the same rate as the Sun progresses over the same period, together with the corresponding Ascendant. The significant aspects are listed below:

⊙ p.n. con. ☍ MC p.n.
♀ a.n. con. ☐ Asc. p.n. and con.
(Asc. p.n. con. ♂ ☊ r.)
(♂ a.n. con. ♂Asc. a.n.)
⊙ a.n. p. ☍♃ a.n. △♄ a.n.
♀ p.n. p. △☿ r.
♀ a.n. con ⚹ ☊ a.n.
♂ p.n. p. ⚹ ♀ r.

In addition, the following aspects between the monthly and yearly factors are present:

Monthly ⊙ a.n. con. ☍ Yearly ☽ a.n. ⚹ Yearly ♄ a.n.
Monthly ♀ p.n. p. ♂ Yearly Asc. p.n. in ♎

These daily progressions are not quite so numerous or so emphatically indicative of marriage when considered on their own without reference to the main configurations present in the lunar figures or to the weekly progressions. Nevertheless, when they are so considered and when due account has been paid to the indications present in the postnatal lunar return and its equivalent figure already examined, the total picture may be regarded as a convincing testimony of the usefulness of the lunar return as an aid to prognostication and of the necessity of assessing its significance by taking into account its relationship to the appropriate complementary figure and of applying the weekly and daily series of progressions in order to determine the precise day on which the major effects are likely to be discharged. Once again the reader may judge for himself the relative merits of the figures cast with and without an allowance for precession, and he may well come to the conclusion, on the basis of the evidence presented, that there is little to choose between them.

In every case where aspects between the monthly and yearly figures have been listed, only the angular and planetary positions in the revolution itself have been used, and not the progressed positions of the planets and angles. Although there is no reason why the latter should not be taken into account, effective results may be obtained by confining the attention to the basic revolutional positions. Aspects formed between monthly and yearly figures taken on their own often seem to give sufficiently clear indications of the time when an event will fall due.

In order to simplify the comparison between the composite monthly and yearly revolutional figures, the former have, in every case, only been compared with the corresponding type of solar figure. The postnatal Lunar Revolution and its antenatal equivalent have been compared with the postnatal Solar Revolution and its antenatal equivalent; similarly, the antenatal Lunar Revolution and its postnatal equivalent have been compared with the antenatal Solar Revolution and its postnatal equivalent.

The Composite Lunar Revolution has, in each case, been made up of the postnatal Lunar Revolution or Equivalent and the corresponding antenatal Lunar Equivalent or Revolution falling the same number of days *before* birth. Because the Solar Revolution may be progressed both forwards and backwards in time, there is no reason why the current postnatal Lunar Revolution should not be combined with the Lunar Revolution or equivalent figure measured the same number of days *backwards* from the day of the *current* postnatal birthday anniversary, or why the current antenatal Lunar Return should not similarly be combined with the corresponding Lunar Return or equivalent figure measured *forwards* in time from the corresponding antenatal birthday anniversary. Students who wish to experiment with Composite Lunar Revolutions constructed according to this formula will find that the results obtained are equally as effective as those arrived at by the other methods used here.

14.

THE PROGRESSED
LUNAR REVOLUTION

In the same way that it is possible to construct a Solar Revolution on the basis of the Sun's Annual Return to its progressed position in the secondary progressed horoscope, it is also possible to construct a Lunar Revolution on the basis of the Sun's monthly return to its place in the secondary progressed horoscope. In a preceding chapter we examined the Progressed Solar Revolution and directions derived from it and found that in the example under consideration most convincing results were obtained. There is every reason to suppose, therefore, that just as the ordinary Solar Revolution may be considered in conjunction with subsidiary lunar figures, so the progressed Solar Revolution may be considered in conjunction with a similar kind of lunar figure, based on the position of the Moon at the exact moment for which the secondary progressed horoscope should properly be cast. This moment is based on the position of the progressed Midheaven, which moves at exactly the same rate as the progressed secondary Sun, so that the distance between angle and luminary always remains constant.

In Chapter 3 an example was given of the way in which the time of the progressed horoscope for any year may be calculated. Once again using the nativity of Ann Harding as an example, we can calculate the position of the secondary progressed Moon by using the time already calculated in Chapter 3 for the moment of the progressed horoscope for the 25th year, that is, 9.01.05 p.m. GMT, 31 August 1902. Due allowance should be made for lunar acceleration or deceleration when calculating the progressed lunar position, according to the method given in Chapter 13. This is 19° 51′ 38″ Leo.

The position of the secondary converse Moon may be calculated in exactly the same way for the 25th year, according to the time of the secondary converse horoscope already calculated as an example in Chapter 3. This time was 9.19 p.m. GMT on 14 July 1878, and the position of the Moon at this moment was 17°40′45″ Scorpio.

If it is required to calculate the secondary progressed Lunar Revolution covering the period of Ann Harding's marriage on 21 October 1926, it is necessary to find the nearest day to this date when the Moon is in 20° Leo. The moment of the return may then be calculated according to the method explained in Chapter 3. The day of the progressed lunar return is 2 October 1926. The Moon returns to its progressed position at 11.14 a.m. GMT. The corresponding day before birth is 11 June 1878, but the day of the Moon's return to its secondary converse position is 12 June 1878. This raises the point as to whether an antenatal equivalent figure should be constructed as the counterpart of the postnatal return, on the lines of the figure constructed for the ordinary lunar returns. In this case, however, as there are not more than 24 hours between the time of the antenatal equivalent and the secondary converse lunar figure, the strong sympathy existing between the progressed and converse lunar figures makes it unnecessary to look further for a complementary figure and we can consider the two lunar returns together.

These returns may also be computed with an allowance for precession, as in the case of the secondary progressed Solar Returns. The positions of angles and planets in the progressed and converse lunar returns, together with the natal positions, are set out below in tabular form for easy reference. Precessional positions are given in brackets.

	MC	Asc.	☉	☽	☿	♀	♂	♃	♄	♅	♆	♇
Nativity	27° ♍	14° ♐	10° ♌	6° ♎	10° ♌	15° ♋	12° ♋	12° ♒	23°R ♑	17°R ♐	2° ♋	19° ♓
Postnatal (Progressed) Lunar Revolution	0° ♋ (10° ♋)	0° ♎ (8° ♎)	8° ♌	19° ♌ (20° ♌)	18° ♌	25° ♍	19°R ♑	17°R ♒	23° ♏	27° ♓	26° ♌	15° ♓
Antenatal (Converse) Lunar Revolution	17° ♒ (8° ♒)	12° ♓ (2° ♓)	21° ♓	17° ♏ (17° ♏)	29° ♑	9° ♑	23° ♋	6°R ♒	2° ♈	26° ♌	8° ♑	26° ♑

These are the main configurations (those involving the angles of the precessional figures are given in brackets):

MC a.n. ☍☉ r., ☽ p.n. ☌♃ p.n. ⚹ ♅ r. △♇ r.
Asc. p.n. ☍♄ a.n.
Asc. a.n. ⚹ ☉ r. △♃ r.
(MC p.n. ☌♀, ♂ r. ⚹ ♀ Ψ a.n. ☌♇ p.n.)
(MC a.n. △☉ p.n. ☌♃ a.n. □♀ Ψ a.n.)
(Asc. p.n. ☌☉ p.n., ☽ r. in ♎ △♃ a.n.)
(Asc. a.n. ⚹ ♄ a.n.)
☉ a.n. ☍♅ r. ⚹ ♅ a.n. ⚹ Ψ p.n. ☌♇ r.
☽ p.n. ⚹ ☿ p.n. □♂ p.n. ☍♃ p.n.
☽ a.n. △♀ r. ☍♂ p.n. △♂ a.n. □♃ p.n.
♀ p.n. ☌MC r. ☍♅ p.n.
♂ a.n. △♄ p.n. ☍♄ r. △♅ p.n. ⚹ ♇ a.n.

As the progressed Lunar Revolution is an extension of the major progressed Solar Revolution, it is important to relate the positions in the monthly figure to those in the yearly figure, in so far as the major aspects are concerned. These are the main configurations formed:

Monthly MC a.n. ☍ Yearly ♀ p.n.
Monthly Asc. a.n. ☌ Yearly ♀ a.n.
Monthly ☉ a.n. (☍ Yearly MC p.n.)
Monthly ☽ p.n. ☌ Yearly ♀ p.n. □♂ p.n. ☍♃ p.n.
    □♄ p.n.
Monthly ♃ p.n. ☍ Yearly MC p.n.
Monthly ♃ a.n. ☌ Yearly Asc. a.n.

The majority of these aspects are in keeping with the nature of the event, which occurred 19 days after the day of the progressed Lunar Return. The weekly series of directions, based on the planetary positions three days before and after the days of the Lunar Returns, contain the following significant aspects:

MC a.n. p. ☍☽ p.n. □♂ p.n. p. △♇ r.
MC a.n. con. ☍☉ r.
Asc. p.n. p. in ♎ ☍♄ a.n.
Asc. a.n. p. ⚹ ☉ r.
(MC p.n. p. ☌midpoint ♀, ♂ r. ⚹ ♀ a.n. p.)
(MC a.n. p. △☉ p.n. p. ☌♃ r.)
(MC a.n. con. △☉ p.n. con. in ♎ ☌♃ a.n.)
(Asc. p.n. p. ☌☉ p.n. p. in ♎ △♃ r.)
(Asc. p.n. con. ☌☉ p.n. con. ☌☽ r. in ♎)
(Asc. a.n. p. △☽ r.)

(Asc. a.n. con. ☌ ☿ a.n. △♀ p.n. p.)
☉ a.n. con. ☌ ♇ r.
♀ p.n. con. △♄ r. ✶ ♄ p.n. con.
♀ a.n. p. ✶ ♂ r.

The following contacts are also formed:

Monthly MC a.n. p. ☌ Yearly ♃ p.n.
Monthly Asc. a.n. p. ☌ Yearly ♀ a.n.
Monthly ☉ a.n. p. (☍ Yearly MC p.n.)

Here the aspects involving the precessional angles are clearly the more indicative of marriage. Several of the directions formed represent the completion of aspects already noted as being within orbs in the main configurations previously tabulated, while the general character of the progressions is quite in keeping with the nature of the event. Our final operation is to examine the daily directions, the directional days being 21 October and 13 September 1926, and 1 July and 23 May 1878. The principal progressed aspects are these:

MC p.n. p. ✶ ☉ p.n. con. □♀ p.n. p. ✶ ♂ p.n.
MC p.n. p. △♃ r.
MC a.n. con. □☉ p.n. p. in ♎
Asc. p.n. p. in ♎ ☍♀ a.n. con. △♃ p.n.
Asc. p.n. con. ✶ ♀ r. △♂ p.n. p.
Asc. a.n. con. ☌ ♂ a.n.
(MC p.n. con. ☌☉ a.n.)
(MC a.n. p. △☉ p.n. p. in ♎ ☍ ♅ a.n. ♆ p.n.)
(MC a.n. con. △☉ p.n. con. △♂ p.n.)
(Asc. p.n. p. □♂ a.n.)
(Asc. p.n. con. ✶ ♂ a.n. ✶ ♄ p.n.)
(Asc. a.n. p. ☌☉ a.n.)
(Asc. a.n. con. □♂ a.n. p. □♃ a.n. p.)
(☉ a.n. p. ☌MC p.n. ☌♂ a.n. con.)
(♀ p.n. con. □ Asc. a.n.)
(☉ a.n. con. ☌Asc. ✶ ♄ a.n.)
♀ a.n. con. ✶ MC a.n. ✶ ♅ r.
♀ a.n. p. △ Asc. p.n. ✶ ♄ a.n. con.
♀ p.n. p. in ♎ △♇ r.
♂ p.n. con. ☍☽ a.n. □♃ p.n.

In addition we have also to consider the following aspects:

Monthly ♀ p.n. p. △ Yearly ♃ p.n.
Monthly ♂ a.n. p. ☍ Yearly Asc. a.n.
Monthly ♃ a.n. p. ♂ Yearly Asc. a.n.

This impressive list of progressed aspects contains very few which are not immediately recognizable as being in keeping with the nature of the event and many which stimulate sensitive points in the main configurations or in the weekly series of directions.

As there is no essential difference between progressed and converse directions, either in the yearly, monthly, weekly or daily series, it is possible to cast a lunar return for the moment *before* birth when the Moon returns to its progressed position by yearly secondary direction *after* birth and for the moment *after* birth when the Moon returns to its converse position by yearly secondary direction. In the case of Ann Harding, the day of such a lunar return after birth does not coincide with the day of the corresponding return before birth, owing to the fact that certain eccentricities in the Moon's orbit cause its apparent speed, viewed from the earth, to vary considerably at different times of the month. The day of the Moon's return after birth to its secondary converse position in our example horoscope is 9 October 1926. The corresponding directional day before birth is 4 June 1878, but the Moon's return before birth to its secondary progressed position takes place on 6 June 1878. It is therefore necessary to construct complementary antenatal and postnatal equivalent figures in order to obtain a complete picture.

The angular and planetary positions in the postnatal 'Converse' Lunar Revolution and in the complementary antenatal equivalent, together with the positions of the radical planets and angles are given below in tabular form.

	MC	Asc.	☉	☽	☿	♀	♂	♃	♄	♅	♆	♇
Nativity	27° ♍	14° ♐	14° ♌	6° ♎	10° ♌	15° ♋	12° ♋	12° ♒ R	23° ♑ R	17° ♐ R	2° ♋	19° ♓
Postnatal Converse Lunar Revolution	26° ♎ (6° ♏)	1° ♉ (10° ♉)	15° ♎	17° ♏ (18° ♏)	29° ♎	4° ♎	18° ♑ R	17° ♑ R	23° ♏	26° ♓	26° ♌	16° ♋
Antenatal Equivalent	27° ♌ (17° ♌)	16° ♏ (9° ♏)	14° ♓	2° ♌ (2° ♌)	20° ♑	1° ♑	18° ♋	7° ♒ R	1° ♈	25° ♌	8° ♑	25° ♑

In order to obtain the angles of the precessional figures, the positions of which are given in brackets, the necessary amount of precession has been added to the longitude of the secondary converse Moon, as the return takes place after birth. The principal configurations which appear in the complete Lunar Revolution are these:

MC p.n. ⚹ ♅ a.n. ♆ p.n.
MC a.n. □♄ p.n. ☌♅ a.n. ☌♆ p.n. □♇ a.n.
Asc. p.n. △♀ a.n. □♄ a.n. ☍♆ r.
Asc. a.n. ☌☽ p.n. ☍☿ a.n. △♀ r. ☍♂ p.n. △♂
    a.n. □♃ p.n. △♇ p.n.
(MC p.n. □☽ a.n. ☍♀, ♆ a.n.)
(MC a.n. ☌☉ r., □♂ p.n. ☍♃ p.n. △♅ r.)
(Asc. p.n. ☍♀, ♂ r. ☍♇ p.n. ☍♂ a.n.)
(Asc. a.n. ☍♀, ♆ a.n.)
☉ p.n. in ♎ □♀ r. △♃ p.n.
☉ a.n. ☍Asc. r. △♃ r. ☍♅ r. ☌♇ r.
♅ p.n. ☍MC r.
♀ p.n. in ♎ ☌☽ r. △♃ a.n. ☍♄ a.n.

Configurations involving the yearly progressed Solar Revolution (in this case the Postnatal Converse Solar Revolution and the Antenatal Equivalent) are as follows:

Monthly MC a.n. ☍ Yearly ♃ p.n.
(Monthly Asc. a.n. ☍ Yearly ♆ a.n.)
Monthly ☉ p.n. ☌ Yearly ☽ a.n. in ♎
Monthly ☽ p.n. ☍ Monthly ♂ p.n. ☌ Yearly Asc. a.n.,
    ♄ p.n.
Monthly ☽ a.n. ☍ Yearly Asc. a.n. △ Yearly ♄ a.n.
Monthly ♀ p.n. in ♎ ☌ Yearly Asc. p.n.
Monthly ♀ a.n. △ Yearly ♅ a.n.
Monthly ♂ a.n., ♇ p.n. (☍ Yearly Asc. p.n.)

These aspect groupings, both in their nature and in their number, compare favourably with the results obtained with other types of lunar return and if suitable directions are formed in the weekly and daily series, these will serve to confirm the efficacy of this type of figure. The wedding took place twelve days after the day of the lunar return, so that the weekly directional days will fall nearly two days before and after the days of the revolutional figures. The following directions are produced:

MC a.n. p. △♀ a.n. con.
MC a.n. con. ♂♅ a.n. ♆ p.n.
Asc. p.n. p. ☐♀ p.n. con. in ♎ △♀ a.n. p. ☍♆ r.
Asc. a.n. p. ♂☽ p.n. ☍♂ p.n. △♂ a.n.
Asc. a.n. con. △♀ r., ♇ p.n.
(MC p.n. p. ☍♆ p.n.)
(MC a.n. p. ⚹ ♇ r.)
(MC a.n. con. ⚹ ☉ p.n. in ♎ ⚹ ☉ a.n. p.)
(Asc. p.n. p. ☍♂ r.)
(Asc. a.n. con. ☐♃ a.n.)
☉ p.n. p. in ♎ △♃ p.n. ⚹ ♅ r.
☉ p.n. con. in ♎ ⚹ Asc. r.
☉ a.n. con. △♃ r.
♀ p.n. p. in ♎ ♂☽ r. △♃ a.n.

In addition the following aspects are formed:

Monthly ♀ p.n. con. in ♎ ♂ Yearly Asc. p.n.
Monthly ☉ a.n. p. △ Yearly ☽ a.n. in ♎
Monthly ☉ a.n. con. ⚹ Yearly ♀ a.n.
Monthly ♂ a.n. con. (☍ Yearly Asc. p.n.)

The majority of these aspects are in keeping with the nature of the
event and several represent the completion of aspects already
previously noted in the main configurations. The daily aspects fall
due twelve days before and after the day of the revolutional
figures, on 27 September and 21 October 1926, and on 23 May
and 16 June 1878. These are the principal directions formed:

MC p.n. p. ☍♆ p.n.
MC p.n. con. in ♎ ⚹ ☉ r. △☉ a.n.
Asc. p.n. p. ☍♂ r.
Asc. a.n. p. ♂♄ p.n. p. ☍♇ a.n.
Asc. a.n. con. ☍♆ a.n.
(MC p.n. p. ♂☽ p.n. ☍♂ p.n.)
(MC a.n. con. ⚹ ☽ r. ☍♃ a.n.)
(Asc. p.n. p. ♂♄ r. ⚹ ♄ p.n.)
(Asc. p.n. con. △♀ a.n. ☐♄ a.n.)
(Asc. a.n. p. ☐♃ p.n.)
☉ p.n. p. in ♎ ⚹ MC a.n.
♂ p.n. p. ☍Asc. a.n.
♂ a.n. p. ☐ MC p.n. △ ♅ p.n.

(♀ a.n. con. △ MC a.n. △♅ r.)
(♂ a.n. con. ☍Asc. p.n.)
☉ p.n. con. in ♎ ☌♀ p.n.
☉ a.n. con. ⚹ ☽ a.n. ⚹ ♄ a.n.
♀ p.n. p. in ♎ △♇ r.
♀ p.n. con. △♂ p.n. con. □♇ r.
♀ a.n. p. □☉ r.

Also, the following contacts between the monthly and yearly figures occur:

Monthly MC p.n. con. ♂ Yearly ☽ a.n. in ♎
Monthly ☉ p.n. p. in ♎ △ Yearly ♃ p.n.
Monthly ☉ a.n. con. △ Yearly Asc. p.n. in ♎
Monthly ♀ p.n. p. in ♎ ☍ Yearly ♂ p.n.
Monthly ♀ a.n. p. △ Yearly ♂ a.n.

These numerous aspects are nearly all consistent in character with the nature of the event and several stimulate sensitive points in the basic configurations and in the weekly directions already listed above. In order to conclude our survey of progressed and converse lunar returns we have now to examine the figure for the return of the Moon to its secondary progressed position which took place on 6 June 1878, and its complementary postnatal equivalent, calculated for 7 October 1926. The positions of the planets and angles in these two figures, together with the natal planets and angles, are set out below in tabular form. The precessional increment should be subtracted from the longitude of the secondary progressed Moon in order to obtain the precessional horoscope, the angles of which, together with the lunar positions, are included in brackets in the table.

	MC	Asc.	☉	☽	☿	♀	♂	♃	♄	♅	Ψ	♇
Nativity	27° ♍	14° ♐	14° ♌	6° ♎	10° ♌	15° ♋	12° ♋	12°R ♒	23°R ♑	17°R ♐	2° ♋	19° ♓
Antenatal Progressed Lunar Revolution	6° ♐ (28° ♏)	17° ♒ (5° ♒)	15° ♓	19° ♌ (19° ♌)	21° ♑	2° ♑	19° ♋	7°R ♒	1° ♈	25° ♌	8° ♑	25° ♑
Postnatal Equivalent	18° ♋ (26° ♋)	15° ♎ (22° ♎)	13° ♎	19° ♎ (20° ♎)	26° ♎	2° ♎	19°R ♑	17°R ♒	23° ♏	26°R ♓	26° ♌	16° ♋

These are the principal configurations:

MC p.n. ☌♀, ♂ r. ☌♂ a.n. ☌♇ p.n.
MC a.n. ✶☽ r. ✶♀ p.n. ✶♃ a.n.
Asc. p.n. ☌☉ p.n., ☽ p.n. in ♎ △☉ a.n. △♃ r. and
  p.n. ✶♅ r. △♇ r.
Asc. a.n. ☍☉ r. ☍☽ a.n. □♂ p.n. ☌♃ p.n. ✶♅ r.
  △♇ r.
(MC p.n. △♄ p.n. △♅ p.n.)
(MC a.n. ☌♄ p.n. □♅ a.n. □♆ p.n. ☍♇ a.n.)
(Asc. p.n. ☌☽ p.n. □♄ r.)
(Asc. a.n. △☽ r., ♀ p.n. ☌♃ a.n.)
♅ p.n. ☍ MC r. ✶♇ a.n.
☉ a.n. ☍Asc. r. △♃ p.n. ☍♅ r. ☌♇ r.
♀ an. ✶♆ r.
♀ p.n. □♆ r.

The following configurations, formed between the monthly and the corresponding yearly figures must also be taken into account:

Monthly MC p.n. ☌ Yearly ☉ p.n.
(Monthly MC p.n. ☍ Yearly ♃ a.n.)
Monthly Asc. p.n., ☉ p.n. in ♎ ☌ Yearly ☽ a.n.
Monthly ☽ a.n. ✶ Yearly ♀ p.n. ✶ Yearly ♂ p.n.
Monthly ♀ p.n. in ♎ ☌Yearly Asc. p.n.
Monthly ♂ p.n. (☍ Yearly Asc. a.n.)
Monthly ♂ a.n. (☍ Yearly Asc. p.n.)
Monthly ♄ p.n. ☌ Yearly MC a.n.

Except for one or two of the aspects involving the angles of the precessional figures, these configurations are all very much in conformity with the nature of the event and, taken as a whole, compare very favourably with the indications given by the other types of lunar revolution already reviewed.

We can now turn our attention to the weekly directions measuring to the event which took place 14 days after the day of the postnatal equivalent. The weekly directional days therefore fall two days before and after the days of the revolutional figures. These are the main directions formed:

MC p.n. con. ✶ ♀ p.n. p. in ♎
MC a.n. p. ☌♂ a.n.
MC a.n. con. ☌♀ r., ♇ p.n.
Asc. p.n. p. △☽ p.n. in ♎ ☍☽ a.n. △♇ r.

Asc. p.n. con. ☍☉ r. △☉ p.n. △☉ a.n. con.
Asc. a.n. p. △♃ p.n. ✶ ♅ r.
Asc. a.n. con. ✶ ☉ r. ♂☉ p.n. in ♎
(MC a.n. con. ☍♇ a.n.)
(MC p.n. con. △♄ p.n.)
(Asc. p.n. con. □♀ a.n.)
(Asc. a.n. con. ♂☽ p.n. △♇ r.)
☉ p.n. p. ♂Asc. p.n. in ♎
♂ a.n. con. ♂MC p.n.
(♀ a.n. p. □ Asc. a.n.)
☉ p.n. con. in ♎ △♃ r.
☉ a.n. p. △♃ p.n. ☍♅ r.

In addition the following aspects are formed:

Monthly ☉ p.n. p. in ♎ ♂ Yearly ☽ a.n.
Monthly ☉ p.n. con. in ♎ (♂ Yearly ☽ a.n.)
Monthly ☉ a.n. con. □ Yearly ☽ p.n. □ Yearly ♂ a.n.
Monthly ♀ p.n. con. ☍ Yearly ♅ p.n.
Monthly ♀ a.n. con. △ Yearly ♅ a.n.
Monthly ♂ a.n. p. ♂ Yearly ☉ p.n.

These aspects are all appropriate in character to the nature of the event and several of them complete aspects already in orbs that have been noted above in the list of special configurations.

In order to complete our survey we have now only to take note of the directions formed in the daily series of progressions. The directional days fall on 21 October and 23 September 1926, and on 20 June and 23 May 1878. These are the principal aspects:

MC p.n. p. ✶ ♀ p.n. in ♎
MC a.n. p. ✶ ☽ p.n., ♀ p.n. p. in ♎ ☍♇ r.
MC a.n. con. ♂♄ p.n.
Asc. p.n. p. ♂☉ p.n. p. ♂☿ p.n. in ♎ ✶ ♅ a.n. ♆ p.n.
Asc. a.n. p. ✶ ♆ a.n.
Asc. a.n. con. ☍♂ a.n. p.
(MC p.n. con. ♂♂ r.)
(MC a.n. p. ✶ ♃ r.)
(MC a.n. con. □☉ r. △ midpoint ♀, ♂ r. ✶ ♀
   p.n. con.)
(Asc. p.n. p. ☍♀ a.n.)
(Asc. p.n. con. □♂ a.n. con.)

(Asc. a.n. p. ☍ ♅ a.n., ♆ p.n. □ ♇ a.n.)
(Asc. a.n. con. □ ☽ p.n., ♀ p.n. p. in ♎ ☍ ♂ a.n.
  △ ♂ p.n.)
♀ p.n. con. □ Asc. r.
♀ a.n. con. ✶ Asc. a.n., ♃ a.n. △ ♅ r.
☉ a.n. con. △ ☿ p.n. con., ♀ p.n. in ♎
♀ a.n. p. ☌ ♂ p.n. ✶ ♂ a.n.
♂ p.n. p. ✶ ♀ r., ♇ p.n.

Also the following aspects are formed between factors in the monthly and yearly figures:

Monthly ☉ p.n. p. in ♎ △ Yearly ♃ p.n.
Monthly ☉ p.n. con. ☍ Yearly ♅ p.n.
Monthly ☉ a.n. con. △ Yearly Asc. p.n. in ♎
Monthly ♀ p.n. p. in ♎ ☍ Yearly ♂ p.n.
Monthly ♀ p.n. con. ☌ Yearly ♂ a.n.
Monthly ♀ a.n. p. (☍ Yearly Asc. a.n., ♄ p.n.)
Monthly ♂ a.n. p. ☍ Yearly ♃ a.n.

Nearly all these aspects will be immediately recognizable as being in conformity with the nature of the event and several of them stimulate sensitive points in the basic configurations already noted or in the weekly series of directions. The indications of the event furnished by the several progressed lunar revolutions examined demonstrate very clearly the value of this type of figure and the extra trouble involved in their calculation is shown to be well worthwhile.

15.

THE MONTHLY NEW MOON

It was demonstrated in Chapter 11 that a figure cast for the moment of the annual return of the Sun to the place held by the Moon at birth (the Annual New Moon Horoscope) gives highly significant indications of the course of events during the ensuing twelve months. It is possible to construct a corresponding monthly figure by calculating a horoscope for the periodical return of the Moon to the place of the Sun at birth. In relation to the nativity such a figure will represent a monthly New Moon horoscope.

As in all other series of revolutional horoscopes, the postnatal figure should be considered in conjunction with its antenatal counterpart. Only in rare cases will the postnatal revolutional day coincide exactly in time with the antenatal revolutional day and it will be necessary to construct the appropriate postnatal and antenatal equivalent figures in order to obtain a complete picture.

It would appear logical to consider the monthly New Moon as an extension of the yearly New Moon and to regard as most significant that monthly figure which most nearly reproduces the main characteristics of the yearly figure. As in the case of the yearly New Moon figure, the monthly New Moon horoscope may be calculated with or without precession. Naturally, the monthly figures without precession should be compared with the yearly figures calculated on the same basis.

The calculation of the monthly New Moon horoscope and its complementary equivalent is carried out in exactly the same way as the calculation of the ordinary Lunar Revolution except that the point of return is the longitude of the radical Sun and not the longitude of the radical Moon. As an example of this type of figure, let us examine the monthly New Moon covering the period of Ann Harding's marriage on 21 October 1926.

The postnatal figure falls due just after midnight on 1-2 October 1926, when the Moon passes over 14°23'33" Leo, the longitude of the radical Sun. The theoretical speed of the Moon at midnight is 5°55'50" (in terms of 12 hours' motion) and the return takes place at 12.09 a.m. GMT. The Sidereal Time at Chicago is 18 hours 56 minutes, giving a Midheaven of 13° Capricorn for the New Moon figure and an Ascendant of 24° Aries. The corresponding antenatal equivalent has a Midheaven of 11° Gemini and an Ascendant of 14° Virgo and is cast for 5.10 p.m. GMT 11 June 1878.

The antenatal monthly New Moon for the same period occurs on 5 June 1878 when the Moon returns to the exact longitude of the radical Sun at 7.43 p.m. GMT. The Moon's theoretical speed is 13°31'27" and the Sidereal Time at Chicago is 6 hours 47 minutes, giving a Midheaven of 11° Cancer and an Ascendant of 9° Libra. The corresponding postnatal equivalent has a Midheaven of 13° Sagittarius and an Ascendant of 28° Aquarius and is cast for 9.32 p.m. GMT, 8 October 1926.

The postnatal monthly New Moon calculated with an allowance for precession will also fall on 2 October 1926. This day is 24 years 56 days after the day of birth and a precessional increment of 20'13" must therefore be added to the longitude of the radical Sun, bringing it to 14°43'46" Leo. As a visual inspection of the Ephemeris shows that the Moon's arrival at this point will not be substantially later than in the case of the figure cast without making an allowance for precession, the same rate of progress may be used as in the former case. The time of the return is 12.50 a.m. GMT and the corresponding Sidereal Time at Chicago is 19 hours 38 minutes, giving a Midheaven of 22° Capricorn and an Ascendant of 11° Taurus. The antenatal equivalent based on this figure has a Midheaven of 1° Gemini and an Ascendant of 6° Virgo and is cast for 4.28 p.m. GMT, 11 June 1878.

The ante-natal monthly New Moon, cast with an allowance for precession, falls on 5 June 1878, which is 24 years 63 days before birth. The precessional increment for this period of time is 20'15" and therefore this amount of arc must be subtracted from the longitude of the radical Sun in order to arrive at the correct point of return for the antenatal figure. The Sun's adjusted longitude is thus 14°03'18" Leo. The Moon returns to this position at 7.08 p.m. GMT when its theoretical speed is approximately 13°51'24" (in terms of 24 hours' motion). The Sidereal Time at Chicago is

6 hours 13 minutes and the Midheaven is 3° Cancer and the Ascendant 2° Libra. The corresponding postnatal equivalent falls on 8 October 1926, with a Midheaven of 21° Sagittarius and an Ascendant of 12° Pisces and is cast for 10.07 p.m. GMT.

For easy reference the position of the planets and angles in the postnatal monthly New Moon, its complementary antenatal equivalent and the nativity are set forth in tabular form below.

	MC	Asc.	☉	☽	☿	♀	♂	♃	♄	♅	♆	♇
Nativity	27° ♍	14° ♐	14° ♌	6° ♎	10° ♌	15° ♋	12° ♋	12°R ♒	23°R ♑	17°R ♐	2° ♋	19° ♓
Postnatal Monthly New Moon	13° ♉ (22° ♉)	24° ♈ (11° ☿)	8° ♎	14° ♌	17° ♎	25° ♍	19° ♑	17°R ♒	23° ♏	27°R ♓	26° ♌	16° ♋
Antenatal Equivalent	11° ♓ (1° ♓)	14° ♍ (6° ♍)	20° ♓	7° ♍	28° ♑	8° ♑	22° ♋	6°R ♒	2° ♈	26° ♌	8° ♑	25° ♑

The principal configurations are listed below. The aspects shown in brackets are those involving the figures calculated with an allowance for precession. The planetary positions given in the table will serve for both types of figure, since there is only a difference of about 40 minutes in the timing of the two figures.

MC p.n. ☍♀, ♂ r. ☍♇ p.n.
Asc. p.n. △♅ a.n. △♆ p.n.
MC a.n. △♃ r.
(MC p.n. ☍♂ p.n.)
(Asc. p.n. ☍☽ a.n. ♂♀, ♆ a.n.)
☉ p.n. ♂☽ r. in ♎ △♃ a.n.
☽ p.n. ♂☉ r. □♂ p.n. ☍♃ p.n.
☉ a.n. ♂♇ r. △♃ p.n.
☽ a.n. ☍♀ a.n. □♃ a.n. ☍♇ a.n.
♀ p.n. ♂ MC r. △♂ p.n. ⚹ ♄ p.n. △♄ r. ☍♅ p.n.
  △♇ a.n.

In addition the following aspects are formed between the monthly and yearly New Moon figures:

(Monthly MC a.n. ☍ Yearly ☽ a.n.)
(Monthly Asc. p.n. ♂ Yearly ♀, ♆ a.n.)

Although there is only one striking cross-aspect between the lunar figures and the major Annual New Moon figures it is perhaps

significant that the monthly New Moon figure falls due only two
days after the yearly figure, cast for 30 September 1926. Especially
notable in the configurations listed above is the fact that, at the
time the lunation Moon was in conjunction with the radical Sun,
the lunation Sun was also in conjunction with the radical Moon
and in both cases the luminaries were in aspect to Jupiter, ruler
of the radical Ascendant.

Now let us examine the directions in the lunar horoscopes
measuring to the time of marriage, which took place on 21
October 1926, 19 days after the day of the monthly New Moon.
The weekly directions will therefore be represented by the aspects
formed by the planets three days before and after the days on
which the monthly lunar figures fell due. Here are the aspects for
the event:

MC p.n. p. ☍♀ r.
(♀ a.n. p. ♂Asc. p.n.)
(Asc. a.n. p. △♀, Ψ a.n.)
♀ p.n. p. ♂MC r.
☿ a.n. con. △♀ p.n. ♂♄ r.
♂ a.n. p. □ Asc. p.n.

The following aspect is also formed:

Monthly ♂ a.n. p. ⚹ Yearly ♀ p.n.

These directions are not so numerous as the weekly ones furnished
by the lunar returns dealt with in Chapter 13 but the activity of
Venus in the progressed aspects noted above is sufficient to focus
attention on the possibility of marriage during the period,
bearing in mind the special emphasis in this direction suggested
by the nature of the basic configurations in the monthly New
Moon figure and its complementary equivalent.

We may now turn our attention to the daily series of
progressions formed by the planets 19 days before and after the
day of the lunar figures. The significant aspects in this series are
listed below:

Asc. p.n. p. △♀ p.n. ♂♇ a.n.
Asc. p.n. con. □♀ p.n. △Ψ p.n. con.
Asc. a.n. p. ☍♅ p.n. con.
(MC p.n. p. ♂♃ r.)

(Asc. p.n. p. ✶ ♂ a.n. p. △♃ a.n. p.)
(Asc. p.n. con. ☍☉ p.n., ☽ r. in ♎ ✶ ♃ a.n.)
(MC a.n. p. ♂♇ r. △♀ p.n.p. in ♎)
☉ p.n. con. ☐♇ r.
☉ a.n. p. ✶ ☽ a.n. ✶ ♀ a.n. ✶ ♆ a.n.
☉ a.n. con. ✶ ♄ a.n. ☐♀ p.n. con.
♀ a.n. con. △♅ r.

The following aspects must also be taken into account:

Monthly ☉ p.n. con. △ Yearly ♂ p.n.
Monthly ☉ a.n. p. ☍ Yearly MC a.n.
Monthly ♀ p.n. p. in ♎ (♂ Yearly MC p.n.)
Monthly ♃ a.n. con. ✶ Yearly Asc. a.n.

These directions bear eloquent witness to the usefulness of the monthly New Moon figure and its complementary equivalent and to the weekly and daily directions based on these figures. But we still have to examine the testimony of the antenatal Monthly New Moon and its counterpart, the postnatal New Moon equivalent. For easy reference the positions of the planets and angles in these two figures are set out below in tabular form:

	MC	Asc.	☉	☽	☿	♀	♂	♃	♄	♅	♆	♇
Antenatal Monthly New Moon	11°♋ (3°♋)	9°♎ (2°♎)	15°♓	14°♓ (14°♌)	20°♑	2°♑	19°♋	7°♒R	1°♈	25°♌	8°♑	25°♑
Postnatal Equivalent	13°♐ (21°♐)	28°♒ (12°♓)	14°♎	6°♏ (7°♏)	28°♎	3°♎	18°♑R	17°♒R	23°♏	28°♓R	25°♌	16°♋

Once again we should first take stock of the main configurations present in these figures and any connection they may have with the principal factors in the nativity. They are as follows:

MC p.n. △☉ r.
MC p.n. ♂Asc. r. ☍☉ a.n. ✶ ♃ r.
Asc. a.n. ♂☉, ♀ p.n. ♂☽ r. in ♎ △♃ a.n.
Asc. p.n. ☍♅ a.n. ☍♆ p.n. △☿ p.n. in ♎
(Asc. a.n. ♂☽ r. ♂♀ p.n. in ♎ ☍♄ a.n.)
(MC p.n. ☍☉ a.n. ♂♅ r. ☍♇ r.)
(Asc. p.n. △♂ r.)
☉ p.n. in ♎ ✶ ☽ a.n. △♃ p.n. and r.

☉ a.n. ⚹ ☽ a.n. △♃ p.n. and r.
☽ p.n. ☍♀, ♆ a.n. □♃ a.n.
♅ p.n. ☍ MC r.

These numerous configurations are nearly all appropriate to the event and, in addition, the following configurations are formed between factors in the monthly and the corresponding yearly figures:

Monthly Asc. p.n. ☌ Yearly ♃ p.n.
Monthly Asc. a.n. ☌ Yearly ☉ a.n. in ♎
(Monthly MC p.n. ☍ Yearly ☉ p.n.)
(Monthly Asc. a.n., ♀ p.n. ☌ Yearly ♂ a.n. in ♎)
Monthly ♂ p.n. △ Yearly ♀ p.n.
Monthly ♂ a.n. ⚹ Yearly ♀ p.n.
Monthly ♀ p.n. ☌ Yearly ☉, ♂ a.n. in ♎
Monthly ♀ a.n. △ Yearly Asc. a.n.
Monthly ♇ p.n. △ Yearly Asc. p.n. △ Yearly ☽ a.n.
Monthly ♅ p.n. (☌ Yearly Asc. p.n. ☍ Asc. a.n.)
Monthly ♅ a.n., ♆ p.n. ☌ Yearly MC p.n.

Now let us examine the directions in this second pair of lunar horoscopes measuring to the time of marriage (21 October 1926), 13 days after the day of the postnatal equivalent figure. The weekly directions will therefore be represented by the aspects formed by the planets two days before and after the days on which the lunation figures fall due. Here are the aspects for the event:

MC a.n. p. ☌♂ r.
MC p.n. p. ☍☉ a.n.
Asc. p.n. con. ☍♅ a.n. ☍♆ p.n.
Asc. a.n. p. in ♎, △♃ r.
Asc. a.n. con. in ♎ △♃ a.n.
(MC p.n. con. ☍♇ r.)
(Asc. p.n. p. △♀ r.)
☉ p.n. p. in ♎ △♃ p.n. ⚹ ♅ r.
☉ p.n. con. in ♎ △♃ r.
☉ a.n. p. △♃ p.n. ☍♅ r.
☉ a.n. con. △♃ r.
♀ p.n. p. ☌☽ r. in ♎

Also the following aspects are formed between the monthly and yearly figures:

(Monthly MC p.n. p. ☍ Yearly ☉ p.n.)
Monthly ♀ p.n. p. in ♎ ♂ Yearly a.n. ☉
Monthly ♂ a.n. p. △ Yearly ☽ a.n., ♄ p.n.

The last part of our investigation concerns the aspects formed in the daily series of directions, formed by the planets 13 days before and after the day of the lunar figure and the moving angles progressed according to the system already explained in previous chapters. The significant aspects are listed below:

Asc. a.n. p. in ♎ △♇ r.
Asc. a.n. con. △☽ p.n. con.
Asc. p.n. p. ⚹ ♄ r. △♄ p.n.
Asc. p.n. con. △☽ r. in ♎ ♂♃ a.n.
(☉ a.n. con. △ Asc. a.n. in ♎)
(MC a.n. p. ♂♀ r.)
(Asc. a.n. p. △♃ r. ⚹ ☽ a.n.)
(MC a.n. con. ♂♇ r.)
(Asc. p.n. p. ☍☽ r. in ♎ ⚹ ♃ a.n.)
(Asc. p.n. con. △♇ r.)
☿ p.n. con. in ♎ △♃ a.n.
☉ p.n. p. in ♎ △☽ a.n. p.
☽ a.n. p. ♂♃ r.
♀ a.n. con. △♅ r.
♂ a.n. con. ♂ MC a.n.
♀ p.n. con. □♅ r.

The following additional aspects must also be taken into account:

(Monthly Asc. p.n. p. ☍ Yearly ☉ a.n. in ♎)
Monthly ☉ p.n. p. in ♎ ♂ Yearly MC a.n.
Monthly ☉ p.n. con. in ♎ □ Yearly Asc. a.n.
Monthly ☉ a.n. con. △ Yearly ♂ a.n. in ♎
Monthly ♂ p.n. p. ☍ Yearly Asc. p.n.

16.

THE MONTHLY
MOONRISE HOROSCOPE

We have seen how a figure calculated for the moment of the exact return of the Sun to the position held by the Ascendant at birth contains sufficient indications of the experiences that are to befall the native during the following twelve months. We have seen also that the Solar Revolution appears to discharge its effects in accordance with the indications contained in the Lunar Revolutions that fall in the subsequent year. Similarly, the yearly New Moon horoscopes operate most strongly under the stimulus of the monthly New Moon horoscopes. The monthly figure corresponding to the Annual Sunrise horoscope should therefore be one based on the periodical return of the Moon to the exact degree, minute and second of the rising degree, as determined by the correct Prenatal Epoch.

The monthly Moonrise horoscope may be treated in exactly the same way as the other types of Lunar Revolution and calculated with or without an allowance for precession. The method of calculation is the same as that given in Chapter 13 except that the return must be calculated for the moment of the Moon's conjunction with the natal Ascendant and not for its return to its own place at birth.

The postnatal monthly Moonrise figure covering the period in which Ann Harding's marriage occurred is cast for 11 October 1926, when the Moon passes over the longitude of the radical Ascendant, 14°40′56″ Sagittarius. The Moon reaches this position at 9.30 p.m. GMT, when its theoretical speed is 6°26′10″ in terms of 12 hours' motion. The corresponding Sidereal Time at Chicago is 16 hours 57 minutes, giving a Midheaven of 15° Sagittarius and an Ascendant of 2° Pisces. The antenatal equivalent of this figure falls on 2 June 1878, and is cast for 7.56 p.m. GMT, Midheaven 8° Cancer; Ascendant 7° Libra.

The horoscope covering the same period but cast for the return of the Moon to the place of the radical Ascendant, plus an increment of 20'15" to compensate for the precessional movement of the equinoxes in the 24 years and 9 weeks that had elapsed since the native's birth, is cast for 10.08 p.m. GMT, when the Moon returns to 15°01'11" Sagittarius, its theoretical speed being 6°26'19" in terms of 12 hours' motion. The corresponding Sidereal Time at Chicago, 17 hours 35 minutes, gives a Midheaven of 24° Sagittarius and an Ascendant of 19° Pisces. The antenatal equivalent, which also falls on 2 June 1878, is cast for 7.20 p.m. GMT and has a Midheaven of 29° Gemini and an Ascendant of 29° Virgo.

The precessional increment for the antenatal Moonrise figure is not exactly the same as that used for the postnatal figure because only in rare instances will the postnatal Moon arrive at its conjunction with the radical Ascendant on the day corresponding with that on which the antenatal Moon arrives at the same conjunction. Only if the radical Moon is within a few degrees of the Descendant is such a coincidence possible. In this case the native was 24 years and 54 days old when the antenatal Moonrise figure fell due and the appropriate increment of 24'14" subtracted from the longitude of the radical Ascendant gives 14°20'42" Sagittarius as the adjusted longitude of the radical Ascendant. The Moon reaches this point at 7.28 a.m. GMT on 14 June 1878, when its theoretical speed is 13°47'37" in terms of 24 hours' motion. The Midheaven is 15° Capricorn and the Ascendant 28° Aries. The postnatal equivalent, which falls on 29 September 1926, is cast for 9.51 a.m. GMT and has a Midheaven of 9° Gemini and an Ascendant of 12° Virgo.

The antenatal Moonrise horoscope, cast without an allowance for precession, has a Midheaven of 23° Capricorn and an Ascendant of 12° Taurus. The GMT of the return is 8.03 a.m., when the Moon's theoretical speed is 13°47'23". The corresponding Sidereal Time at Chicago is 19 hours 41 minutes. The equivalent postnatal figure falls on 29 September 1926, at 9.23 a.m. with a Midheaven of 0° Gemini and an Ascendant of 5° Virgo.

In order to facilitate a study of the various configurations present in the combined monthly Moonrise horoscopes, the position in the postnatal Moonrise figure and its antenatal equivalent, together with the positions of the angles and planets in the nativity are set out below in tabular form:

	MC	Asc.	☉	☽	☿	♀	♂	♃	♄	♅	♆	♇
Nativity	27° ♍	14° ♐	14° ♌	6° ♎	10° ♌	15° ♋	12° ♋	12°R ♒	23°R ♑	17°R ♐	2° ♋	19° ♓
Postnatal Moonrise Horoscope	15° ♐ (24° ♐)	2° ♓ (19° ♓)	17° ♎	14° ♐ (15° ♐)	3° ♏	7° ♎	18°R ♑	17°R ♒	24° ♏	26°R ♓	26° ♌	16° ♋
Antenatal Equivalent	8° ♋ (29° ♓)	7° ♎ (29° ♍)	12° ♓	4° ♋ (3° ♋)	18° ♑	28° ♈	17° ♋	7°R ♒	1° ♈	25° ♌	8° ♑	26° ♑

The principal configurations are these:

MC p.n. ♂Asc., ♅ r. ☍☉ a.n. ♂☽ p.n. △☉ r.
MC a.n. ♂♀, ♂ r. ♂☽ a.n. □♀ p.n.
Asc. p.n. △☽ a.n., △♀ r.
Asc. a.n. ♂☽ r., ♀ p.n. in ♎ △♃ a.n.
(Asc. a.n. ☍♅ p.n. △♇ a.n.)
♅ p.n. ☍MC r.
☉ p.n. in ♎ △♃ p.n.
☉ a.n. ☍☽ p.n. △♃ p.n.
☿ a.n. ⚹ ♂ a.n. ♂♂ p.n.
♂ a.n. ♂♀ r. ♂♇ p.n.

In addition the following configurations occur between the monthly and the corresponding yearly figures:

Monthly MC p.n., ☽ p.n. ☍☉ a.n. ♂ Yearly ☉ p.n.
  ♂ Yearly MC a.n.
Monthly Asc. p.n. ♂ Yearly ♃ a.n. ☍ Yearly ☽ p.n.
Monthly Asc. a.n., ♂☽ p.n. in ♎ ♂ Yearly ☽ a.n.
  ☍ Yearly ♄ a.n.
(Monthly Asc. p.n. ♂ Yearly ♅ p.n.)
Monthly ☉ p.n. in ♎ △ Monthly ♃ p.n. (⚹Yearly
  MC a.n.)
Monthly ☉ a.n. △ Yearly ♂ a.n.
Monthly ♂ a.n. □ Yearly ☉ a.n.
Monthly ♃ a.n. △ Yearly Asc. p.n. ♂ Yearly ☽ a.n.
  ☍ Yearly ♄ a.n.

All these interchanges between monthly and yearly positions are within a degree of exactitude.

Having established that the main configurations present in the monthly Moonrise figure are consistent in their general nature with the character of the event we may now proceed to survey the weekly and daily directions measuring to the time of the event which took place 10 days after the day of the postnatal Moonrise figure. This period of 1½ weeks will therefore be represented by the passage of a day and a half before and after the days of the Moonrise figures. The principal directions in force are these (those involving the angles of the precessional figures are shown in brackets):

MC p.n. p. ⚹ ☉ p.n., ♃ p.n. ☌ ♅ r.
MC p.n. con. ☌ Asc. r. △☉ r. ☌ ☽ p.n.
Asc. a.n. con. ☌ ☽ r. in ♎ △♃ a.n.
(Asc. p.n. con. △♀ r., ♇ p.n.)
(Asc. a.n. p. in ♎ ☍ ♄ a.n.)
☉ p.n. p. in ♎ ☍ ♇ r.

These directions are fewer in number than those usually thrown up by this method of progression, which is probably accounted for by the fact that the event followed only just over one directional day after the Moonrise horoscope. All the aspects therefore will have been closely within orbs in the revolutional figures. Progressions in the daily series measure to 10 days before and after the lunar revolutional days. These are the principal directions formed:

MC p.n. p. △♅ a.n., ♆ p.n.
MC a.n. p. □☉ p.n. in ♎ □♀ a.n. con. ☌ ♂ a.n.
Asc. p.n. p. □☉ a.n. p.
Asc. p.n. con. ☌ ♃ p.n.
Asc. a.n. p. in ♎ ⚹ ☉ r. □♀ r., ⚹ ☽ p.n.
(MC p.n. con. ☌ Asc. r. △☉ r. 150° ♀ r. ☌ ☽ p.n.)
(MC a.n. con. ☌ ♇ r.)
(Asc. p.n. p. ☍ ♀ p.n. in ♎)
(Asc. a.n. p. ☌ ♀ p.n. in ♎ △♃ a.n.)
(Asc. a.n. con. □☉ a.n. p.)
☉ p.n. con. △♃ a.n. ☌ ♀ p.n., ☽ r. in ♎
♂ a.n. con. ☌ MC a.n.
♀ p.n. p. △♇ r.

In addition, the following aspects are formed:

(Monthly MC p.n. con. ☌ Yearly ☉ p.n.)
Monthly Asc. p.n. p. ☌ Yearly ♅ p.n.

(Monthly Asc. a.n. con. ☍ Yearly ♅ p.n.)
Monthly ⊙ p.n. con. in ♎ ♂ Yearly Asc. p.n.
Monthly ⊙ a.n. con. △ Yearly ♀ p.n.
Monthly ♀ a.n. p. ⚹ Monthly ♂ a.n. con. (△ Yearly
   Asc. p.n.)
Monthly ⊙ a.n. p. □ Yearly ♅ p.n.

All these progressed aspects are in character with the nature of the event and can be regarded as a satisfactory demonstration of the usefulness of this type of lunar horoscope. In order to complete our survey of the combined Moonrise horoscope we must now turn our attention to the antenatal Moonrise figure for the month, together with its postnatal equivalent. For easy reference the positions of the planets and angles in these two horoscopes are set out below in tabular form (precessional positions in brackets):

	MC	Asc.	⊙	☽	☿	♀	♂	♃	♄	♅	♆	♇
Antenatal Moonrise Horoscope	23° ♄ (15° ♄)	12° ♈ (28° ♈)	23° ♓	14° ♐ (14° ♐)	2° ♓	11° ♈	24° ♋	6° ♒	2° ♈	27° ♌	9° ♈	25° ♈
Postnatal Equivalent	0° ♓ (9° ♓)	5° ♍ (12° ♍)	5° ♎	12° ♋ (13° ♋)	13° ♎	22° ♍	$19°_{SR}$ ♋	17° ♒	22° ♏	$27°_R$ ♓	26° ♌	15° ♋

The principal configurations are these:

MC p.n. ☍♄ a.n.
MC a.n. △♀ p.n. ☍♂ a.n. ☌♄ r. △♂ p.n. ⚹♄ p.n.
   △♇ a.n.
Asc. a.n. ☌♀ a.n., ♆ a.n. ⚹ ♂ r., ☽ p.n., ☌♂ p.n.
(MC a.n. ☍☽ p.n. ☍♀, ♂ r. △♀ a.n. ☍♇ p.n.)
(Asc. p.n. △♂ a.n. △♀, ♂ r. △♇ p.n.)
♀ p.n. ☌MC r.
♀ p.n. ☌☽ r. in ♎ △♃ a.n.
♀ a.n. △♂ a.n. □⊙ p.n. ⚹ ♂ p.n. ⚹ ♄ a.n. △♇
   p.n. △♄ r. □♇ r.

In addition the following configurations occur:

Monthly Asc. p.n. △ Yearly ☿ p.n. ☌ Yearly ♅ p.n.
Monthly Asc., ♀ a.n. ☌ Yearly ☽ a.n.
Monthly ☽ a.n. △ Yearly ⊙ p.n. ☌ Yearly ♀ p.n.

Monthly ♂ p.n. ☌ Yearly MC p.n.
Monthly ♅ a.n., ♆ p.n. ☌ Yearly Asc. p.n.

The wedding took place 22 days after the day of the monthly postnatal equivalent, so that the weekly series of directions will fall due three days before and after the days of the monthly figures. The following are the principal directions formed in this series:

MC p.n. con. ⚹ ♅ p.n.
MC a.n. p. △♀ p.n. p. ☍♂ a.n. p. ⚹ ♅ p.n.
Asc. p.n. con. ⚹ ♆ r.
Asc. a.n. p. ☌♀ a.n. p.
(MC p.n. p. △♃ r.)
(MC p.n. con. △☉ p.n., ☽ r. in ♎ △♃ a.n.)
(MC a.n. p. △♀ p.n. con.)
(MC a.n. con. ☍☽ p.n. △♀ a.n. ☍♂ r.)
(Asc. p.n. p. △♀ a.n. p.)
(Asc. p.n. con. △♀ a.n.)
(Asc. a.n. p. ⚹ ♆ r.)
(Asc. a.n. con. ⚹ ☉ a.n. □♄ r.)
☉ p.n. con. in ♎ ☍♄ a.n.
☉ a.n. p. ⚹ ♅ a.n., ♆ p.n.
☿ p.n. con. ☌☽ r. in ♎
♀ a.n. con. ☌♆ a.n.

Also, the following aspects are formed:

(Monthly MC a.n. con. ☍ Yearly ♆ p.n.)
Monthly ☉ a.n. con. (☍ Yearly Asc. a.n.)
Monthly ♀ p.n. p. ☍ Yearly ♄ a.n. ♅ p.n.
Monthly ♀ p.n. con. ⚹ Yearly ♂ a.n.
Monthly ♂ a.n. p. △ Yearly ♄ a.n., ♅ p.n.

These directions are nearly all in character with the nature of the event and several stimulate sensitive points in the basic configurations already noted. On this occasion the number of aspects involving the precessional angles is especially noteworthy, the benefics figuring prominently in these contacts.

The daily series of directions, for which the directional days are 21 October and 7 September 1926 and 6 July and 23 May 1878 are as follows:

MC p.n. p. ☌☉ a.n. □♀ p.n.
MC p.n. con. □♂ a.n. p. ☌♆ a.n.
Asc. p.n. p. ☌♀ p.n. ✶♄ p.n.
MC a.n. p. ☍☉ r. ✶☽ a.n.
Asc. p.n. con. △♀ a.n. con. ☍♃ p.n. △♅ r.
Asc. a.n. con. ☍☉ p.n. in ♎ ✶♃ a.n. p.
(MC p.n. con. ☍♂ p.n.)
(MC a.n. p. △☉ p.n. △♀ a.n. p. ☌♃ a.n.)
(MC a.n. con. △♀ p.n. con.)
(Asc. p.n. con. ☌♀ p.n. con. ☌♅ a.n., ♆ p.n. □♇ a.n.)
(Asc. a.n. con. □♇ r.)
(☉ a.n. p. ☍MC a.n.)
(☉ ☽ p.n. con. △MC a.n.)
☿ a.n. con. ☌Asc. a.n. ✶♂ r., a.n. con.
♀ p.n. p. in ♎ △♇ r. △♃ p.n. con.
♂ p.n. p. and p.n. con. ✶☿ a.n. p., ♀ r., ♇ p.n.

In addition to these numerous aspects, the great majority of which are in character with the nature of the event, the following aspects have also to be taken into account:

(Monthly MC p.n. con. ☍ Yearly ♂ a.n.)
(Monthly Asc. a.n. con. △ Yearly ♂ a.n.)
Monthly ☉ ☽ p.n. con. □ Yearly ☉ a.n.
Monthly ♀ p.n. con. ☌ Yearly Asc. p.n.
Monthly ♀ a.n. con. ☌ Yearly ☉ p.n.

Several of the progressed aspects in the daily series fall either on sensitive points in the basic configurations already noted or on the degrees tenanted by angles or planets in the weekly directions.

Although all types of lunar figures, considered in conjunction with the major solar figures to which they relate appear to give most satisfactory results, readers may be inclined to believe, as I do, that the monthly, weekly and daily series of progressions based on the Composite Solar Revolutions fulfil the same function and entail considerably less labour in their calculation!

17.
THE DUODECIMAL
SOLAR REVOLUTION

In mundane astrology, considerable importance is attached to a figure cast for the exact moment of the Sun's entry into the four cardinal signs of the zodiac. There is a tradition that the Spring Ingress, when the Sun enters Aries, sets the pattern for the whole year, although a more recent school of thought is inclined to place the emphasis on the Winter Solstice horoscope, when the Sun enters Capricorn. Whichever figure is reckoned to be of greater importance, the remaining three cardinal ingress horoscopes are regarded as being of subsidiary importance. The entry of the Sun into the eight remaining signs is not often singled out for special mention, although these intermediate ingress figures have a bearing upon the events of the year and may be used to determine more closely at what time the events foreshadowed by the main ingress figure are likely to be precipitated.

The main cardinal ingress figure for the year is exactly the same in principle as a Solar Revolution. The yearly return of the Sun to its own place in the nativity is the equivalent of a 'personal ingress' figure, with the Sun's radical position fulfilling the role of a personal 0° Capricorn or 0° Aries. If the parallel is a truly significant one it should be possible to calculate a horoscope based on the Sun's position in the nativity which is the equivalent of the intermediate ingress figures of mundane astrology. These figures also should bear a subsidiary relationship to the main Solar Revolution and indicate by their nature the times when the experiences promised by the major figure are most likely to come about. By measuring off from the position of the natal Sun successive arcs of 30°, the Sun's monthly progress may be arranged to produce a 'personal ingress' figure for each month. Cyril Fagan and others have demonstrated the efficacy of three-monthly figures, forming a personal 'cardinal ingress', calculated in terms of the Sidereal Zodiac and only taking into account postnatal positions of the planets. I propose to demonstrate that it is valid to take into account all the intermediate figures produced by the Sun's monthly arrival at points successively 30° further on from the exact position of the natal Sun and that such figures attain their maximum effectiveness when considered in conjunction with the corresponding figures formed before birth. These figures are equally striking, whether they be cast with an allowance for precession or not.

As an example, let us calculate the monthly Solar Return measuring to the time of Ann Harding's marriage, which took place on 21 October 1926. The following procedure is recommended:

(1) Find the date of the Monthly Solar Return.

Note the Sun's degree on 21 October 1926		27° ♎
Subtract degree of radical Sun		14° ♌
2 signs		13°

Add the number of whole signs traversed to the longitude of the radical Sun.

Sun's longitude at birth	14° 23′ 33″ ♌
Plus 2 signs	14° 23′ 33″ ♎

The Sun passes over this point on 8 October 1926

(2) Calculate the amount of arc between the Solar Return point and the Sun's position at noon on 8 October 1926.

Sun's position at noon	14° 26′ 51″ ♎
Sun's position at Solar Return	14° 23′ 33″ ♎
	0° 03′ 18″

(3) Calculate Sun's daily speed.

Sun's longitude at noon, 8 October	14° 26′ 51″ ♎
Sun's longitude at noon, 7 October	13° 27′ 35″ ♎
	0° 59′ 16″

(4) Calculate the time needed by the Sun to travel 3′17″.
    0°03′17″ divided by 0°59′16″
    is equivalent to 0.0547222/0.9877777
                or 0.0553993;
    multiply by 24 to give 1.3295838 or 1hr 19m 46.5s.

(5) Calculate equivalent Sidereal Time at Chicago.

From Sidereal Time at noon on 8 October 1926		13 05 27
Subtract amount of time before noon that the Duodecimal Return falls due		1 19 45
Also subtract correction for Sidereal Time		0 00 13
		11 45 29
Subtract allowance for difference in longitude between Chicago and Greenwich		5 50 36
Also subtract correction for Sidereal Time		0 01 17
Sidereal Time of Duodecimal Return		5 53 36

This gives a Midheaven of 28° Gemini and an Ascendant at Chicago of 28° Virgo.

The antenatal Duodecimal Return is calculated in exactly the same way except that the number of whole signs added to the Sun's radical position to obtain the position of the Sun for the postnatal monthly figure must be subtracted from the position of the radical Sun to obtain the Sun's position in the antenatal figure. The increment of two signs subtracted from the Sun's natal longitude gives a position of 14°23′33″ Gemini and the corresponding day before birth when the Sun passes over this degree is 5 June 1878. The return falls due at 5.48 a.m. GMT and the figure calculated for Chicago has a Midheaven of 14° Sagittarius and an Ascendant of 0° Pisces.

In order to facilitate the examination of the principal configurations in the figures themselves and between the planets and angles in the returns and in the nativity, the necessary positions are set out below in tabular form.

	MC	Asc.	☉	☽	☿	♀	♂	♃	♄	♅	♆	♇
Nativity	27° ♍	14° ♐	14° ♌	6° ♎	10° ♌	15° ♋	12° ♋	12°R ♒	23°R ♑	17°R ♐	2° ♋	19° ♓
Postnatal Duodecimal Return	28° ♓	28° ♍	14° ♎	1° ♏	27° ♎	3° ♎	18°R ♑	17°R ♒	23° ♏	26° ♓	26° ♌	16° ♋
Antenatal Duodecimal Return	14° ♐	0° ♓	14° ♓	6° ♌	20° ♑	1° ♑	18° ♋	7°R ♒	1° ♈	25° ♌	8° ♑	25° ♑

The principal configurations are as follows:

MC p.n. ♂ ☌ r.
Asc. p.n. ☌ midpoint ☉ p.n. ☽ r. in ♎
MC a.n. ☌ Asc. r. ☍ ☉ a.n.

⊙ a.n. and p.n. Δ♃ p.n. and r.
☽ p.n. ☍♀ a.n.
☽ a.n. ☍♃ a.n.
♅ p.n. ☍MC r.
♃ a.n. Δ☽ r.

In addition, the Moon in the postnatal monthly figure falls close to the opposition of Mars in the postnatal yearly figure, and Mars in the postnatal monthly figure falls close to the position of Venus and the trine of Saturn in the postnatal revolution for the year. All those factors characteristic of marriage that appear in the major Solar Revolutions will not necessarily appear in the monthly revolutions, although a fair proportion of them may be expected to do so.

The marriage took place 13 days after the date on which the postnatal Duodecimal Revolution fell due. The day-for-a-week progressions will therefore be represented by the planetary positions 2 days before and after the day of the Duodecimal Returns. The following significant directions are formed by this measure:

Asc. p.n. p. ☌⊙ p.n. con. in ♎ Δ♃ r.
⊙ a.n. con. Δ♃ r.
⊙ p.n. p. ☐♀ r. ☐♇ p.n.
♀ p.n. p. ☌☽ r. in ♎

The daily series of directions, represented by the planetary positions 13 days before and after the day of the Duodecimal Returns contain these important configurations:

♂ a.n. p. ☌MC p.n. major Solar Revolution
♂ a.n. con. ☐ Asc. p.n.
MC a.n. p. ☍⊙ a.n. p. ☐♅ p.n.
Asc. a.n. con. ☌♃ r.
♀ a.n. p. ☌♂ p.n. p.
⊙ p.n. con. in ♎ ☍♄ a.n.
♀ p.n. con. ☐♅ r.
♀ p.n. p. in ♎ Δ♇ r.
♀ a.n. con. Δ♅ r.

All the interplanetary configurations formed by postnatal progressed planets and by antenatal converse planets will be common to the daily series of progressions of all yearly and monthly figures that cover the period of this event.

In order to calculate the Duodecimal Solar Returns, making an allowance for precession, it is necessary to take into account not only the amount of precession for the number of whole years of the native's age but also the number of months that have elapsed since the last birthday. In this case the return falls due 24 years and 2 months after birth, so that the increments for 24 years (20′06″) and 2 months (approximately 9 weeks = 00′09″) are added together and then added to the Sun's longitude as calculated for the same return without precession (14°23′33″ Libra) to give the adjusted solar position. This is 14°43′48″ Libra. The Sun returns to this position at 6.53 p.m. GMT on 8 October 1926, giving a Midheaven at Chicago of 4° Scorpio and an Ascendant of 9° Capricorn.

In order to determine the correct solar position for the antenatal return, making an allowance for precession, it is necessary to deduct the increment for 24 years and 9 weeks (20′15″) from the Sun's longitude as calculated for the same antenatal return without precession (14°23′33″ Gemini). The adjusted solar longitude is therefore 14°03′18″ Gemini. The Sun returns to this position at 9.21 p.m. GMT on 4 June 1878, giving a Midheaven at Chicago of 3° Leo and an Ascendant of 28° Libra.

Except for the Moon, there will be little difference between the positions of the planets in the figure calculated with an allowance for precession and that calculated without. There will therefore be hardly any difference in the interplanetary aspects formed. The major variation will occur in the different positions of the Midheaven and Ascendant and in order to compare the relative merits of the two systems it is only necessary to observe which configurations are now angular and what aspects are formed by the progressed angles of the new figures. Important configurations involving the angles of these returns are listed below:

MC p.n. ☍ ☌ p.n. Major Solar Revolution ☍ ♀, Ψ a.n.
    ♂ ☽ p.n.
MC a.n. ☍ ♃ a.n.
Asc. a.n. ☍ ♀ a.n.

The presence of both benefics close to angles is a typical feature of returns indicating the likelihood of marriage.

The weekly series of directions, represented by the planetary positions two days before and after the day of the returns, contain the following significant aspects:

♀ a.n. con. ☍ Asc. a.n. in ♎
♀ a.n. p. ♂♂ p.n. Major Solar Revolution ☍MC p.n. con.
Asc. a.n. con. in ♎ ⚹ ♅ a.n. ⚹ ♆ p.n.

In the daily series of progressions, falling due thirteen days before and after the day of the returns, the following angular directions are appropriate to the event:

☉ p.n. p. ♂Asc. a.n. in ♎
Asc. p.n. p. ♂♄ r.
Asc. p.n. con. ☍☉ a.n. p. ☐♅ p.n. △♅ a.n.
　△♆ p.n.
MC a.n. con. ☐♀ p.n. p. in ♎
Asc. a.n. p. ☍♆ a.n.
Asc. a.n. con. △♃ p.n.

It will thus be seen, judged from the standpoint of the number of significant angular configurations, both in the return itself and in the weekly and daily series of progressions, that there is little to choose between the indications given by the Duodecimal Returns calculated on the basis of the Sun's natal longitude and the same class of figure calculated with an allowance for precession. Both types of figure, however, give eminently satisfactory results and demonstrate that the principle according to which they are constructed is a sound one. A similar series of figures may also be constructed using the longitude of the radical Moon and the longitude of the radical Ascendant as starting-points.

18.

THE SYNODICAL LUNATION

Comparatively little has been written about these figures in modern times and it may be that the lack of attention paid to this type of horoscope is due more to the extra trouble involved in calculation rather than to any lack of merit in the figure itself. Some writers have suggested that the synodical lunation is only of secondary importance and that its indications are not as clear-cut as those given by other methods. It may well be that the fashion of neglecting this class of horoscope has prevented astrologers from gaining enough practical experience in its use. After experimenting with combined postnatal and antenatal lunations, I feel that few astrologers have really done justice to the merits of these figures.

As the Sun and Moon progress in the zodiac on the days after the native's birth, they will periodically re-establish the same relationship between themselves, in terms of longitudinal elongation, that existed at the moment of birth. In other words, if the luminaries were in conjunction at birth, the moment of the next conjunction between them after birth would be the moment for which the first synodical lunation should be calculated. If the luminaries were in opposition at birth, every subsequent opposition between the Sun and Moon would mark the time of successive synodical lunations. Whatever the zodiacal distance between the luminaries at birth, the recurrence of the same longitudinal elongation between them as they progress through the signs signals the beginning of a new synodical lunation. Each synodical lunation has rule over one year of life and the actual period of time elapsing between one lunation and the next is about 29½ days. At the rate of a day-for-a-year this corresponds very closely with the time taken by Saturn to complete a circuit of the zodiac and it may well be that the indications of the synodical lunation have some special link with karmic factors in the life.

All the synodical lunations relating to a life of normal duration will therefore occur within six or seven years of the day of birth, measured both backwards and forwards in time. It has been said that the first seven years of life are the truly formative period, governing the whole course of the subsequent life. This idea receives some confirmation in the compressed time-scale of the synodical lunations!

As in the case of the various types of Solar Revolution, it is necessary to consider the antenatal figure in conjunction with the postnatal figure if the best results are to be obtained.

These figures, although not strictly speaking of the same family as Solar Revolutions, since they are not calculated on the basis of current planetary positions, may nevertheless be interpreted according to the same principles. Because the basis of this type of figure is the recurrence of a relationship between two moving bodies, and because a period of 29½ days is symbolically equated to the passage of a year, there is no question of making any allowance for precession in the calculations.

The monthly re-occurrence of the same relationship between the Sun and Moon means that it is also possible to treat this figure in the same way as a monthly lunar return, regarding it as having a bearing upon the events happening during the actual calendar month in which the lunation takes place. To distinguish this class of figure from the major synodical lunations that are equated to one year, they are referred to as 'current' synodical lunations. Synodical lunations have also been called 'Embolismic Lunations' or 'Lunar Progresses'.

The calculation of the synodical lunation figure is slightly more complicated than the calculation of the Solar Revolution, because the acceleration or deceleration of the Moon has to be considered in relation to the apparent speed of the Sun. To this end it is necessary to take into account the speed of the Moon's motion during the twelve-hour period immediately preceding and following the twelve hours in which the moment of the synodical lunation actually occurs, so that the changing speed of the Moon during the crucial middle period may be more accurately computed. This accuracy is necessary in order to determine as correctly as possible the Midheaven and Ascendant of the synodical figure because once again the whole emphasis of the figure is governed by the nature of those planets which are placed on the angles and also because the position of the progressed

angles is one of the most important factors in timing the events
of the period.

As an example, let us calculate the postnatal synodical lunation
for Ann Harding's 24th birthday. The following procedure is
recommended:

(1) Calculate the day on which the synodical
    lunation for the required year takes place.
    Age of native   24 years
    Extract from Tables in Appendix II the number of years and
    days after birth that the lunation falls due   1 year 344 days
    Count 1 year 344 days forward from the date of
    birth   17 July 1904
    (As the tables are only approximate, it may be necessary to look
    on either side of the day indicated to find the actual day of the
    lunation.)

(2) Calculate the difference in longitude between
    the positions of the radical Sun and Moon.
    From longitude of radical Moon (as this
        luminary is further advanced in the zodiac) 6° 29′ 21″ ♎
    Subtract longitude of radical Sun   14° 23′ 33″ ♌
                                       1 sign   22° 05′ 48″

(3) Estimate approximately the time when the Sun
    and Moon will be 1 sign 22°05′48″ apart.
    Moon's position at midnight,
        16/17 July 1904   16° 01′ 14″
    Sun's position at midnight, 16/17 July 1904   23° 57′ 43″
    Difference   1 sign   22° 03′ 31″

    This is 02′17″ short of the required distance; therefore,
        the luminaries will be the required distance apart
        shortly after midnight.

(4) Calculate the excess of the Moon's motion over
    the Sun's motion at the estimated time of the
    synodical lunation (taking into account lunar
    acceleration or deceleration).
    From the Moon's position at midnight,
        16/17 July 1904   16° 01′ 14″ ♍
    Subtract Moon's position at noon,
        16 July 1904   8° 42′ 52″ ♍
    Theoretical speed of Moon (in terms of
        twelve hours' motion) at 6.00 p.m.
        16 July 1904   7° 18′ 22″

Subtract Sun's motion over same period	0° 28′ 38″

Excess of lunar over solar speed at
  6.00 p.m. (A)   6° 49′ 44″

From Moon's position at noon, 17 July 1904   23° 16′ 19″ ♍
Subtract Moon's position at midnight,
  16/17 July 1904   16° 01′ 14″ ♍

Theoretical speed of Moon (in terms of
  twelve hours' motion) at 6.00 a.m.,
  17 July 1904   7° 15′ 05″
Subtract Sun's motion over same period   0° 28′ 38″

Excess of lunar over solar speed at
  6.00 a.m. (B)   6° 46′ 27″

The $\dfrac{A + B}{2}$ = theoretical excess of lunar over solar speed

at midnight, 16/17 July 1904   (A) 6° 49′ 44″
                                      (B) 6° 46′ 27″
                                          ─────────────
                                           13° 36′ 11″
                                      ÷ 2 6° 48′ 05″

The actual time of the lunation is so close to midnight as to
  render further adjustments in the speed unnecessary.

(5) Using the theoretical excess of lunar over solar
    speed already calculated, find how soon after
    midnight the Moon will have gained the
    required 02′16″ over the Sun.
       Moon's gain over Sun in 12 hours   6° 48′ 00″
       Moon's gain over Sun in 12 minutes   0° 06′ 48″
       Divide 12 minutes' gain by 3   0° 02′ 16″
         = gain in 4 minutes
       Time of synodical lunation = 12.04 a.m. GMT 17 July 1904.

(6) Find the equivalent Sidereal Time at Fort Sam
    Houston, Texas (the birthplace) (29° N 47′, 95° W 20′)
       To the Sidereal Time at noon, 16 July 1904   7 35 35
       Add time after noon when lunation falls due 12 04 00
       Also add correction for Sidereal Time   0 02 01
                                                    ─────────────
                                                    19 41 36
       Subtract allowance for difference in longitude
         between Greenwich and Fort Sam
         Houston (95° W 20′)   6 21 20
       Also subtract correction for Sidereal Time   0 01 03
                                                    ─────────────
       Sidereal Time at Fort Sam Houston   13 19 13

This Sidereal Time gives a Midheaven of 21° Libra and
an Ascendant, at Fort Sam Houston, of 5° Capricorn.

The corresponding Synodical Lunation before birth falls on 29
August 1900 at 10.16 p.m. GMT. The Sidereal Time at Fort Sam
Houston is 14.25.20, giving a lunation Midheaven of 8° Scorpio
and an Ascendant of 21° Capricorn.

As a first step towards examining whether the indications given
by these Synodical Lunation figures are appropriate to the event
of marriage, which took place during the year to which they relate,
a table is given below containing the positions of the angles and
planets in the nativity and in the postnatal and antenatal
Synodical Lunations.

	MC	Asc.	☉	☽	☿	♀	♂	♃	♄	♅	♆	♇
Nativity	27° ♍	14° ♐	14° ♌	6° ♎	10° ♌	15° ♋	12° ♋	12° ♒ R	23° ♉	17° ♐ R	2° ♋	19° ♓
Postnatal Synodical Lunation	21° ♎	5° ♉	24° ♋	16° ♍	2° ♌	26° ♋	11° ♋	28° ♈	19° ♒ R	27° ♐ R	6° ♋	21° ♓
Antenatal Synodical Lunation	8° ♏	21° ♉	6° ♍	28° ♎	20° ♌	21° ♋	13° ♋	2° ♐	28° ♐ R	8° ♐	29° ♓	17° ♓

As in the case of Solar Revolutions, the whole emphasis of these
figures is determined by the positions of the planets in relation
to the angles. The closer a planet is to the Midheaven or the
Ascendant (or the opposition of these two points) the more effect
it will have on the pattern of events during the ensuing year. The
system of using a number of predetermined 'event configurations' that was applied to the interpretation of Solar Revolutions
(see Chapter 5) cannot be applied in quite the same way but the
following aspects formed between the various planets and angles
in the three charts are sufficient testimony to the usefulness and
significance of the Synodical Lunation figures:

Asc. a.n. ☍♀ a.n. ☍☉, ♀ p.n. ♂♄ r.
MC p.n. ☍♃ p.n. ♂☽ a.n. in ♎ (♃ p.n. △♅ p.n.
     ☍☽ a.n. △♄ a.n. ✶♆ a.n.)
Asc. p.n. ☍♆ p.n. △☉ a.n.
♂ a.n. and p.n. ♂♂ r.
♄ p.n. △♇ r. in seventh house
♇ a.n. ☍♅ r.

The presence of both benefics on angles is a typical feature of horoscopes operative during the marriage year.

The wedding took place on 21 October 1926, 75 days after the 24th birthday. The rate of progression usually employed in the directing of synodical lunations is based on the fact that about 29½ days actual motion of the planets is equivalent to one year of life. This means that one day's actual motion is equivalent to about 12½ days of the life. Using the same time-scale it will be found that 2½ degrees of the Sun's progress and about 32½ degrees of lunar progress are equivalent to one month of life. Applying these rates of progression to the case under review, we find that 75 days of life are represented by six days actual motion measured from the day of the lunation. This period may be measured both backwards and forwards in time, and from the moment of both the postnatal and the antenatal synodical lunations. The Midheaven of each figure may also be progressed at the same speed as the Sun progresses, as in the case of all other types of figure. We have therefore to look at the planetary positions on 23 and 11 July 1904, and on 4 September and 23 August 1900, to see what lunation directions were operative. They were as follows:

MC p.n. (progressed) $\delta\,\mathcal{Y}$ p.n.
Asc. p.n. con. $\Delta\mathcal{Y}$ p.n. $\delta\,\hbar$ a.n. $\delta\,\Psi$ a.n.
δ p.n. p. $\delta\,♀$ r.
$♀$ p.n. p. $\delta\,\odot$ r.
Asc. a.n. (converse) $\delta\,♀$ r.
$\odot$ a.n. con. $\Delta\mathcal{Y}$ p.n. (applying)
δ a.n. p. $\delta\,♀$ a.n. con.
$♀$ a.n. p. $\delta\,♀$ p.n.

The general tenor of these aspects, with both benefics figuring prominently and the aspects between Venus and Mars, are fairly typical of the event.

Let us now make an experiment, regarding the synodical lunation as if it were a current Solar Revolution, casting it for the latitude and longitude of Chicago, where Ann Harding was domiciled at the time of her marriage. The difference between the longitude of Fort Sam Houston and Chicago is 7°41′, so that the Midheaven at Chicago will be 29° Libra in the postnatal figure, and the Ascendant 3° Capricorn. The adjusted antenatal synodical lunation has a Midheaven of 16° Scorpio and an

Ascendant of 21° Capricorn. It will be observed that while Venus still remains on the angle of the antenatal figure, Jupiter, significantly, is much nearer the IC of the postnatal figure.

Now, as a further experiment, let us apply the day-for-a-month, day-for-a-week and day-for-a-day series of directions that we have already applied to the progression of the Solar Revolution. Seventy-five days is 2½ months and by adjusting the Midheaven of the antenatal lunation by the amount of the Sun's progress in 2½ days, the progressed Ascendant of this figure is brought to the exact opposition of the Sun in the postnatal figure, having at the same time just passed the conjunction of the radical Saturn. A similar progression of the postnatal Midheaven gives a corresponding Ascendant which is trine the antenatal lunation Sun and opposition postnatal Neptune. The converse postnatal Venus has moved back to the position of the Sun in the postnatal lunation, while the progressed antenatal Venus has almost reached the same position.

The day-for-a-week progressions fall eleven days before and after the lunation dates, on 28 and 6 July 1904, and 18 August and 9 September 1900. The following directions are formed:

Asc. p.n. p. $\vartheta\odot$, $\venus$ p.n. con. $\vartheta\venus$ a.n. con. $\vartheta\mars$ r.
$\mars$ a.n. con. ϑ Asc. p.n.
$\odot$ con $\mars\,\mathrm{\text{☽}}$ p.n. $\times\,\venus$ r.
MC p.n. con. in $\libra$ $\triangle\,\pluto$. r.

These are strikingly typical of the event and suggest that there are some grounds for regarding the experiment as successful.

We can continue the experiment by calculating the day-for-a-day directions which will fall due 75 days before and after the lunations days. The directional days will therefore be 30 September and 3 May 1904, and 12 November and 15 June 1900. The following directions are formed:

$\venus$ p.n. p. in $\libra$ $\times\,\mars$ p.n. p. $\times\,\saturn$ a.n. $\triangle\,\neptune$ a.n.
$\vartheta\,\jupiter$ p.n.
Asc. p.n. p. $\times\,\pluto$ p.n. $\square\,\venus$ a.n.
$\odot$ p.n. p. $\mars\,\text{☽}$ r. in $\libra$
MC p.n. p. $\vartheta\,\mars$ p.n.
MC a.n. con. $\mars\,\odot$ a.n.
$\jupiter$ p.n. con. $\triangle\,\odot$ r. $\triangle$ Asc. r.
$\odot$ p.n. con. $\times\,\mars$ r.

⊙ a.n. p. 8 ☾ p.n. con.
♀ p.n. con. Δ ☾ a.n. p.
♀ a.n. p. in ≏ ⚹ ♅ a.n. p.
♃ a.n. p. Δ⊙ r. ☌ Asc. r.
♀ a.n. con. ☌⊙ p.n. 8 ♄ r.

Such an array of typical aspects, all measuring to the day of marriage, especially when considered in conjunction with the testimonies afforded by the monthly and weekly progressions of the synodical lunations, make it appear probable that this method of determining when the major effects of these figures fall due is a perfectly valid one. Although it must be conceded that such a method appears to be assailable on logical grounds in that the time-measures applied make it necessary to take into account a much wider period of time than that covered by the 29½ days of the lunation period itself, it must be remembered that I made the suggestion in *The Technique of Prediction* that it was probable that as well as being able to equate the passage of a day with that of a year, a month, a week or a day of the actual life, the same period could also be equated to an hour, a minute or a second of actual time. Such a procedure, again, would mean that planetary positions far outside the span of a normal lifetime would have to be taken into account. Experiments of various kinds with directional astrology and time-measures have convinced me that most astrologers take a much too narrow and stereotyped view of time, the true nature of which is yet to be fully established. For this reason a special chapter on the phenomenon of time has been included in this volume. In the last analysis, however great the theoretical support or opposition for or against any system may be, the final proof of the pudding is in the eating and the example we have just examined bears ample testimony to the validity of the system proposed.

A further point now arises. It is possible to calculate monthly lunar returns having a special relationship to the yearly solar return. It is also possible to calculate a current synodical lunation figure having a relationship to the actual month in which it occurs. Presumably such a figure should bear the same relationship to the synodical lunation for the year as the monthly lunar return bears to the solar return for the year. The parallel is by no means exact, however, as the solar return for any year is a current figure, while the synodical lunation is not. Nevertheless we have shown that in the case of secondary directions there is a definite sympathy between the current 'day-for-a-day' directions and the symbolical 'day-for-a-year' directions covering the same period of time. The various current lunation horoscopes and the daily horoscope form a more specific background against which to assess the impact of the various transiting planets. It appears reasonable to suppose that a similar sympathy may exist between current synodical lunations and the longer-term lunations formed during the earliest years of life, as that which exists between solar and lunar returns and between major secondary directions and the current daily measure.

The current synodical lunation covering the period of Ann Harding's marriage fell after birth on 11 October 1926. An inspection of the Ephemeris shows that on this date Venus was in conjunction with the radical Moon and we are reminded of the direction formed by the progressed Sun in the major postnatal lunation when, moved at the rate of a day-for-a-day, it also formed a conjunction with the radical Moon. Any conjunction between the luminaries, either in the lunation figure itself or as a result of aspects formed by progression, is especially significant in this type of horoscope as it derives its origin from the original relationship between the luminaries in the nativity. In this instance the conjunction occurs in the marriage sign Libra, as it must when the radical Moon is involved, and is also joined by Venus in the current lunation figure, a most suitable configuration for indicating the possibility of marriage. In addition, Mars at the time of the current lunation joins the position of the converse postnatal Mars in the daily series of progressions, which had formed an opposition to the antenatal progressed Sun in the same series. The corresponding current antenatal synodical lunation occurring on 5 June 1878 also shows signs of a special sympathy with the major lunations and their progressions, through the positions of the Sun, the Moon and Uranus.

In order to examine the effects of the current synodical lunations in greater detail it is necessary to calculate the exact moment of the return in terms of the longitude of Chicago. Also, because over the years, the eccentricities of the Moon's orbital motion cause it to vary ever more from the mean position, there is a tendency for the postnatal lunation day not to coincide exactly with the antenatal lunation day in terms of the native's precise age. In the case under review we find that the antenatal lunation falls three days before the postnatal lunation. In order to compensate for this it is necessary to calculate a corresponding postnatal and antenatal equivalent figure as in the case of other types of revolutional horoscope where the postnatal and antenatal figures do not coincide in point of time. For easy reference, the positions of the planets and angles in the postnatal synodical lunation and the antenatal equivalent, together with those in the nativity, are set out below in tabular form.

	MC	Asc.	☉	☽	☿	♀	♂	♃	♄	♅	♆	♇
Nativity	27° ♍	14° ♐	14° ♌	6° ♎	10° ♌	15° ♋	12° ♋	12°$_R$ ♒	23°$_R$ ♑	17°$_R$ ♐	2° ♋	19° ♓
Postnatal Synodical Lunation	17° ♋	15° ♎	17° ♎	9° ♐	2° ♏	7° ♎	18°$_R$ ♑	17°$_R$ ♒	24° ♏	26°$_R$ ♓	26° ♌	16° ♋
Antenatal Equivalent	6° ♐	17° ♒	12° ♓	9° ♋	18° ♑	29° ♈	17° ♋	7°$_R$ ♒	1° ♈	25° ♌	8° ♑	25° ♑

The following configurations are worthy of special notice:

MC p.n. ☌ ♂ a.n. ☌ ♇ p.n. ☌ ♀ r.
Asc. p.n. ☌ ☉ p.n. in ♎ △ ♃ p.n.
Asc. a.n. ☌ ♃ p.a. △ ☉ p.n.
☽ r. ☌ ♀ p.n. △ ♃ a.n.
♅ p.n. ☍ MC r.

The marriage took place ten days after the lunation fell due. The converse Ascendant of the postnatal lunation had then moved back by daily motion to the conjunction of the radical Moon and the lunation Venus in Libra, all within about a degree of the converse postnatal Sun on the directional day (1 October 1926). On the same day Venus was in sextile to the lunation Saturn. Ten days measured forward from the time of the antenatal equivalent, which fell on 3 June 1878, gives 13 June as the daily progressed directional date, when Mars is in 24° Cancer, conjunct the Sun in the major postnatal synodical lunation and sextile the daily converse Venus of the current postnatal synodical lunation. On 23 May 1878, the converse daily directional day of the antenatal equivalent, Venus was in 17° Aries, opposing the rising Sun in the current postnatal lunation figure.

In order to complete our study we may now consider the current antenatal synodical lunation, together with its postnatal equivalent, the planetary and angular positions of which are set out below in tabular form.

	MC	Asc.	☉	☽	☿	♀	♂	♃	♄	♅	♆	♇
Antenatal Current Synodical Lunation	17 ♐	5° ♓	14° ♓	6° ♌	20° ♑	1° ♑	18° ♋	7°R ♒	1° ♈	25° ♌	8° ♑	25° ♑
Postnatal Equivalent	7° ♋	6° ♎	14° ♎	2° ♏	27° ♎	3° ♎	18°R ♑	17°R ♒	23° ♏	26°R ♓	26° ♌	16°R ♋

The following configurations should be noted:

MC a.n. ♂ ♅ r.
Asc. p.n. ♂♀ p.n. ♂☽ r. in ♎
☉ a.n. ☍ Asc. r.
☽ a.n. ⚹ ♀ p.n. ☍ ♃ a.n.
☽ p.n. ☍ ♀ a.n.

The marriage took place thirteen days after the day represented by the antenatal lunation when the converse daily Ascendant of the antenatal figure had moved back to the opposition of the radical Sun. On 23 May, the corresponding converse directional day, Venus in 17° Aries was in trine to the radical Uranus and the Midheaven of the antenatal lunation, while Venus on the progressed directional day, 18 June 1878, was in 16° Taurus, on the IC of the major antenatal synodical lunation for the year. The daily progressed Ascendant of the postnatal equivalent forms a trine with Jupiter in the same figure, having just passed the conjunction of the Sun in Libra. Mars on 21 October 1926, the progressed directional day of the postnatal equivalent (and also the actual day of the marriage) had also reached 16° Taurus and was therefore in conjunction with the daily progressed Venus of the complementary lunation figure and the IC of the major antenatal synodical lunation for the year. The daily converse Ascendant of the postnatal equivalent figure is in opposition to the postnatal Uranus. In the converse daily directions of the equivalent figure, Venus is in trine to Mars and forms a T-square with the radical Uranus–Pluto opposition.

It will be apparent from the foregoing scrutiny of some of the principal features and progressions of the major and minor synodical lunations measuring to the time of Ann Harding's first marriage that not only does this type of figure produce excellent indications of the nature of the event to be expected but that very satisfactory results can be gained by treating the major synodical lunations as if they were current solar revolutions, that is, casting them for the current place of residence and progressing them at the rate of a day-for-a-month, a day-for-a-week and a day-for-a-day. In addition, the current synodical lunations, with their appropriate equivalent figures, may be used in conjunction with the major synodical lunations for the year in order to determine when their effects are most likely to become manifest.

As in the case of other similar types of figure, the Part of Fortune will often give a valuable clue to the trend of events during the year, a special emphasis being placed on any planet or group of planets with which it is in strong close aspect. Because the synodical lunation figure depends upon the maintenance of a fixed relationship between the positions of the luminaries, the Part of Fortune in the lunation figure will only vary from its position in the nativity by the amount of arc that the lunation Ascendant is distant from the radical Ascendant. The positions of the Parts of Fortune in the yearly and current lunations we have been considering are listed below, together with the planets closely in aspect to them.

Major p.n. Lunation PF 27° ♒ ⚹ ♃ p.n. ⚹ ♄ a.n. ⚹ ♅
  p.n. △♆ a.n.
Major a.n. Lunation PF 14° ♓ △♂ a.n. △♀, ♂ r.
Current p.n. Lunation PF 7° ♐ ♂☽ p.n. ⚹ ♀ p.n., ☽ r. in
  ♎ ⚹ ♃ a.n.
Current a.n. Equivalent PF 10° ♈ ☍♀ p.n. ⚹ ☉ a.n.
Current a.n. Lunation PF 28° ♈ ☍☿ p.n. in ♎ ♂♀ a.n.
Current p.n. Equivalent PF 28° ♏ □♅ a.n. △♅ p.n.
  □♆ p.n.

19.

THE YEARLY LUNAR REVOLUTION

Just as each synodical lunation after birth can be taken to represent each succeeding year after birth, so each lunar return after birth can be regarded as symbolic of the native's experiences during the corresponding year after birth. It is a recognized astrological principle that cycles of differing lengths may be equated to each other and so it is that in secondary directions the day is equated to the year. A day is the time taken by the earth to rotate on its axis and thus turn full circle in relation to the Sun. A year is the time taken by the earth to circle round the Sun in its orbit, thus completing another type of revolution. By equating a Lunar Revolution to a Solar Revolution we are thus following well-established astrological practice, and indeed, the Church of Light use such a measure as 'minor directions' in their method of secondary directions. I propose to treat this lunar revolution in the same way as the synodical lunation, already discussed in the previous chapter. This means that the postnatal and antenatal horoscopes must be considered together in conjunction with the nativity. Also, they must be cast for the place where the native actually is on the birthday for the year to which the lunar return measures. The resultant figures, cast for the time of the Moon's actual return to its radical position, should then be progressed in the usual way at the rate of a day for a month, a day for a week and a day for a day.

In passing it may be mentioned that the system of tertiary directions, discovered by E. H. Troinski, is also based on the Lunar Revolution but in this case, each day after birth is taken to represent the passage of time covered by one lunar revolution after birth, a day for a lunar month. It will be apparent therefore, that this measure is based on standard astrological practice. It is in fact only slightly different in timing from my monthly series of secondary directions explained in *The Technique of Prediction* in which a day was equated, not to a lunar month but to a calendar month. This measure is in the ratio of one to thirty and is roughly the equivalent of equating a Solar Revolution (a year) to one revolution of Saturn (29½ years). Although the method of derivation of tertiary directions does not qualify them for inclusion here, it may be mentioned in passing, that converse tertiaries, measured backwards from the day of birth, are equally effective and need to be considered in conjunction with progressed tertiaries if the system is to yield completely satisfactory results.

Let us now examine the indications given by the Composite Yearly Lunar Revolution for the year of Ann Harding's marriage. The twenty-fourth lunar revolution after birth and the twenty-fourth lunar revolution before birth measure to the event in question. A mean lunar revolutional period is about 27 days 7 hours 43 minutes, so that thirteen lunar revolutions will occur in the space of a year. In order to simplify the calculation of the yearly lunar revolution, a table is given in Appendix III showing approximately the number of years, months and days before or after birth that the lunar revolution for any given year falls due. Because of the Moon's comparatively fast speed and the small amount of precessional increment involved, there is little point in calculating a precessional lunar revolution.

The first notable feature of the lunar figures for the event in question becomes apparent before any calculations are made. The dates on which the figures fall due are 24 May 1904 and 21 October 1900. We recognize 21 October as the day of the wedding in 1926, though the corresponding day before birth was 23 May 1878. This discrepancy is due to the fact that 1900 was not a leap year so that an extra day has to be counted backwards from birth in order to compensate for this. The time of the postnatal lunar revolution is 10.51 p.m. GMT and of the corresponding antenatal revolution, 2.33 p.m. GMT and the planetary positions of each figure, together with the angles for Chicago, are given in the table below, which also includes the positions of the natal angles and planets.

	MC	Asc.	☉	☽	☿	♀	♂	♃	♄	♅	♆	♇
Nativity	27° ♍	14° ♐	14° ♌	6° ♎	10° ♌	15° ♋	12° ♋	12° ♒ R	23° ♑ R	17° ♐ R	2° ♋	19° ♓
Postnatal Yearly Lunar Revolution	14° ♌	6° ♏	3° ♓	6° ♎	17° ♈ R	21° ♈	4° ♓	19° ♈	21° ♒	29° ♐ R	4° ♋	19° ♓
Antenatal Yearly Lunar Revolution	8° ♍	21° ♏	27° ♎	6° ♎	20° ♏	14° ♍	14° ♌	10° ♐	0° ♑	10° ♐	29° ♓	17° ♓

These are the principal configurations:

MC p.n. ♂ ☉ r. ♂ ♂ a.n. ☍ ♃ r.
MC a.n. ♂ ♀ p.n.
Asc. a.n. ♂ ☿ a.n. ☍ ♀ p.n. ⚹ ♄ r. □ ♄ p.n.
☉ p.n. △ ☽ r. in ♎ ♂ ♂ p.n.
☉ a.n. in ♎ ☍ ♃ p.n. △ ♄ p.n. ⚹ ♄ a.n. ⚹ ♅ p.n. △ ♆ a.n. △ ♀ r.
☽ a.n. ⚹ ♃ a.n. ♅ a.n.
♀ a.n. □ Asc. r.
♂ a.n. △ Asc. r. △ ♃, ♅ a.n.
♃ p.n. △ ♅ r. ⚹ ♇ a.n.

The general tenor of these aspects is in character with the nature of the event and we may therefore examine the monthly aspects based on the two lunar figures with a reasonable expectation of finding a number of appropriate planetary contacts. The event took place 75 days after the 24th birthday, that is in about 2½ months and we may progress the lunar figures by 2½ days, both before and after the day of the revolution, in order to obtain the monthly directions, which are these:

MC p.n. p. △ ♅ r. ⚹ ♇ a.n.
MC p.n. con. ♂ ♂ a.n. con. ☍ ♃ r.
Asc. p.n. con. △ ♆ p.n.
Asc. a.n. con. ☍ ♀ p.n.
♀ p.n. p. ☍ Asc. a.n.
☉ p.n. p. △ ☽ r. in ♎ ♂ ♂ p.n. p.
☉ a.n. p. ⚹ ♄ a.n. ⚹ ♅ p.n. △ ♆ a.n.
♀ a.n. p. □ ♅ r.
♀ a.n. con. ⚹ ♂ r.
♂ p.n. con. ♂ ☉ p.n.

Several of these progressions represent the forming of exact aspects between planets already noted above as being within orbs of a significant contact. The general nature of these directions is in keeping with the character of the event.

We may now review the weekly directions which fall due 11 days before and after the two revolutional days. These are the principal progressed aspects in this series:

MC p.n. con. ⚹ ☉, ♂ p.n. ⚹ ♀ p.n. p.
MC a.n. con. □♂ p.n. con.
Asc. p.n. p. △ midpoint ♀, ♂ r. ⚹ ♀ a.n.
Asc. a.n. con. △♀ r.
☉ p.n. p. ☍Asc. r. ⚹ ♂ a.n.
♀ p.n. con. △ MC a.n. ☍Asc. p.n.
♀ a.n. p. ☌MC r. △ p.n. con.
☉ a.n. con. in ♎ △♇ a.n. ⚹ ♅ r.
♂ p.n. p. △♃ r. ☍♃ a.n. p.
♂ a.n. p. △♃ p.n. ⚹ ♇ r.
♂ a.n. con. △♃ a.n. con.
♃ p.n. con. △♅ r.

Several of these aspects touch off sensitive points in the basic configurations already noted and in the monthly series of progressions previously listed. All the directions formed are suitable to the nature of the event and provide a striking demonstration of the validity of this type of progression.

The daily series of directions fall due 75 days before and after the two revolutional days. The dates are 7 August and 10 March 1904, 4 January 1901 and 7 August 1900. The following are the principal progressed aspects formed:

MC p.n. p. in ♎ ⚹ ♃ a.n. p. ⚹ ♅ p.n. p.
MC p.n. con. ☍♃ a.n. con.
☉ p.n. p. ☌MC p.n. ☌☉ r. ☌♂ a.n. △♀ a.n. p., ♅ a.n. p.
☉ a.n. con. ☌MC p.n. ☌☉ r., etc.
♀ a.n. p., ♅ a.n. p. ☌Asc. r. △☉ r.
☉ p.n. con. □♇ r.
☉ a.n. p. ☍midpoint ♀, ♂ r. △♀ a.n.
♀ p.n. con. △♇ r.
♂ a.n. p. ⚹ ♂ r.
♂ a.n. con. △☉ a.n. in ♎ ☍♄ a.n. con. ☌♆ a.n. con.
♃ a.n. p. ⚹ ☉ a.n. in ♎ ☍♆ a.n. p.
♄ a.n. p. △MC a.n. ☍♀ a.n. con.

These daily directions are equally impressive, especially those involving the natal Sun and Ascendant. One point open to criticism is that the progressed daily angles do not make many significant contacts although one or two are within a degree or so of such aspects. If the figure were cast for the birthplace the consequent adjustment of the angles would not produce better results. As in the case of the daily progressions applied to the synodical lunation, the directional days for all but the first 27 days of the year fall outside the actual period of one lunar month that elapses between one lunation and the next but the above example shows that it is possible to obtain striking results by extending the daily directions beyond the actual duration of the figure, both before and after the day of the lunar revolution. Readers who may feel inclined to raise objections to such a procedure on logical grounds are referred to Chapter 21 in which the whole question of time in relation to the progression of the horoscope is discussed in detail.

Because there is no essential difference in nature between the Lunar Revolution, the monthly New Moon figure and the Monthly Moonrise figure, these two latter types of horoscope may also be used as yearly lunar figures as well as for current figures, each successive New Moon and Moonrise figure immediately before and after birth being regarded as symbolic of the pattern of events in each successive year.

20.
THE TOTAL PICTURE

In the foregoing chapters we have examined a number of different types of yearly and monthly horoscopes, all constructed on the basis of the periodical return of the Sun or Moon to a given fixed point in the nativity or, in the case of synodical lunations, constructed on the basis of a re-establishment of the relationship between the luminaries that existed in the nativity. Each of these figures considered in conjunction with its appropriate antenatal or postnatal counterpart, has yielded satisfactory indications of the native's marriage and in each case the timing of the event has been most adequately shown by the various series of directions developed from the revolutional figures. Each horoscope, whether it be the Solar Revolution, the Annual New Moon, the Annual Sunrise horoscope, the Synodical Lunation, the Yearly Lunar Revolution or the various monthly lunar figures, has added its testimony to the existence of an ordered pattern in the life of the individual, a pattern which can be determined and demonstrated through the study of astrology. This testimony becomes even more striking when we attempt to find a common denominator or series of such denominators running through all the revolutional figures covering the period.

In order to find such a group of common denominators we should first go to the nativity, the source of all the various annual and monthly returns and the essential frame of reference for all the derivative figures. In the nativity will be found certain configurations which have a bearing on marriage and all the various circumstances surrounding the event and we shall expect to find these configurations prominently linked with the revolutional figures in such a way as to enhance their significance and to allow them the maximum opportunity for expression. In a woman's horoscope, the Sun and Mars, according to their position by sign, house and aspect, are the principal indicators of the opposite sex and of the type of experiences which the native is likely to meet with in courtship and marriage. Venus is the planet governing the ability to live in harmony with others, while planets close to the first and seventh cusps play a major part in indicating the native's attitude towards others and consequently to the responses she is likely to evoke from them. Planets in Libra show the native's underlying and, to a certain extent, subconscious attitude towards all matters involving partnership. Bearing these points in mind we can see that in our example horoscope the Sun forms part of a very potent configuration, for it is in trine to the rising Uranus and sextile to the setting Pluto. It is also in conjunction with Mercury and in opposition to Jupiter. The Moon in Libra can be regarded as joining in this configuration by virtue of its applying trine to Jupiter, an aspect strengthened by the much closer trine of the Moon to the Part of Fortune, itself in conjunction with Jupiter.

The second planetary combination of importance is the conjunction between Venus and Mars, falling just within the seventh house, and its wide opposition to Saturn. These two configurations between them account for nine out of the ten planets. The remaining planet is Neptune, hardly near enough to Mars to form a conjunction, yet not to be overlooked as it is domiciled in the seventh house. From the two main basic groups we may pick out the following degree areas as those most likely to figure prominently in the revolutional horoscopes for the marriage year:

12° – 15° ♌ ♒ (☉ ♃)
12° – 16° ♋ ♑ (♀ ♂)
14° – 19° ♊ ♐ (Asc. ♅ ♇)
6° – 7° ♈ ♎ (☽)

Schedule I below shows how each of these important degree areas is emphasized in the various types of yearly figure, either by angular prominence or by being tenanted by a planet in one of these figures.

I	12°-15° ♌ ♒ (☉, ♃)	12°-16° ♋ ♑ (♀, ♂)	14°-19° ♊ ♐ (Asc., ♅, ♇)	6°-7° ♈ ♎ (☽)
Solar Revolution	(Asc. p.n. 16° ♒)	♀ p.n. 17° ♋ ♀ a.n. 14° ♋ ♇ p.n. 15° ♋	(MC a.n. 17° ♐)	
Progressed Solar Revolution	MC p.n. 15° ♌ ♀ p.n. 16° ♌ ♀ a.n. 12° ♌		(MC p.n. 24° ♐)	(☽ a.n. 11° ♎)

Converse Solar Revolution	♂ a.n. 13° ♌	(Asc. p.n. 17° ♑) p.n. 14°♋ (MC a.n. 17°♋) (☽ a.n. 12° ♑)	♀ p.n. 18° ♊ ♀ a.n. 15° ♊	
Annual New Moon	p.n. e. 14° ♌	MC a.n. e. 9° ♑ p.n. e. 13°♋	MC p.n. 14° ♊ a.n. e. 22° ♊	
Annual Sunrise Horoscope	(MC a.n. e. 17° ♌) ☽ p.n. e. 13°♒ ♂ p.n. e. 11°♒ ♂ a.n. e. 13°♒	(Asc. p.n. 10° ♑) ♇ p.n. 14°♋ ♇ p.n. e. 12°♋	MC a.n. e. 16° ♐ (Asc. a.n. 19° ♐)	Asc. p.n. 6°♎ (MC a.n. 11°♎) ☽ a.n. 9°♎
Synodical Lunation		♂ p.n. 11°♋ ♂ a.n. 13°♋		
Annual Lunar Revolution	MC p.n. 14° ♌ ♂ a.n. 14° ♌		♃ a.n. 10° ♐ ♅ a.n. 10° ♐	

It will be noticed that there is not a particularly marked emphasis on the lunar degree and that the synodical lunations only produce one special emphasis on the selected radical positions. The radical Sun–Jupiter opposition is the most consistently stimulated area, which is what we would expect to find.

Schedule II below shows how these same zodiacal areas are stimulated by the monthly, weekly and daily series of progressions based on the same yearly figures.

II	12°-15° ♌ ♒ (☉, ♃)	12°-16° ♋ ♑ (♀, ♂)	14°-19° ♊ ♐ (Asc., ♅ ♇)	6°-7° ♈ ♎ (☽)
Solar Revolution	Monthly ☉ a.n. con. 12° ♌ ☉ p.n. con. 12° ♌ Weekly (MC a.n. p. 17° ♌) Asc. a.n. con. 17°♒ Daily (MC p.n. p. 18°♒)	♀ a.n. con. 11°♋ MC p.n. con. 13°♋	MC a.n. p. 19° ♐ Asc. p.n. p. 15° ♐ Asc. a.n. con. 14° ♐	 MC p.n. p. 6°♎ MC a.n. con. 5°♎
Progressed Solar Revolution	Monthly MC p.n. con. 14° ♌ Weekly (MC a.n. con. 15° ♌) Daily (MC p.n. p. 14°♒) ☿ p.n. con. 15° ♌	 (Asc. a.n. con. 15° ♑)	 (MC p.n. con. 17° ♐) Asc. p.n. p. 14° ♐ ♀ p.n. con. 15° ♊	 MC p.n. p. 5°♎

Progressed Solar Revolution (cont'd)			(Asc. a.n. p. 16° ♐) ⊙ a.n. p. 15° ♐ ♀ a.n. p. 16° ♐	
Converse Solar Revolution	Monthly ♂ a.n. p. 14° ♌ ♀ a.n. con. 14° ♌ ♂ a.n. con. 12° ♌ Weekly Asc. a.n. p. 15° ♒ ☿ a.n. p. 15° ♒ Daily ♀ a.n. p. 16° ♌	(Asc. p.n. con. 13° ♑) MC p.n. p. 16° ♋	♀ p.n. con. 15° ♓ MC p.n. con. 20° ♓ Asc. a.n. con. 16° ♐ Asc. p.n. p. 17° ♐ (Asc. p.n. p. 15° ♓)	Asc. p.n. p. 5° ♎ MC p.n. p. 9° ♎
Annual New Moon	Monthly Weekly Daily (MC a.n. con. 15° ♌) (Asc. p.n. e. p. 15° ♌) ⊙ a.n. p. 16 ♒ ⊙ p.n. e. con. 16° ♒	☿ p.n. e. p. 13° ♋ (MC a.n. p. 12° ♋) MC a.n. e. p. 12° ♑ (Asc. p.n. e. p. 13° ♑) ⊙ a.n. e. p. 12° ♋ ☿ a.n. e. p. 12° ♋	(MC a.n. con. 20° ♓) MC p.n. p. 17° ♓ MC a.n. con. 13° ♓ MC a.n. e. con 19° ♐	(Asc. p.n. e. p. 6° ♈)
Annual Sunrise Horoscope	Monthly MC a.n. p. 12° ♒ Asc. a.n. e. con. 17° ♒ Weekly (MC p.n. e. con. 15° ♌) ♀ p.n. e. con. 12° ♒ Daily	(Asc. a.n. p. 14° ♉) ♃ p.n. con. 15° ♉ (Asc. p.n. e. p. 15° ♋)	(Asc. a.n. con. 14° ♐) MC p.n. e. p. 16° ♓ (Asc. p.n. e. p. 18° ♐) ♂ p.n. p. 17° ♐ ♀ p.n. con. 14° ♐ (Asc. p.n. e. con. 20° ♓)	☿ p.n. e. con. 7° ♈
Synodical Lunation	Monthly Weekly	Asc. a.n. p. 15° ♉ ⊙ p.n. con. 12° ♋ ♀ p.n. con 12° ♋ ♀ a.n. con. 14° ♋	Asc. p.n. con. 18° ♐	

	Daily			
Synodical Lunation (cont'd)	♄ p.n. p. 14° ♒	☿ a.n. con. 12° ♋	♃ a.n. p. 15° ♐	Asc. p.n. p. 7° ♈ p.n. p. 6° ♎
Annual Lunar Revolution	Monthly MC p.n. con. 12° ♌ a.n. con. 12° ♌ Weekly Daily	☉ a.n. p. 13° ♉	☉ p.n. p. 13° ♓ ♀ a.n. p. 15° ♐ ♅ a.n. p. 14° ♐	

Once again the lunar degree is the least stimulated, while the solar area and that tenanted by the rising and setting planets in the nativity receive an almost equal emphasis. It must be remembered that the above table has been expressly constructed to demonstrate the build-up on certain specific points in the nativity and it cannot be used to compare the respective merits of the various revolutional figures, especially as only the conjunctions and oppositions of the selected degrees have been included.

III	12°-15° ♌ ♒ (☉, ♃)	12°-16° ♋ ♉ (♀, ♂)	14°-19° ♓ ♐ (Asc., ♅, ♇)	6°-7° ♈ ♎ (☽)
Lunar Revolution		Asc. a.n. 17° ♋ (Asc. a.n. 10° ♋) Asc. p.n. e. 17° ♋ MC a.n. e. 14° ♉	(MC p.n. 19° ♓) ☉ a.n. 18° ♓ ☉ a.n. e. 17° ♓	
Progressed Lunar Revolution	Asc. a.n. 17° ♒ ♃ p.n. 17° ♒ ☽ p.n. 19° ♌ ☽ a.n. 19° ♌	(MC p.n. 10° ♋) MC p.n. e. 18° ♋ ♇ p.n. 16° ♋	☉ a.n. 15° ♓	(Asc. p.n. 8° ♎) ☉ p.n. 8° ♎
Converse Lunar Revolution	MC a.n. 17° ♒ (MC a.n. e. 17° ♌) ♃ p.n. 17° ♒	(Asc. p.n. 10° ♉)	Asc. a.n. 12° ♓ ☉ a.n. 21° ♓ ☉ a.n. e. 14° ♓	
Monthly New Moon		MC p.n. 13° ♉ MC a.n. 11° ♋	MC p.n. e. 13° ♐ (MC p.n. e. 21° ♐) MC a.n. e. 11° ♓ ☉ a.n. 15° ♓ ☉ a.n. e. 20° ♓	Asc. a.n. 9° ♎
Monthly Moonrise Horoscope		☽ p.n. e. 13° ♋ ♂ a.n. e. 17° ♋ ♇ p.n. 16° ♋	MC p.n. 15° ♐ ☉ a.n. 12° ♓	Asc. a.n. e. 7° ♎ ☉ p.n. e. 5° ♎ ♀ p.n. 7° ♎
Synodical Lunation		MC p.n. 17° ♋ ♂ a.n. e. 17° ♋ MC p.n. 12° ♋ (Asc. p.n. 9° ♉)	MC a.n. 17° ♐ ☉ a.n. 14° ♓ ☉ a.n. e. 12° ♓	Asc. p.n. e. 6° ♎ ♀ p.n. 7° ♎
Duodecimal Return		♂ a.n. 18° ♋ ♇ p.n. 16° ♋	MC a.n. 14° ♐ ☉ a.n. 14° ♓	Asc. p.n. 10° ♎

Schedule III on page 221 shows how the same areas are stimulated in the various lunar and monthly figures.

Here, the accentuation of the natal Sun–Jupiter opposition is less pronounced, only occurring in the Progressed and Converse Lunar Revolutions, while the accentuation of the radical Moon is slightly more pronounced than in the case of the yearly figures.

We may now observe how these same zodiacal areas are stimulated by the planets and angles in the weekly and daily progressions of the various monthly figures set out below in Schedule IV.

IV	12°-15° ♌ ♒ (☉, ♃)	12°-16° ♋ ♑ (♀, ♂)	14°-19° ♓ ♐ (Asc., ♅, ♇)	6°-7° ♈ ♎ (☽)
Lunar Revolution	**Week**	Asc. a.n. con. 16° ♋ (Asc. a.n. p. 12° ♋) MC a.n. e. p. 16° ♑ MC a.n. e. con. 12° ♑ Asc. p.n. e. con. 15° ♋	MC p.n. con. 12° ♓ (MC p.n. con. 17° ♓) ☉ a.n. con. 16° ♓ ☉ a.n. e. p. 19° ♓ ☉ a.n. e. con. 16° ♓	(Asc. a.n. e. con. 5° ♈) ☉ p.n. e. con. 8° ♎
	Day	(Asc. p.n. e. con. 11° ♋) ♂ a.n. con. 11° ♋	(MC a.n. e. con. 20° ♐) ☿ a.n. e. p. 16° ♓	
Progressed Lunar Revolution	**Week** Asc. p.n. e. con. 14° ♒	(MC p.n. p. 13° ♋) MC a.n. con. 16° ♋	☉ a.n. p. 17° ♓	(Asc. p.n. con. 6° ♎)
	Day	(MC p.n. e. con. 12° ♋)	MC a.n. p. 19° ♐	
Converse Lunar Revolution	**Week** MC a.n. con. 14° ♒ (MC a.n. p. 11° ♒) (MC a.n. e. con. 15° ♌)	(Asc. p.n. p. 12° ♑)		♀ p.n. p. 7° ♎
	Day MC a.n. e. con. 16° ♌	Asc. p.n. p. 12° ♑	Asc. p.n. con. 21° ♐	
Duodecimal Return	**Week**	MC p.n. p. 14° ♋	MC a.n. p. 15° ♐ a.n. p. 16° ♓	♀ p.n. p. 5° ♎
	Day Asc. a.n. con. 10° ♒ (MC a.n. p. 15° ♌)			☿ p.n. con. 6° ♎

Monthly New Moon	Week	MC p.n. p. 15° ♉ MC a.n. p. 13° ♋	MC p.n. e. p. 15° ♐ MC a.n. e. p. 14° ♓ (MC p.n. e. con. 19° ♐) ☉ a.n. e. con. 17° ♓ ☉ a.n. p. 17° ♓	Asc. a.n. con. 7° ♎ ♂ p.n. e. p. 7° ♎
	Day (MC p.n. p. 11° ♒)	(MC a.n. p. 15° ♋)	(MC a.n. con. 20° ♓) (MC a.n. e. p. 19° ♓)	(Asc. p.n. con. 8° ♈) (Asc. p.n. e. p. 7° ♈) ☿ p.n. e. con. 7° ♎
Monthly Moonrise Horoscope	Week	(MC a.n. con. 12° ♉)	MC p.n. p. 17° ♐ MC p.n. con. 14° ♐ (MC p.n. e. p. 12° ♓)	Asc. a.n. e. p. 8° ♎ Asc. a.n. e. con. 6° ♎
	Day Asc. p.n. con. 16° ♒ MC a.n. p. 14° ♒		(MC p.n. con. 14° ♐)	(Asc. p.n. p. 8° ♈) (Asc. a.n. e. p. 8° ♎) ☉ p.n. con. 8° ♎
Current Synodical Lunation	Week Asc. a.n. e. con. 15° ♒	MC p.n. con. 16° ♋	MC a.n. p. 18° ♐ MC a.n. con. 15° ♐ ☉ a.n. p. 16° ♓ ☉ a.n. e. p. 14° ♓	Asc. p.n. e. p. 7° ♎ ♀ p.n. e. p. 6° ♎
	Day Asc. a.n. con. 14° ♒		MC a.n. e. p. 16° ♐	Asc. p.n. con. 6° ♎ ☉ p.n. e. p. 7° ♎ ☿ p.n. e. con. 7° ♎

Once again the accentuation of the radical Sun–Jupiter opposition is less pronounced probably because the majority of the figures are based on a lunar and not a solar return.

Just as the nativity is the common source of all the derivative annual and monthly figures, so the planetary positions on the wedding day, 21 October 1926, and on the corresponding directional day before birth, 23 May 1878, represent the common meeting ground of all the postnatal progressed and antenatal converse daily directions measuring to the time of the event. These will therefore be the final stimulating factors which trigger off the major directions indicating the event and we shall therefore expect to find that a fair proportion of the degrees tenanted by planets on these two days are involved with significant directions already formed and in conjunction or opposition with significant points in the several revolutional figures. The following schedules show how the positions of the planets on 21 October 1926 and 23 May 1878 are accentuated by the positions of the angles and planets in the various solar and lunar figures and by the directions based on those figures. (See pages 225-34.)

In the same way it can be demonstrated that no important event occurs without a similar kind of emphasis on the positions of all the planets on the day of the event and on the corresponding day before birth in the day-for-a-day series of progressions. The significance of such an emphasis would appear to be that no event of any magnitude will take place except at a time when there is a convergence or intersection of many different cycles of influence, each supporting and reinforcing the other in such a way as to produce an overwhelming 'build-up' in favour of some particular course of action or some important development in the individual destiny. Each of the various solar and lunar cycles are probably linked in some subtle way with the intellectual, emotional, psychic and physical states of the native and the simultaneous arrival of a similar type of peak condition in each cycle sets the stage for some appropriate external manifestation or significant experience, just as the correct arrangement of a number of dials on the outside of a safe makes it possible for the door to be opened with the minimum of effort.

The existence of such a complicated and delicately interwoven pattern of interlocking and lunar cycles makes it difficult to believe that events just 'happen' haphazardly without the existence of some preconceived master-plan. This need not mean that the 'quality' of the event or the nature of the native's psychological reactions to the effects of the event are subject to any external conditioning. It does, however, appear to support the belief held by astrologers — that the general broad trends of the individual's life may be discerned from the state of the heavens at the moment of his birth and that the natal horoscope is the blueprint which indicates what the pattern of his development is likely to be. It suggests, moreover, that the directions and cyclic revolutions based on that horoscope will show the times when opportunities will be afforded for the individual to make the most effective efforts towards the fulfilment of that pattern of development, together with the times when periods of trial and testing will arise in order to determine whether the native's efforts towards self-development have been successful and rightly directed.

21 October 1926	Solar Revolution	Progressed and Converse Solar Revolution	Annual New Moon	Annual Sunrise Horoscope	Synodical Lunation	Annual Lunar Revolution
☉ 27° ♎			Revolution MC a.n. 27° ♎	Month (MC p.n. con. 26° ♎)	Revolution ☽ a.n. 28° ♎ Week MC a.n. con. 28° ♎ Day ♃ p.n. p. 27° ♈	Revolution ☉ a.n. 27° ♎ Day MC p.n. 26° ♎
☽ 6° ♉			Week ♀ a.n. e. con. 7° ♉	Revolution (MC p.n. 6° ♏) (☽ a.n. 7° ♉) Week (Asc. p.n. e. con. 7° ♏) Day (Asc. a.n. e. con. 7° ♏)	Month MC a.n. con. 6° ♏	Revolution Asc. p.n. 6° ♏
☿ 17° ♏			Revolution (☽ a.n. 16° ♏) Month Asc. p.n. e. p. 18° ♉ ♀ p.n. e. p. 18° ♉ Day ♂ p.n. con. 16° ♉	Revolution ♂ a.n. 18° ♏ Month (MC p.n. p. 17° ♏) (Asc. a.n. e. p. 17° ♏)		Revolution ☿ p.n. 17° ♉
♀ 20° ♎	Month Asc. p.n. p. 21° ♎ Day (MC a.n. p. 19° ♎)	Converse Revolution ♂ p.n. 19° ♈ Week (Asc. a.n. p. 20° ♎)	Revolution MC p.n. 18° ♎ Month (MC p.n. p. 19° ♎)	Day Asc. a.n. con. 19° ♎	Revolution MC p.n. 21° ♎ Month MC p.n. con. 19° ♎	Revolution ☿ p.n. e. 21° ♎ Day (MC p.n. e. p. 18° ♈)

21 October 1926	Solar Revolution	Progressed and Converse Solar Revolution	Annual New Moon	Annual Sunrise Horoscope	Synodical Lunation	Annual Lunar Revolution
			Week ☿ p.n. p. 19° ♎ ☿ a.n. p. 19° ♎ Day MC p.n. e. con. 19° ♈			
♂ 15° ♉			Revolution Asc. p.n. e. 15° ♏ Week MC a.n. p. 16° ♏	Revolution ♂ p.n. 16° ♏ ♀ a.n. 15° ♉ Day Asc. p.n. con. 15° ♏	Day Asc. a.n. con. 16° ♏	Week Asc. p.n. p. 14° ♏ Asc. a.n. con. 16° ♏
♃ 17° ♒	Week Asc. a.n. con. 17° ♒ (MC a.n. p. 17° ♌) Day (MC p.n. p. 18° ♒)		Day ☉ a.n. p. 16° ♒ ☉ p.n. e. con. 16° ♒	Revolution (MC a.n. e. 17° ♌) (☽ p.n. e. 17° ♒) Month Asc. a.n. e. con. 17° ♒	Week ♄ p.n. p. 18° ♒	
♄ 25° ♏	Day (MC a.n. con. 25° ♉)	Progressed Revolution MC a.n. 25° ♏ Day (MC a.n. con. 24° ♉) Converse Month MC a.n. con. 26° ♏ Week (MC p.n. p. 26° ♏)	Week (Asc. a.n. e. p. 24° ♏) ☿ p.n. e. con. 24° ♉ Day MC p.n. con. 24° ♉ ♄ p.n. e. con. 25° ♏	Revolution ♄ p.n. e. 25° ♏ Month MC p.n. e. p. 25° ♉ (Asc. p.n. e. con. 23° ♏) Day Asc. a.n. con. 25° ♉	Day ☿ p.n. con. 26° ♉	Revolution Asc. a.n. 24° ♏ Month Asc. a.n. p. 26° ♏ ♀ p.n. p. 24° ♉ Day MC a.n. p. 24° ♏

21 October 1926	Solar Revolution	Progressed and Converse Solar Revolution	Annual New Moon	Annual Sunrise Horoscope	Synodical Lunation	Annual Lunar Revolution
		Day (MC a.n. con. 27° ♉) ♄ p.n. con. 25° ♏				
♅ 26° ♓	Week Asc. a.n. p. 25° ♓		Revolution (Asc. a.n. 25° ♍) Week ♀ p.n. p. 27° ♍ Day (MC a.n. c. p. 25° ♍)	Month Asc. p.n. con. 27° ♍		Day Asc. a.n. con. 25° ♍
♆ 26° ♌		Converse Revolution ♃ p.n. 26° ♒	Revolution MC p.n. c. con. 26° ♌ ♃ p.n. c. 27° ♒ Week (Asc. p.n. c. con. 26° ♒) ♀ a.n. con. 26° ♌ Day ♀ p.n. c. con. 27° ♌	Day Asc. p.n. p. 27° ♌	Month ☿ a.n. p. 27° ♌ Day MC a.n. con. 27° ♌	Week MC a.n. con. 27° ♌
P 16° ♋		Converse Week MC p.n. p. 16° ♋ Day MC a.n. p. 17° ♄		Day (Asc. p.n. c. p. 15° ♋)		

21 October 1926	Lunar Revolution	Progressed and Converse Lunar Revolution	Monthly New Moon	Monthly Moonrise Horoscope	Current Synodical Lunation	Duodecimal Return
☉ 27° ♎	Revolution Asc. a.n. e. 26° ♈	Progressed Day Asc. p.n. e. p. 26° ♎	Revolution ☿ p.n. e. 28° ♎	Revolution (Asc. a.n. 28° ♈) ♀ a.n. e. 28° ♈	Revolution ☿ p.n. e. 28° ♎ a.n. e. 29° ♎	Revolution (Asc. a.n. 28° ♎) ☿ p.n. 27° ♎
☽ 6° ♉	Week ♀ a.n. e. 6° ♉ Day (Asc. a.n. e. p. 5° ♉)		Revolution ☽ a.n. e. 7° ♏ Week (Asc. p.n. con. 6° ♉)			Week (MC p.n. p. 6° ♏) Day (Asc. a.n. 7° ♏)
☿ 17° ♏	Day ♂ p.n. e. con. 18° ♉		Day ♂ p.n. con. 17° ♉	Revolution ☿ a.n. e. 18° ♉ Day (MC p.n. e. con. 17° ♉)	Revolution ☿ a.n. e. 18° ♉ Week ☿ a.n. e. con. 18° ♉	Week ☿ a.n. con. 18° ♉ Day (MC p.n. p. 17° ♏)
♀ 20° ♎	Revolution ☿ p.n. e. 21° ♎ Day (MC p.n. e. p. 18° ♈)		Day Asc. a.n. p. 19° ♎	Week ☉ p.n. p. 19° ♎	Week ☉ p.n. p. 18° ♎	
♂ 15° ♉			Week (Asc. p.n. p. 15° ♉) Day ♀ a.n. p. 16° ♉	Week Asc. a.n. p. 16° ♉	Week ☿ a.n. e. con. 16° ♉ Day ♀ a.n. p. 16° ♉	Day ♀ a.n. p. 15° ♉
♃ 17° ♒				Day Asc. p.n. e. con. 18° ♌	Revolution Asc. a.n. e. 17° ♒	

21 October 1926	Lunar Revolution	Progressed and Converse Lunar Revolution	Monthly New Moon	Monthly Moonrise Horoscope	Current Synodical Lunation	Duodecimal Return
♄ 25° ♏	Revolution ☿ p.n. 23° ♈ ☿ a.n. 25° ♈ Week ☿ a.n. e. p. 26° ♈ Day MC p.n. con. 25° ♈ ♀ a.n. p. 25° ♈		Week ☿ a.n. e. con. 24° ♈ Day Asc. p.n. p. 24° ♈	Week MC p.n. e. con. 27° ♈	Day MC a.n. e. con. 26° ♏	
♅ 26° ♓	Revolution MC a.n. 27° ♓ MC p.n. e. 26° ♓ Week MC a.n. con. 25° ♓ ♀ p.n. e. con. 25° ♍ Day Asc. p.n. p. 25° ♍ ☉ p.n. con. 27° ♍		Revolution ♀ p.n. 25° ♍		Day Asc. p.n. e. con. 25° ♍	
♆ 26° ♌		Progressed Day (Asc. a.n. p. 25° ♒) Converse Day (MC a.n. p. 26° ♒)				Week Asc. a.n. con. 27° ♒
♇ 16° ♋					Week MC p.n. con. 16° ♋ ♂ a.n. e. con. 16° ♋	

23 May 1878	Solar Revolution	Progressed and Converse Solar Revolution	Annual New Moon	Annual Sunrise Horoscope	Synodical Lunation	Annual Lunar Revolution
☉ 2° ♊	Day (Asc. p.n. con. 3° ♐)		Revolution ☿ a.n. e. 1° ♊	Month (Asc. p.n. e. p. 2° ♐) Week (Asc. p.n. con. 3° ♐) Day (Asc. p.n. p. 2° ♐)	Revolution ♃ a.n. 2° ♐ Day ♃ a.n. con. 3° ♐	Revolution ☉ p.n. 3° ♊ Month ♂ p.n. con. 3° ♊ Week Asc. a.n. p. 2° ♐ Day MC p.n. con. 1° ♊
☽ 24° ♒ and ♅ 25° ♌		Progressed Month MC a.n. con. 25° ♌		Week MC p.n. p. 24° ♌ Day MC p.n. con. 25° ♌	Week ☉ a.n. con. 25° ♌ Day ♂ a.n. p. 25° ♌	Week MC p.n. p. 25° ♌
☿ 11° ♉	Day MC p.n. con. 11° ♉	Progressed Week MC a.n. con. 11° ♏ Day Asc. a.n. con. 11° ♏	Month Asc. p.n. e. con. 12° ♏ Day (Asc. p.n. e. con. 13° ♏)	Revolution ☽ a.n. 11° ♉ Month MC p.n. e. con. 12° ♉ Day Asc. a.n. p. 11° ♏ ☿ p.n. con. 11° ♏	Month MC a.n. p. 11° ♏ Day ☉ p.n. con. 12° ♉ Asc. a.n. p. 11° ♉	
♀ 17° ♈		Progressed Day ♂ p.n. con. 17° ♈ Converse Month ♂ p.n. con. 17° ♈	Revolution Asc. a.n. e. 17° ♈	Revolution ☉ p.n. e. 17° ♈ ☉ a.n. e. 16° ♈ Month (MC a.n. p. 17° ♎)		

23 May 1878	Solar Revolution	Progressed and Converse Solar Revolution	Annual New Moon	Annual Sunrise Horoscope	Synodical Lunation	Annual Lunar Revolution
♂ 11° ♋		Progressed Week (MC a.n. con. 10° ♋)		Revolution (Asc. p.n. 10° ♉)	Month Asc. a.n. con. 10° ♉ ♂ a.n. con. 11° ♋	
♃ 7° ♒		Progressed Month Asc. a.n. p. 5° ♒ — Converse Day (MC p.n. con. 7° ♉)	Day (Asc. p.n. con. 5° ♒) ♃ p.n. e. con. 7° ♒			
♄ 0° ♈		Progressed Revolution ♄ a.n. 1° ♈ — Converse Month Asc. p.n. con. 0° ♎	Week ♄ a.n. con. 0° ♈ — Day Asc. p.n. e. p. 2° ♈	Day (Asc. a.n. e. p. 0° ♎)		
♆ 8° ♋	Week (Asc. a.n. p. 9° ♏) ♂ p.n. p. 7° ♋	Progressed Month Asc. p.n. p. 8° ♏ — Converse Month (MC p.n. con. 9° ♏)	Month ♀ p.n. e. con. 9° ♋ — Day (MC p.n. p. 9° ♏)	Revolution (Asc. a.n. e. 9° ♏)	Revolution MC a.n. 8° ♏	Month Asc. p.n. p. 8° ♏ — Week ♀ p.n. con. 8° ♋
♇ 25° ♋	See column for (♄ 25° ♏) in table for 21 October 1926					

23 May 1878	Lunar Revolution	Progressed and Converse Lunar Revolution	Monthly New Moon	Monthly Moonrise Horoscope	Current Synodical Lunation	Duodecimal Return
☉ 2° ♊			Revolution (MC a.n. e. 1° ♊)	Revolution ☿ a.n. 2° ♊ Week MC p.n. e. p. 3° ♊	Day MC a.n. con. 1° ♐	
☽ 24° ♒ and ♅ 25° ♌		Progressed Day (Asc. a.n. p. 25° ♒)	Week Asc. p.n. e. con. 25° ♒	Day (Asc. p.n. e. con. 25° ♌)		
☿ 11° ♉			Revolution (Asc. p.n. 11° ♉) Week ♀ a.n. e. p. 11° ♉	Revolution Asc. a.n. 12° ♉ ♀ a.n. 11° ♉		
♀ 17° ♈	Week ☿ p.n. e. con. 17° ♎ Day (MC p.n. e. p. 18° ♈)	Progressed Week Asc. a.n. p. 17° ♎ Day Asc. p.n. e. p. 16° ♎	Revolution ☿ p.n. 17° ♎ Week ☉ p.n. e. p. 16° ♎	Revolution ☉ p.n. 18° ♎	Revolution ☉ p.n. 17° ♎ Week Asc. p.n. p. 16° ♎ ☉ p.n. p. 18° ♎ ☉ p.n. e. p. 17° ♎ Day Asc. p.n. e. p. 17° ♎ ☿ p.n. con. 16° ♎	Week ☉ p.n. p. 16° ♎ Day (Asc. a.n. con. 17° ♎)

23 May 1878	Lunar Revolution	Progressed and Converse Lunar Revolution	Monthly New Moon	Monthly Moonrise Horoscope	Current Synodical Lunation	Duodecimal Return
♂ 11°♋	Revolution (Asc. a.n. 10°♋)	Progressed Revolution (MC p.n. con. 10°♋) Converse Revolution (Asc. p.n. 10°♑)	Week MC p.n. con. 10°♑	Week MC a.n. e. p. 10°♋		Week MC p.n. con. 10°♋ (Asc. p.n. p. 10°♑)
♃ 7°♒				Day (MC a.n. p. 6°♒)		
♄ 0°♈	Day Asc. a.n. e. con. 0°♎	Progressed Revolution Asc. p.n. 0°♎	Week (Asc. a.n. con. 0°♎) ♀ p.n. e. con. 1°♎	Day (Asc. p.n. e. p. 0°♎) (Asc. a.n. e. p. 1°♎)		Week ♀ p.n. con. 0°♎
♆ 8°♉	Week ♀ a.n. p. 8°♉	Progressed Revolution Asc. a.n. con. 8°♏ Converse Revolution ♀ a.n. 9°♉ Day MC p.n. p. 8°♉	Revolution ☽ p.n. e. 7°♏ ☽ a.n. e. 7°♏ ♀ a.n. e. 8°♉	Week ♀ a.n. con. 8°♉ Day MC p.n. e. con. 9°♉	Revolution ☽ p.n. e. 8°♏	
♇ 25°♉	See column for (♄25°♏) in table for 21 October 1926					

PART IV:
ON TIME AND CYCLES

21.

THE PHENOMENON OF TIME CONSIDERED IN RELATION TO PREDICTIVE ASTROLOGY

Serious students of astrology are probably attracted to the science because they have not allowed themselves to be confined within the constricting straight-jacket of a dogmatic orthodoxy which regards astrology, at best, as suspect and, at worst, as superstitious nonsense. Yet some astrological students still cling tenaciously to a most elementary and orthodox concept of the nature of time in spite of the fact that a study of directional astrology, with its many different time-measures, is a constant challenge to some of our most fondly cherished ideas about time. Even those acquainted with the teachings of various occult schools of thought, who have perhaps accepted pronouncements that time is very much speeded up on those planes less dense than the material, or that time ceases to exist in the realm of the Absolute, have probably been reluctant to allow these ideas to influence their attitude towards time as it is understood on the material plane.

The astrologer is made aware at a very early stage in his studies that the passage of each year of life after birth can be symbolically and effectively related not only to the passage of each four minutes of time after birth (as in primary directions) and to the passage of each twenty-four hours after birth (as in secondary directions) but also to the passage of each synodical month after birth (as in the system of synodical lunations). The suggestion was made by Alan Leo, in *Casting the Horoscope*, that primary directions were related to the intuitional world, secondary directions to the mental world, synodical lunations to the emotional world and transits to the natural world (physical plane). It should be added, perhaps, that it is impossible to have an experience on one plane without there being repercussions on the other planes and this explains why it is possible to use the various systems, whichever level they may be related to, and get results that reflect events that may be related to planes other than the one to which the system specifically relates.

It will be observed that in terms of the intuitional plane, a whole life's experiences would take place (at the rate of four minutes per year) within about six hours of the moment of birth. In terms of the mental world (secondary directions) the life-experiences would be contained within a span of some eighty or ninety days on either side of the birthdate, while the synodical lunations covering a whole lifetime would not extend to more than about eight years on either side of the birthdate.

The student is not only confronted with the hypothesis that greater cycles of time can be equated with very much lesser cycles but also with the idea that, in the astrological sense, time can move backwards as well as forwards. Not only are there progressed primary directions but also converse primaries. There are converse as well as progressed secondaries. There are converse synodical lunations and converse transits (the 'day-for-a-day' measure as explained in *The Technique of Prediction*). Because of a desire to cling to an orthodox concept of the time-measure there are still some astrologers who appear to be reluctant to accept the idea of converse directions (measured backwards in time before birth) on the grounds that they are 'contrary to nature'. When we know more about the real world (remembering the manifest world which we cognize with our waking consciousness is, to all intents and purposes, a world of illusion) such objections will be found to be without real foundation.

It is easy to test the efficacy of converse directions by a critical examination of a number of cases. Many examples of converse secondary directions are given in *The Technique of Prediction*. The cumulative evidence of such examples alone is sufficient to argue a strong case for the validity of converse directions. But to the enquiring mind such evidence cannot be regarded as conclusive unless some kind of rationale accompanies it in order to give a semblance of logicality to the process. I shall therefore attempt to provide, in the following paragraphs, some explanation of the reasons why the movements of the planets before as well as after birth are taken into account when assessing future tendencies.

Time, as the ordinary mortal perceives it, consists of an historical past, in which definite events are known to have happened, stretching backwards to remote periods of antiquity, and an unknown and seemingly endless future in which certain possible lines of development may be guessed at but about which very little can definitely be known. Between these two stands the present, the ever-now, continuously and dispassionately eating into the future and as dispassionately and ceaselessly spewing it out again onto the refuse heap of the past. That which is past is known to man (at least in part). That which is to come is unknown. Experience of things past is but a memory; experience of things to come but a vision. The only vivid, living experience is that of the ever-present now, the perpetual (but illusory) dividing line between present and future.

According to Ouspensky, time as a dimension only exists because human consciousness is limited in its ability to be aware of more than three dimensions at one and the same time. A reel of film, when run through a cinematograph projector, will produce a moving image upon a screen, giving the impression of reality. Such a reel of film will consist of a very large number of 'still' pictures and the projection of these pictures at speed creates the illusion of continuous movement. In much the same way, man records his conscious impressions of the world about him. He cannot record past, present and future all at once because his 'camera' cannot cope with so many dimensions. If it could, past and future would merge imperceptibly into 'present' and 'time' as we know it would cease to exist. Because man is only able to cope simultaneously with three dimensions, time to him partakes of the nature of the infinite.

There are an infinite number of points in a line. There are an infinite number of lines in a plane surface. There are an infinite number of plane surfaces in a solid. And yet a line, a plane surface and a solid can all be of finite proportions. Infinity, therefore, is a matter of relativity. A being whose perceptions were only capable of experiencing simultaneously one dimension (a line) could only become cognizant of a two-dimensional world by registering a series of lines, one after the other, and so this second dimension would, for him, partake of the nature of time. A being with two-dimensional awareness, who was capable of registering only area (and not mass) simultaneously, could only become aware of mass by registering a series of areas, one after the other as the mass passed through his plane of awareness, and so for him this third dimension would partake of the nature of time. Man, as we know him, is capable of registering three dimensions simultaneously but he can only cope with the line of events in sequence. For him, therefore, the line of events partakes of the nature of time. There are gifted individuals who can to a greater or lesser extent 'tune in' on the line of events, be they past or future, but at the present stage of human development, this ability is rare.

If it is possible to tune in to the line of events, this raises the question of whether events are preordained and inevitable. If there were only four dimensions, this conclusion would appear to be inescapable. There are, however, further dimensions which relate to the possibility of the variation of events through the exercise of choice and to the eternal repetition of such events or such possibilities. Astrology relates specifically to these dimensions and so it is contrary to the nature of the science to forecast in absolute terms what will happen. To do so ignores the possibility that alternative choices are frequently open to man.

A simultaneous and comprehensive awareness of any given dimension must necessarily give a much more accurate understanding of the true nature of the phenomena that belong to that dimension than a sequential and partial awareness of an infinite number of 'cross-sections' of that dimension. Man, owing to the limitation of his consciousness, is denied the ability to comprehend the true nature of time, for in order to do so he would need to become aware of his whole lifetime in one flash of consciousness. Moments of high crisis can bring into play man's higher faculties, just as danger brings about a release of adrenalin to mobilize physical activity to an enhanced degree. Occultists state that before the reincarnating ego finally comes to birth there will stretch out before him a picture of the whole life about to be lived out on the physical plane. Usually the ego is given a choice of lives, so that even at this stage there is no absolutely rigid pattern to be followed. Lives offer opportunities, which may be capitalized upon or squandered. Only in the transcendental stages of birth and death, it appears, can ordinary man cast off the limitations of his normal state of consciousness.

Astrology is a key by which we may discern something of the purpose behind the life of each human being and the relationship which that life bears to every other life in the solar system. Astrology is therefore a means whereby we may gain some idea of the total picture of our own world and the system of which it is a part. Such a total picture is composed of more dimensions than we, as human beings, are able to cope with simultaneously or understand completely. If we understood more about the true nature of time we should appreciate more fully the reasons for measuring backwards as well as forwards in time from the moment of birth. The astrologer who only takes account of directions formed after birth is proceeding on the assumption that his awareness of the time dimension enables him to know all he needs to know about time. But the stars in their courses move in a multidimensional field and if we are to interpret their message to the best advantage it behoves us to make an attempt to handle the time dimension not from the narrow standpoint of human awareness but with a greater regard for the true nature of the time-factor and the part which it plays in shaping the appearance of the material world.

If it is true that everything happens at once, although our consciousness only enables us to perceive events in sequence, then all the planets must perform their revolutions around the Sun at once, while the Sun moves simultaneously around a greater Sun carrying its system with it. The track of each planet would therefore not be a circle but a spiral. Thinking only in terms of our own solar system we can visualize a solid composed of a number of spirals, all twining around a great luminous curving line, which is the Sun's path in space. The spiral representing the path of Mercury will be nearest to the Sun and, because it travels fastest in its orbit, the number of turns in the spiral will be greater than in any of the other planetary spirals. The greater the diameter of the planet's orbit, the fewer turns there will be in the spiral, so that in the spiral of Pluto (which will be on the 'outside' except at one or two points when it will come within the spiral of Neptune) the coils will be fewest. There may, of course, be other planets beyond the orbit of Pluto!

By visualizing such a solid we have, in a sense, translated time into space, a dimension with which we are more familiar. In order to locate a point in space we need two co-ordinates if we are dealing with a plane surface, or three co-ordinates if we are dealing with a point in a solid. If we regard our mass of spirals as a solid figure we should be able to locate any point on (or in) it with reference to three co-ordinates. In the astrological sense our three co-ordinates are the nativity (time present), progressed directions (time future) and converse directions (time past as actually measured from the time of birth). The analogy is not perfect but serves to convey that the time-factor is more complicated than human consciousness is capable of perceiving by ordinary means. All those planes that lie outside human consciousness become fused together in a conglomerate which we label 'time'. Such a concept of time as we have outlined suggests that birth is a kind of vortex brought about by the interplay of time past and time future and that death is a similar kind of vortex occurring through the interplay of corresponding factors at the end of the time-pattern we recognize as a human life.

We can approach the problem from a slightly different angle if we regard it solely from the point of view of the solid figure of spirals we have visualized, which has been called the 'Long Body' of the solar system. The form of such a solid is governed by certain set rules and it is possible to determine the shape of any given part of a solid by reference to the shape of the parts around it, which is the equivalent of taking several 'bearings' on a given point. Again, using the spatial aspect of time as a basis, and remembering that there is no such thing as a straight line in nature, we can approach the problem in another way and infer that the line of the sequence of events also cannot be a straight line. In fact it has been said that time is curvilinear so that in theory, at any rate, if we measure a line backwards as well as forwards in time we shall eventually end up at a point where both lines coincide.

If time is curvilinear, as various metaphysical writers have suggested, a lifetime may be seen as a circle, or cycle. Theoretically, a lifetime has been considered as being equivalent to the cycle of Uranus (84 years). Eighty-four is made up of seven twelves, while the biblical three-score and ten is made up of seven tens. It has been suggested that the seven units of ten quoted in the Bible were used as a cipher and that ten actually represented the number twelve in that context. Whether or not this is true it is interesting to reflect that the zodiac was said at one time to contain ten signs, which have now become twelve. Uranus, too has a connection with the transition from one state of awareness to another, such as that which occurs at birth and death. Uranus is exalted in Scorpio.

In secondary directions a day is equated to a year. Both of these periods are the durations of cycles. A day is the time taken by the earth to make a complete rotation on its axis; a year is the time taken by the earth to make a complete revolution around the Sun. If we reflect that in the major series of secondary directions one kind of cycle is equated to another kind of cycle, we can discern the basis of a general principle applicable to many of the directional systems used in Western astrology — that there is a correspondence in nature between greater and lesser cycles which stand in relationship to each other as macrocosm and microcosm so that it is possible to relate any two cycles to each other. This relationship of the greater to the lesser underlies the statement in the Bible that God made Man in His image.

If we equate one earth cycle (one year) to one Saturn cycle (30 years) we establish a ratio of 1:30, which is approximately the equivalent of a day for a month. As the Saturn cycle assumes the role of macrocosm in this relationship, directions based on this measure may have some special connection with *karma*.

By equating the cycle of Jupiter (12 years) to the cycle of Uranus (84 years) we establish a ratio of 1:7, which is the equivalent of a day for a week. Jupiter rules growth and expansion, and Uranus is connected with change, especially with changes of consciousness brought about dynamically through the awakening and development of intuitive understanding. Every seven years the physical body undergoes subtle changes, which are no doubt designed to pave the way for developments in the finer bodies. We may therefore infer that 'day-for-a-week' directions indicate possible lines of self-development through a new orientation of the life brought about by the growth of intuitive understanding.

In primary directions, one degree of R.A.M.C. (4 minutes of time) is equated to the passage of a year. This represents a measure 360 times as fast as the 'day-for-a-year' directional measure of secondary directions, based on the ratio 1:365. The measure of Valentine Naibod (59′08″ of R.A.M.C.) also used in primary directions represents a measure 365 times as fast as the day-for-a-year measure, thus preserving the original ratio of 1:365, based on the correspondence between the minor cycle of the earth's rotation on its axis and the major cycle of the earth's revolution around the Sun. The day-for-a-day measure (transits) is 365 times slower than the day-for-a-year measure (secondaries) which in turn is 365 times slower than the primary measure. According to this method of evaluation it looks as if the term 'tertiaries', which has been applied to a system of directing which depends upon lunar cycles should rightly, or at least logically, be applied to transits!

Because time is in one sense an illusion fostered by our own limited awareness, we should be prepared to abandon an overly rigid concept of its properties and the laws under which it operates. As well as being able to equate a day effectively with a year, a month, a week or with itself (transits) it may well be that we can properly equate a day also with an hour, a minute or a second, the only snag being that in the last case it will be necessary to consider planetary positions millions of years before and after birth. By equating a day with a second, we find that the passage of approximately 240 years is equal to one day of the life. This also conforms fairly closely to the law of cycles in that, according to present calculations, the cycle of Pluto is reckoned to take 248 years. It also coincides with the periodicity of the Mutations Conjunctions of Jupiter and Saturn, which change from one element to another in the same time-span. Apart from the technical difficulties of calculating planetary positions for such remote periods of time, the practical value of such measures would be very small indeed. Speculation of this nature is only useful in so far as it focuses attention upon the possibility of planetary movements that actually take place outside the life-span, being either earlier or later in time, having a bearing upon events which take place within the life-cycle.

The existence of such a possibility paves the way for the application of a new directional method to 'short-term' revolutional figures, such as the Synodical Lunation (see Chapter 18) and the Annual Lunar Return (see Chapter 19) in which periods of about 29½ and 27½ days are equated to a year. Hitherto, directional systems applied to such figures have been placed on a proportional division of the actual time elapsing between the moment of one return and the next, so that in the case of a Lunar Return, which takes place every 27½ days, about 2¼ days are equated to one month, about 8 hours to one week and just over one hour to one day. If, however, we are prepared to concede that it is possible to direct such figures by extending the span of the directional period beyond the actual 27 days between one revolution and the next, we may once more apply the usual day-for-a-week and day-for-a-day measures to these horoscopes, remembering that however illogical such a practice may seem, it will only appear so in the light of our extremely limited perception of the true nature and quality of time.

The student who wishes to enlarge upon his understanding of the nature of time is recommended to read Dr Maurice Nicoll's *Living Time*. Dr Nicoll develops the idea that an individual's past, present and future are always in functional relationship with each other and that not only can past thought and action affect the present but, in some way not comprehensible to ordinary understanding, future thought and action can modify the past. Here is a possible explanation for the fact that the positions of progressed (postnatal: future) and converse (antenatal: past) planets measuring to the same point in life often appear to combine to produce aspects symbolic of the happenings at the time and of the psychological states of the native. It will also be observed that the daily progressed directions of one Solar Revolution will be the converse daily directions of the subsequent Solar Revolution (unfolding in reverse order), suggesting that the actions and psychological states of one year may have a much stronger influence than would normally appear possible, on the events that happen and the attitude of mind adopted during the following year. In a lesser degree, these reversed progressions will operate in exactly the same way in a Lunar Revolution so that the previous month's thoughts and actions will play a large part in determining the events of the following month. Such a connection is comparatively easy to accept as the causes and their effects will cover a relatively short period of time. The general principle, however, must apply to all life-cycles, so that the thoughts and actions registered during the first thirty years of life for instance (the Saturn cycle) must also determine to a large extent the psychological attitudes and happenings of the next thirty years. Because of the importance of the seven-year cycle this may be the reason why the Roman Catholic Church attributes an overriding importance to the training a child receives during the first seven years of its life. In this case the attitudes developed during the first seven years are held to be definitive for the rest of one's life.

Before leaving the subject of time and its connection with the various directional techniques of astrology it may be remarked that if the suggestion put forward by Alan Leo is correct — that primary directions are related to the intuitional world, secondary directions to the mental world and synodical lunations to the emotional world — then, in one sense, primary directions may be regarded as a substitute for intuition. A person with highly developed intuitional awareness is sometimes able to see the trend of future events with surprising accuracy. According to the normal concept of time a feat such as this is regarded as 'seeing into the future'. But if we allow that four minutes of time on the physical plane is the equivalent of a whole year's existence on the intuitional plane, then it will be apparent that for the intuition, functioning consciously on its own plane, the conditions that will be operative one (physical) year hence may be sensed in four (physical plane) minutes of time. Thus the physical 'future' speedily becomes the intuitional 'now' and it is in terms of this 'present consciousness' that the intuition makes its judgements.

Mental awareness and emotional consciousness function at corre-
spondingly slower speeds while on those planes composed of more
rarefied matter than the intuitional, time as we know it becomes
infinitely speeded up in relation to the physical plane until we
arrive at a point where apparently time seems to be annihilated
and everything may be experienced as happening at once.
Astrologically this is represented by Saturn (Father Time) and its
relationship with Uranus (the Lightning Flash). If man possessed
a perfect four-dimensional awareness he would perceive everything as happening at once. Such a state of awareness would place
him at a higher level in the hierarchy than man now occupies.

A rough and ready illustration of the connection between the
different time-values of various planes of consciousness is given by
a figure composed of a number of concentric circles around the
point they share as a common centre. Each circle represents consciousness functioning at a certain level of awareness. If we mark
off a segment of the outer circle and join the extremities of the arc
to the centre we shall also have marked off a segment of each of
the smaller circles but because these circles are smaller, the
marked-off portion along the circumference of each will be
progressively smaller as we approach the centre. If we regard the
circumference of the outer circle as representing the line of events
experienced on the physical plane and the circumference of the
circle next within it as representing the line of events as experienced on the emotional plane, the next circle as representing the
mental plane and so on, the difference in length between the
respective arcs so formed will represent the difference in time
taken to become aware of a given sequence of events on the
respective planes of consciousness, measured in terms of the
passage of time on the physical plane. As the radius of the circles
diminishes so the arc becomes less, until at the centre there is no
arc at all or, in other words, we have again reached a theoretical
state where everything is experienced as happening at once. Time,
therefore seems to be long or short according to the density of the
plane in which the consciousness is functioning. In our waking
life, time can seem to drag or become very much speeded up
according to the part of our consciousness we are centred in. The
passage of a few seconds to a man sitting inadvertently on a red
hot stove might seem to be inordinately prolonged, while the
same man sitting with a beautiful woman on a comfortable sofa
might find the passage of an hour all too short!

Consciousness centred at the physical level is the normal level of man's attainment. Conscious awareness working on the emotional plane for any length of time is a rarer achievement and at the mental and intuitive level rarer still. The astrologer has at his command a way of artificially contacting these higher levels with the assistance of primary and secondary directions and according to his ability to understand and interpret the message of the planetary and zodiacal symbolism, so he will be able to build up a picture of the way in which future events may be shaped. Indeed, by the continual practice of such exercises he may eventually develop within himself the beginnings of a conscious awareness on those planes so that he need at some future date no longer be dependent on any prop or artificial device as a means of obtaining knowledge of the future.

One further comment remains to be made. Alan Leo, in his remarks on the several types of directions and their connections with the various types of consciousness, suggests that primary directions may be regarded as indicating inescapable karma, while secondary directions represent changing mental phases, and synodical lunations transient emotional phases. He regards Solar Revolutions as being related purely to the environmental atmosphere and having no great effect on the inner experiences. I do not agree with this view, firstly because a prolonged acquaintance with the working of secondary directions has led me to the conclusion that they are adequate to account for the native's experiences on any plane of awareness and also because I believe that Solar Revolutions, properly used and understood, are no less inferior in this respect; and secondly because I believe that in spite of the vast and obvious differences that exist between the essential nature of each plane of awareness, there exists between them a profound sympathy, in much the same way as there is a vibrational sympathy between the successive octaves of the piano, so that a cause arising on one plane will produce its inevitable effects on the others. The law of correspondences allows us to apply the maxim 'As above, so below' to all planes of awareness; consequently we can, so to speak, take a bearing on the future equally well by considering the testimony of primary or secondary directions or, as here, by studying the indications contained in the appropriate Solar Revolutions and synodical lunations.

22.

THE ETHICS OF PREDICTION

One of the principal objects of this book (and its companion volume, *The Technique of Prediction*) is to acquaint the student with various techniques whereby he may be enabled to predict to a greater or lesser degree the course of future events. The ability of the astrologer to predict accurately has long been a source of fascination to the interested layman, who is often inclined to regard prediction as the be-all and end-all of astrology. A very much larger section of the community has been eager to condemn astrology as false on the basis of predictions made from time to time by astrologers whose occasional wrong prognostications have, for one reason or another, become public property. While it cannot be denied that astrology can offer no more spectacular achievement than a correctly framed prediction, it must be remembered that providing indications of future trends is only one of the functions of astrology and one which is probably not more valuable than those which permit a character analysis or a diagnosis of illness and the prescription of appropriate remedies to be made from the natal horoscope. Further, to condemn astrology as false because astrologers make wrong predictions is no more logical than to condemn the science of medicine as useless because doctors make wrong diagnoses or prescribe remedies that do harm to their patients. Both astrologers and doctors, being human, are fallible. Yet in both cases their callings are such that it would seem to be much better for the human race if they could achieve a greater measure of infallibility!

When the astrologer fails in his attempt to predict correctly, the reason for his failure probably lies in the fact that he has attempted too much. One of the wisest and most important pieces of advice ever to have been given to the student was undoubtedly that accredited to Claudius Ptolemy, who warned against attempting to predict in too great detail for, while the astrologer might reasonably expect to achieve a high standard of accuracy if he confined himself to a general statement of the type of event to be expected, it was only in rare instances that he could rely upon receiving the degree of inspired guidance needed in order to predict the specific details of some particular happening. One is reminded, when pondering this advice, of the teaching of Ouspensky, who maintained that it is not possible to predict with certainty the actions of any man who is 'awake', an expression he used to indicate an advanced level of self-awareness that only those who have striven long and earnestly have managed eventually to achieve.

The consciousness of the 'unawakened' man is monopolized by a number of different 'I's' all clamouring for their needs to be fulfilled. Some of these needs belong to the intellectual consciousness, others to the emotional consciousness; some are instinctive, others physical. At one time the voice of one need becomes more demanding, at another the voice of a different type of need becomes more insistent, and the unawakened man, not distinguishing clearly between the origins of each clamant demand, responds first to one voice within him, then to another and is predictable because his responses are mechanical. Man 'asleep' or 'unawakened' is an automaton who will respond to a similar set of circumstances as though a button had been pressed and in this way is predictable, whereas man 'awake' or man who has developed his consciousness has also developed the power to choose according to the progress he has made and is therefore less predictable.

There is less chance of a wrong prediction if the native's circumstances and temperament are reasonably well known to the astrologer. Some astrologers prefer to work on a horoscope without any prior knowledge of the native. One such once described a woman with the Moon and Venus rising in Libra as having 'a beautiful peaches and cream complexion, with fine blond hair'. She would have been spared her subsequent embarrassment if she had taken the trouble beforehand to ascertain that the horoscope was that of a black lady! The Dutch astrologer C. Aqua. Libra makes a useful comparison between the probable reactions of a butcher's boy and an exalted philosopher to a progressed aspect of Mars to the Moon. At such a time the butcher's boy, within easy reach of sharp instruments, may well become a nuisance to himself and a menace to those in his immediate vicinity, whereas the philosopher may merely find himself embarking upon some complicated metaphysical speculations which call for strenuous mental effort. A third person, being endowed with a moderate amount of self-control, may find himself involved in spirited arguments under the same progressed aspect. In each case the response would be conditioned to a large extent by the native's evolutionary status and by the environment in which he moved.

In the Middle Ages, families of great wealth and influence employed their own astrologers, who lived with the family, thus having an opportunity to study at first hand the working out of the various directional and revolutional projections of the nativities of each member of the family. Modern conditions do not encourage the present-day continuance of such a practice but even so, the wider the knowledge the astrologer has about the circumstances of his client and the previous reactions of the native to the various planetary stimuli by direction and transit the more accurately he should be able to foresee the probable trends that are likely to manifest themselves as a result of approaching directions and transits.

It is a wise plan not to forecast too far ahead, except in the broadest terms, because any long-term forecast must necessarily be speculative in relation to some departments of the life and so to the options which may be open to the native. Specific developments may take place during the period covered by a long-term forecast which considerably clarify the general picture and enable more detailed predictions to be made for the immediate future.

Sometimes the astrologer is asked to predict the date of the native's death. Although it may be possible for the truly evolved individual to contemplate the predicted date of his death with equanimity, it is given to few to judge whether the native has indeed reached such a point in his evolution. And if he were not able to contemplate such knowledge without a qualm, the psychological effect of being in the possession of such information might substantially alter the balance of his outlook on life, inducing an attitude of morbid despair or even reckless abandon as the predicted date drew nearer, with consequent reactions upon health and behaviour. The consensus of opinion among astrologers is strongly against the practice of predicting the actual time of the native's death — even if there were an infallible rule for predetermining such a date! Nor is there any guarantee that at all times and under all circumstances the length of an individual's life is irrevocably and inexorably fixed.

This being so, if the astrologer is asked to predict the probable events for a period in which it seems likely to him that death may occur, it would be better to refer to such a period as a time of crisis, explaining that such crises are likely to occur from time to time in every life, although with varying frequency, and although one such crisis may ultimately prove to be the final one there is nothing to be gained by regarding this or that crisis as being insurmountable. Instead, the period should be presented as one of trial and testing, in which greater rewards might be gained from reflection rather than from action. Aspects appearing to indicate death formed by direction, especially early in the life, sometimes denote a 'psychological death' in which the native 'dies' to part of himself, as it must be if any sort of 'initiation' is to take place, and such a change will take place, whether through a gradual or a sudden heightening of awareness, bringing with it a new understanding and a new outlook which makes it impossible to hang on to old habits of thinking or feeling, which therefore die.

With these ideas in mind we may now consider the vexed problem with which astrologers are always confronted when they assert that future events may, within limits, be predicted. If it were possible to predict events in the life of an individual, thereby implying that certain things are destined to happen, does this not rule out the possibility of that individual having freedom of choice through the exercise of free will? From the Ouspenskian viewpoint there are very few men who have developed will-power in the full and proper sense of the term. Such a suggestion is so unflattering to the ordinary man that he automatically rejects it, mistakenly believing himself to be guided by his own indomitable will when he is, in fact, more or less completely at the mercy of first one and then another set of desires which insistently demand to be fulfilled, regardless of the true merits of any given situation. If we are really honest with ourselves and successfully make the effort to keep a constant and impartial watch upon ourselves and the urges which motivate our conduct, we shall have to admit that many times we act in response to the dictates of the needs of our physical body, of our emotions or of our intellect. Rarely indeed do we act from a sense of 'wholeness' with the rest of creation, knowing ourselves to be a part of it or, indeed, with a sense of the consciousness of our real destiny, otherwise many of our actions would be different!

Nevertheless, the astrologer is forced to take the world as he finds it and he must concede that there are certain situations in which the individual appears to be free to choose between two or even more possible courses of action, thus confirming, at any rate to outward appearances, that scope for the exercise of free will does exist. There are certain happenings, however, over which the individual appears to have little or no control. His own birth is one. Since the astrologer is aware that the moment of birth has the closest possible connection with the potentialities and trends of the whole life to follow, he may well be excused if he reasons that if the start of a life is outside the native's control and the planetary conditions at that moment largely reflect the subsequent pattern of the life, then fatalism would seem to play an almost over-whelming part in shaping the events of that life.

Viewed from the narrow concept that a single human life begins and ends without any discernible prior cause that may be linked with the native himself and ends without any future opportunity to make amends for past failure, except in some purgatorial after-death state, the fate versus free will dilemma seems to resolve itself very much in favour of predestination. However, according to occult teaching, there is an important factor which throws an entirely different light on the situation. This is the doctrine of reincarnation, which explains that the seemingly haphazard appearance of human beings on the physical plane is governed by an ordered set of laws that exist for the sole purpose of assisting human evolution. A single lifetime is all too short for ordinary man to accomplish the tremendous amount of work necessary to complete his evolution on the physical plane and so he must return again and again, albeit with a fresh personality, to continue his efforts and to correct past mistakes that would otherwise hamper his future progress or even deny it altogether.

Man is a being who feels, thinks, acts and aspires. His task is to learn to control and direct aright his feelings, thoughts, actions and aspirations for, according to the occultist, man's every feeling, thought, action and aspiration produces an effect at the appro-priate level of consciousness. Negative feelings, turbulent emo-tions, distorted thoughts, harmful actions and misdirected aspirations may all be regarded as causes which set in motion vibrations of a type which can produce effects that are registered as unpleasant by the individual who experiences them and who is, in fact, merely reaping the harvest of what he has sown.

The span of one lifetime is all too short for the multitude of various feelings, thoughts, actions and aspirations indulged in by the individual to have their final repercussions upon him and so the results of many of the causes set in motion during one lifetime are not made manifest until the next. Truly we reap the harvest of what we have sown but, especially in cases where painful results have been brought about, the reaping may not take place until several lives have made us strong enough to bear the vicissitudes that must eventually fall to our lot as the inevitable outcome of causes set in motion in some previous incarnation.

Here, then, is a key which can open up a new understanding of the problem of fate versus free will. Leaving aside the question of the corporate destiny of the human race, we can appreciate that through the operation of the law of cause and effect, each of us shapes his own destiny by the quality and nature of his feelings, thoughts, actions and aspirations. We may choose how we feel, how we think, how we act and how we aspire and by making our choice we are moulding the pattern of our future. Our present has already been determined by our past choices, for now we are paying off our debts to the past and reaping our rewards for any previous right effort we have made. This, then, is our fate, but it is a fate we have fashioned for ourselves through the previous exercise of free will. By the present exercise of our free will we can influence the course of our future destiny. The only snag is that we are such creatures of habit that we tend over and over again, to indulge in the same types of emotional reaction, to pursue the same trends of thought, to act according to the same patterns of behaviour and to direct our aspirations towards the same kind of goal. Only by occasionally being confronted with circumstances and situations that shock us out of our habitual reactions are we given the incentive to make the necessary adjustments to our way of living.

This doctrine of cause and effect, coupled with the idea of reincarnation, enables us to build up a picture in which the working out of fate and the operation of free will may be seen in perspective. The fact that we appear to be powerless to avoid being born at a certain time, that we are unable to choose our relatives, that we cannot avoid bereavement and that sometimes we are handicapped from birth by physical or mental infirmity — in short, the whole pattern of our present destiny — is due to choices we have made in the past through the exercise of our own free will. The present, with all its limitations, is in fact a living monument to the exercise of our free will in previous incarnations. Now, as always, we are perfectly free to feel, think, act and aspire exactly as we wish and by so doing to mould the pattern of our future existence. The impact of calamitous events need not fill us with dread or pessimism nor the presence of precipitous obstacles fill us with dismay or despair. To that extent we are still free agents. Though the broad pattern of our life is predestined, but only by our own previous use or misuse of free will, we may have earned for ourselves the right to a certain limited freedom of action here and now. That much of our future which has not been pre-determined by past habits of thought, feeling and action we may now build for ourselves and we may even modify some of the present and future effects of causes set in motion in the past if only we are able to go about it in the right way.

The astrologer who understands this relationship between the fate and free will of the native will then appreciate the desirability of assessing any future trend of events in terms of the oppor-tunities for self-development that they may afford the native, bearing in mind that the pattern of each life is so arranged that we are provided with the particular variety of experience best calculated to assist us in building up and strengthening within ourselves those qualities and abilities that we need in order to make effective progress along our evolutionary path. Individual difficulties most often arise, not so much because of the absence of certain qualities but, because in past lives one or more qualities may have been overdeveloped in relation to the rest. The prob-lem, therefore, is usually one of overemphasis in one particular direction, with the result that special work is required in order to adjust some imbalance or to develop some particular faculty or ability.

This being so, the astrologer may often render more valuable assistance, not by seeking to predict events in as much precise detail as possible but, by trying to discern what special lessons these events may hold for the native and what attitudes of mind the native may best employ and cultivate in order to make the best use of the new situations that are about to arise. Some events may be recognized as rewards for past or present effort, some as setbacks designed to test the degree to which the native has succeeded in developing certain qualities. Others may appear to fall into no special category but may, in fact, be designed to allow for the entry of some completely new factor into the life, giving the native an opportunity of embarking upon an entirely new line of endeavour in some particular field.

It is not always possible to discern the exact reasons for every event that happens to the native and for the existence of every environment in which he finds himself, nevertheless certain types of happening may, in themselves contain indications of the purpose underlying them. Early loss of one or both parents, for instance, may well mean that the native has to develop independence; typically emotional independence if the mother dies and independence in practical, everyday affairs if he is left fatherless. Serious and prolonged illness or repeated setbacks in his career may indicate the need to cultivate courage and fortitude in adversity or to develop persistence and determination. Involvement in the misfortunes of others may be a means of lessening a pronounced tendency to self-pity, while a predisposition to become involved in emotional problems would suggest a need to develop judgement in such matters so that the heart did not always rule the head. Through a careful study of the nativity and the directions and revolutions in force at the time, the astrologer should be able to discern some of the underlying reasons for the events of the period. In addition it should be possible to suggest, by reference to any helpful configurations in the nativity or in the current directions or revolutional figures, which of those qualities already cultivated by the native might best be used to gain the utmost benefit from periods which favour the native's progress and to minimize the depressing and frustrating limitations experienced during periods of adversity.

It has often been said that the old classification of planets into benefics and malefics is a false one; similarly, the division of aspects into 'good' and 'bad' categories. From the point of view of character analysis there is much to be said for throwing overboard the old classifications, but when it comes to judging the type of event that different planetary configurations are likely to herald, there is every reason to uphold the old classifications. Calamities do not coincide with good aspects involving the benefics, nor do great material benefits derive from bad aspects involving the malefics. If, however, we understand that adversity is often a necessary spur to human evolution and achievement and that too much good fortune can encourage inertia and indolence, then we again arrive at the point where we may question the overall aptness of the terms 'benefic' and 'malefic'. Since it is given to few of us to welcome misfortune as a possible means of improving our spiritual stature or to deplore good fortune as a stultifying experience, the final rejection of the traditional terminology can hardly be contemplated!

A brief guide to the qualities indicated by each of the luminaries and planets when strong and well aspected in the nativity and a suggestion as to the particular kind of test the native is likely to be subjected to when they are afflicted by direction or in the revolution is given below:

	Qualities	*Purpose of Tests*
Sun	Nobility of character; virility; aspiration; creative power.	To help native overcome pride and egotism; to develop independence and to make him consciously aware of his own real self.
Moon	Sensitive awareness of surrounding emotional conditions; ready sympathies; adaptability; solicitude for others; instinctive shrewdness.	To help native gain better control of his feelings, to respect the feelings of others and to respond correctly to the promptings of his instincts.
Mercury	Native wit; reasoning power; adaptability; opportunism; power of interpretation; ability to cope with detail.	To help native develop versatility; to strengthen the power of self-expression or check verbosity; to stimulate the growth of the reasoning powers and to make more flexible on the intellectual plane; to conquer indecision; to curb carelessness; to overcome nervousness.
Venus	Power of devotion; capacity for harmonious co-operation; appreciation of beauty; artistic talent; charm; poise.	To help native in the right development of his affections; to enable him to appreciate the right use of leisure; to overcome sloth and indolence; to curb self-indulgence and pleasure-seeking.
Mars	Energetic drive; initiative, leadership.	To help native use his energies constructively; to control his aggressiveness; to overcome intemperance; to curb passionate impulses and conquer bad temper.

Jupiter	Enthusiasm; generosity; liberality; fair-mindedness; jovial good humour.	To help native curb reckless extravagance; to avoid mistakes of judgement through over-optimism and over-confidence; to combat laziness and to expand his philosophical understanding of life.
Saturn	Integrity; self-discipline; persistence; desire for perfection; ability to husband resources.	To help native to cultivate perseverance and singleness of purpose; to conquer meanness, selfishness and narrowness of outlook; to overcome pessimistic moods; to rise above a purely materialistic evaluation of life.
Uranus	Creative originality; dynamic leadership; independence of thought and action; intuitive awareness.	To help the native to curb eccentric and erratic behaviour; to discipline wilful contrariness and to modify iconoclastic tendencies; to discriminate in the use of power and in his enthusiasm for new ideas, new friends and new methods.
Neptune	Idealism; powers of sympathy and understanding; devoted self-sacrifice; emotional receptivity	To help the native to overcome extravagant emotional moods and a restless craving for emotional fulfilment; to teach him neither to yearn for the unattainable nor to attach false glamour to unworthy objects; to avoid self-deception on all levels; to steer clear of reckless infatuations; to resist the too ready gratification of physical appetites and to help him to appreciate the need for distinguishing at all times between the true and the false and for acting with absolute integrity.
Pluto	Will-power; compelling sense of destiny based on a subconscious realization of man's part in the Divine Plan. Understanding of group psychology and the power to	To help the native mobilize all his powers to achieve a measure of reorientation; to confront him with situations which compelled him to reassess his ideas, particularly in those departments of life ruled by the planets in closest aspect to Pluto and the sign containing Pluto, as a result of which he will either

| inspire group action. Grasp of bedrock essentials. Ability to stand alone. | become increasingly self-reliant or will allow himself to become submerged in a group, being dominated by mass opinion and regimented in accordance with the needs of the community; to develop his resistance to the compelling impact of ideas springing from the group unconscious and to avoid all forms of obsession that are likely to turn him aside from his legitimate aims; to help him to purify himself on all levels, particularly in relation to those states of consciousness represented by the planets in strong close aspect to Pluto. |

Because there appears to be a subtle connection between the native's mental attitudes and the external circumstances in which he finds himself and because the physical reactions of wrong emotional attitudes can be very harmful, the Church of Light have advocated that under certain types of adverse directions the native should be encouraged deliberately to cultivate definite mental and emotional attitudes as an antidote to the nature of the planetary vibrations in force at critical periods of the life. The extent to which the native may be able to take advantage of such advice is problematical. Nevertheless, as so much may depend upon the cultivation of a positive and balanced attitude to life, especially in so far as reactions to severe disappointments and disheartening experiences are concerned, everything should be done to assist the native to guide his thoughts in the right direction. To this end the astrologer should always be on the look out for signs in the nativity of the direction in which the native's special attributes of character may lie so that he may be encouraged to develop and rely upon his own resources in times of crisis.

As a general guide, the following suggestions may prove helpful at a time when a luminary or planet is prominent and afflicted in progressions or revolutions:

Sun
A tendency for the native's power of action to be inhibited. If the affliction is from Saturn or Neptune there is a need to cultivate

a more positive courageous and persevering attitude; if from Mars, Jupiter or Uranus, there is a need to practise much self-control and to cultivate an attitude of calm confidence.

Moon

A tendency for the sympathies to be directed inwards, encouraging the development of difficulties in personal relationships. Cultivate sympathetic thought for others, especially for those in distressed circumstances, and foster the development of the cherishing propensities above all towards the family and then for all sentient life in need of care and protection.

Mercury

A tendency for the mind to become overactive and anxious. Cultivate careful attention to detail, and serenity of purpose. Make a commonsense appraisal of problems and once a decision has been reached, refrain from endlessly turning the matter over in the mind, an energy-wasting process which cannot make any improvement on the final result.

Venus

A tendency to allow emotional disappointments to have a disproportionate effect. An excessive desire for harmony leads to over-sensitivity. Allow reason to rule emotion and endeavour to realize that the very nature of our existence does not make it possible for us to live in perfect harmony all the time. That being so, we are laying ourselves open to emotional difficulties if we are not prepared to accept certain disharmonies as a temporary necessity.

Mars

Problems arise over the right direction of energy. Guard against acting too hastily, too impulsively or too vigorously. At all times the native should 'look before he leaps' and cultivate forethought and solicitude for others, trying to visualize beforehand the probable effect of his behaviour on others. His energies should be consciously directed towards fighting for the rights of those who are unable to prosecute their own cause through lack of privilege or influence and not used forcefully in furtherance of self-interest. Forthright action should only be taken after calm reflection. An interest in looking after those in less fortunate circumstances is best developed at this time.

Jupiter

Just as the faults of Mercury are best counteracted by the virtues of Jupiter, so the shortcomings of Jupiter are best offset by the virtues of Mercury. A tendency towards carelessness, extravagance and over-optimism, arising from a disregard for careful and intelligent forethought should be countered by cultivating an interest in diligently appraising the possibilities of every situation with due regard for the dictates of prudence and common sense.

Saturn

Lack of confidence, courage and determination should be offset by a resolve to act positively and an effort to mix freely with others. An attempt should be made to cultivate a buoyant disregard for obstacles and setbacks but at the same time accepting the need for conservation of effort in the departments of life most affected by the affliction.

Uranus

A lack of serenity and a restless, unsettled attitude is likely to bring difficulties in personal associations. A strong desire to relieve tensions by 'doing something at all costs' should be counteracted by the cultivation of a point of view which is prepared to accept that the irksome circumstances of the moment may ultimately turn out to be of the greatest advantage and that shocks and sudden new departures are sometimes necessary for human evolution in that they act to awaken the individual to new possibilities and to shake him out of his old habits that may, without his having realized it, have stood in the way of his development.

Neptune

An overactive imagination may subtly obscure the real issues of the period and an over-indulgence of the emotions may act to inhibit action and prevent issues being seen in proper focus. The Saturnian virtues of solid, down-to-earth common sense and steady application to the job in hand are the best antidote to the dreamy idealism and vague drifting that may occur during a period of Neptunian affliction. A strongly positive attitude to life should be encouraged.

Pluto

Unusual compulsions of various kinds seem to encourage wrongheadedness. Disruptive tendencies in the individual that have long lain dormant are brought out into the open by a combination of inexorable circumstances and strangely compelling urges that arise from the subconscious. Such a situation will test the extent to which the native has been able to achieve self-integration, and the effectiveness of his personal philosophy. The cultivation of an attitude of calm detachment and a determination to analyse accurately and dispassionately his own motives will help to mitigate some of the more disastrous possibilities of the period.

A life that is difficult in terms of the number of tests and trials that the native is called upon to face may thus be regarded as far more worthwhile than an untroubled life where little happens to disturb the native's smooth and placid existence and, as a general rule, it may be understood that a difficult path is more often chosen by the earnest striver after self-development. An individual, once having chosen, through the agency of the Higher Self, to come to birth at a given time and place in order to gain certain types of experience, any subsequent attempt on his part to side-step such experiences would appear to be a deliberate thwarting of the whole purpose of the life. Yet there are astrologers who deliberately seek ways and means of avoiding the effects of difficult phases in the life indicated by progressions and revolutions showing the likelihood of periods of stress. While it is a moot point whether we can avoid any of the unpleasant events in our outer life (unless perhaps we deserve to avoid them!) we always have it in our power, if we so desire, to regulate our own reactions to the events in which we have to play a part, whether that part be active or passive. The astrologer's task, therefore, is not to counsel those who consult him to seek the best way of avoiding any blows that fate may seem to have in store. Indeed, the story of astrology is full of anecdotes about warnings of such a nature which have proved to be of no avail! Rather should the astrologer seek to prepare the native to react to such events in the best possible way so that he does not become overwhelmed when surrounded by apparent catastrophe and to suggest how he may mobilize his natural resources so that he may be in a position to extract the fullest measure of benefit, from the evolutionary standpoint, that may be derived from his participation in such events and experiences.

23.

CONCLUSION

The object of this work is not so much to produce a comprehensive system of prediction as to show how almost identical results may be obtained by using similar systems based on different points of reference, yet all based on a single common principle, the periodical return of either luminary to one particular place in the horoscope, that is to its own position, to the position of the other luminary or to the position of the Ascendant. Such a concurrence of testimonies, based upon striking similarities between the interplanetary configurations and the angular positions of significant planets in each type of figure, could hardly be arrived at by some conveniently fortuitous accident and must inevitably give the unbeliever some cause to reflect, if he is honest with himself, that such a state of affairs points strongly to the possibility of some kind of underlying plan in each human experience, a plan which can reveal itself, in its broad outlines at least, to the initiated who are versed in the intricacies of astrology.

A comprehensive and completely reliable system of prognostication may be fashioned from the various types of revolutional figure dealt with in the foregoing pages. Normally it will be sufficient to use either the Composite Solar Revolution, the Composite Annual New Moon or the Composite Annual Sunrise Horoscope, applying the various directional measures based on the unit of a day, as required. Except under special circumstances, there should be no need to calculate figures both with and without an allowance for precession and the student will no doubt already have decided for himself which type of figure he prefers. One of the secondary purposes of this work has been to investigate whether revolutional figures calculated with an allowance for precession give better results than those calculated without such an allowance. My own conclusion is that the difference in the two methods is so small as to be negligible.

If, when the progressions of the major revolutional figures have been studied, the reader feels that he requires further evidence on which to base his interpretation, he may then select, from the various methods at his disposal, that category of yearly or monthly figure that he believes is best suited to his purpose.

We may now turn to a consideration of one or two of the special uses to which these revolutional figures may be put. If there should be an error of fifteen minutes in the birthtime, for instance, this will cause the Solar Revolution also to be fifteen minutes out. Because the Solar Revolution can be progressed day by day, it is possible to attempt a rectification of the nativity by carefully studying the progressions involving the revolutional angles. In such cases it will usually be found that over a period of years, revolutions consistently display planets having a significant bearing on important events in conspicuous positions, yet falling short of an exact conjunction of an angle by an almost identical number of degrees. This may well indicate that an adjustment to the nativity is necessary, so as to bring the planets in question exactly on to the angle of the revolutional figures. A further test can then be applied to the revolution by progressing the angles of the adjusted figure and noting whether more suitable aspects are formed by the recalculated angles. Experiments may also be made with the annual New Moon and Annual Sunrise figures, bearing in mind that an error of a few minutes in the birthtime will throw up a greater error in revolutional figures of this type. In the case of the Annual New Moon, a mistake of fifteen minutes in the natal horoscope will cause the position of the radical Moon to be wrong to the extent of some 7′ of arc, a distance which the Sun will take some three hours to cover. Similarly, the birth Ascendant could be some 4° from its true position if there were an error of fifteen minutes in the birthtime, which could throw the Annual Sunrise horoscope out by as much as four days. In such cases it should be possible to detect whether a true or false figure has been obtained, thus further improving the chances of obtaining a correct result.

We can now turn to another matter. The fact that it has been possible to isolate and identify certain types of 'event configuration' in revolutional figures suggests that experience gained in handling these horoscopes may be of great assistance to the student in other branches of astrological research. If, for instance, we can say that Mercury–Neptune aspects combined with the presence of Moon–Uranus configurations is a factor nearly always present in Solar Revolutions at the time of travel, we shall expect to find these configurations present in the horoscopes of much-travelled people. And if we note that Moon–Pluto and Mercury–Mars configurations are nearly always present in the Solar Revolution at the time when the native is involved in divorce proceedings, then we may expect that these factors in the nativity may also be part of the pattern that indicates the 'divorce-prone' type. We can thus learn more about the interpretation of nativities and the meaning of natal planetary complexes by studying the composite Solar Revolution and we can turn to the Solar Revolution for evidence if we wish to conduct research into the horoscopical features associated with various types of event, physical condition or psychological attitude.

Several new types of revolutional figure have been introduced to the reader, and I believe that their effectiveness has been demonstrated, not only by the large number of directions in each case that are appropriate to the event concerned but especially by the schedules at the end of Chapter 20 which show that the number of significant configurations listed under the orthodox figures is matched by the number of similarly derived directions arising from other types of figure. That this is so is a striking proof of the wonderful variety of means by which astrology makes it possible to gain a knowledge of future trends and tendencies. The common testimony of the various solar and lunar figures and the simultaneous climax of key aspects in a number of different horoscopes all derived from the same nativity and all having reference to the same period of life, is indeed a graphic illustration of the wonderful way in which astrology provides ample means for the solving of our problems, if only we care to avail ourselves of them. Thus we may truly say that the very fabric of our existence is built up of wheels within wheels, of circles within circles, of spirals within spirals. Like the mechanism of some intricate celestial clock, fashioned and assembled by a master craftsman, so the Earth, Moon and planets moving in their respective orbits and periodically establishing a similar relationship with each other, combine together to produce by their revolutions the timepiece which registers, for the initiated, the chronological pattern of a lifetime's events. Thus it may truly be said that these revolutions are indeed the Cycles of Destiny.

APPENDICES

APPENDIX ONE
PRECESSIONAL INCREMENTS

The first point of Aries in the Tropical Zodiac moves backwards through the Zodiac of the Constellations at the rate of 50.2572″ per year. If it is desired to calculate a Solar Revolution in terms of the natal Sun's position in relation to the fixed stars it is necessary to calculate how far the Tropical Zodiac has shifted, relative to the Sidereal Zodiac, between the time of the native's birth and the particular anniversary under review. This amount of arc must then be added to the Sun's natal longitude in order to compensate for the precessional movement of the Tropical Zodiac. The Solar Revolution should then be calculated for the Sun's return to the corrected position. In order to correct the Sun's position for Prenatal Solar Revolutions it will, of course, be necessary to deduct the appropriate increment from the position of the radical Sun.

Age of Native	Precessional Increment	Age of Native	Precessional Increment
Years	° ′ ″	Years	° ′ ″
1	0 50	51	42 43
2	1 41	52	43 33
3	2 31	53	44 24
4	3 21	54	45 14
5	4 11	55	46 04
6	5 02	56	46 54
7	5 52	57	47 45
8	6 42	58	48 35
9	7 32	59	49 25
10	8 23	60	50 15
11	9 13	61	51 06
12	10 03	62	51 56
13	10 53	63	52 46
14	11 44	64	53 36
15	12 34	65	54 27
16	13 24	66	55 17
17	14 14	67	56 07
18	15 05	68	56 57
19	15 55	69	57 48
20	16 45	70	58 38
21	17 35	71	59 28
22	18 26	72	1 00 19
23	19 16	73	1 01 09
24	20 06	74	1 01 59
25	20 56	75	1 02 49
26	21 47	76	1 03 40
27	22 37	77	1 04 30
28	23 27	78	1 05 20
29	24 18	79	1 06 10
30	25 08	80	1 07 01
31	25 58	81	1 07 51
32	26 48	82	1 08 41
33	27 39	83	1 09 31
34	28 29	84	1 10 22
35	29 19	85	1 11 12
36	30 09	86	1 12 02
37	31 00	87	1 12 52
38	31 50	88	1 13 43
39	32 40	89	1 14 33
40	33 30	90	1 15 23
41	34 21	91	1 16 13
42	35 11	92	1 17 04
43	36 01	93	1 17 54
44	36 51	94	1 18 44
45	37 42	95	1 19 34
46	38 32	96	1 20 25
47	39 22	97	1 21 15
48	40 12	98	1 22 05
49	41 03	99	1 22 55
50	41 53	100	1 23 46

Months	° ′ ″	Weeks	° ′ ″
1	04	1	01
2	08	2	02
3	13	3	03
4	17	4	04
5	21	**Days**	**° ′ ″**
6	25		
7	29	1–3	00
8	33	4–10	01
9	38	11–18	02
10	42	19–25	03
11	46	26–31	04

APPENDIX TWO
SYNODICAL LUNATIONS

Tables showing approximately the number of years and days to be added to, or subtracted from the day of birth in order to find the Postnatal or Antenatal Synodical Lunation for any year of life.

These tables are based on an average synodical lunation period of 29 days 12 hours 44 minutes 2.7 seconds. The period between one lunation and the next is regarded as covering one year of life, so that one day of the lunation month will represent about 12 days 9 hours of life.

For the purposes of these tables each fourth year has been regarded as a Leap Year.

Age of Native	Add or subtract for Lunation date		Age of Native	Add or subtract for Lunation date	
Years	Years	Days	Years	Years	Days
1		30	51	4	45
2		59	52	4	75
3		89	53	4	104
4		118	54	4	134
5		148	55	4	163
6		177	56	4	193
7		207	57	4	222
8		236	58	4	252
9		266	59	4	281
10		295	60	4	311
11		325	61	4	340
12		354	62	5	5
13	1	19	63	5	34
14	1	48	64	5	64
15	1	78	65	5	93
16	1	107	66	5	123
17	1	137	67	5	153
18	1	167	68	5	182
19	1	196	69	5	212
20	1	226	70	5	241
21	1	255	71	5	271
22	1	285	72	5	300
23	1	314	73	5	330
24	1	344	74	5	359
25	2	8	75	6	24
26	2	38	76	6	53
27	2	67	77	6	83
28	2	97	78	6	112
29	2	126	79	6	142
30	2	156	80	6	171
31	2	185	81	6	201
32	2	215	82	6	231
33	2	245	83	6	260
34	2	274	84	6	290
35	2	304	85	6	319
36	2	333	86	6	349
37	2	363	87	7	13
38	3	27	88	7	43
39	3	57	89	7	72
40	3	86	90	7	102
41	3	116	91	7	131
42	3	145	92	7	161
43	3	175	93	7	190
44	3	204	94	7	220
45	3	234	95	7	249
46	3	263	96	7	279
47	3	293	97	7	308
48	3	322	98	7	338
49	3	352	99	8	2
50	4	16	100	8	31

APPENDIX THREE
YEARLY LUNAR REVOLUTIONS

Tables showing approximately the number of years and days to be added to, or subtracted from the day of birth in order to find the Postnatal or Antenatal yearly lunar revolution for any year of life.

These tables are based on an average lunation period of 27 days 7 hours 43 minutes. At the end of the fourth year an extra day has been included as a Leap Year day.

Age of Native	Add or subtract for Lunation date		Age of Native	Add or subtract for Lunation date	
Years	Years	Days	Years	Years	Days
1		27	51	3	298
2		55	52	3	326
3		82	53	3	353
4		109	54	4	14
5		137	55	4	42
6		164	56	4	69
7		191	57	4	96
8		219	58	4	124
9		246	59	4	151
10		273	60	4	178
11		301	61	4	206
12		328	62	4	233
13		355	63	4	260
14	1	18	64	4	288
15	1	45	65	4	315
16	1	72	66	4	342
17	1	99	67	5	5
18	1	127	68	5	32
19	1	154	69	5	59
20	1	181	70	5	87
21	1	209	71	5	114
22	1	236	72	5	141
23	1	263	73	5	168
24	1	291	74	5	196
25	1	318	75	5	223
26	1	345	76	5	250
27	2	8	77	5	278
28	2	35	78	5	305
29	2	62	79	5	332
30	2	90	80	5	360
31	2	117	81	6	22
32	2	144	82	6	49
33	2	172	83	6	77
34	2	199	84	6	104
35	2	226	85	6	131
36	2	254	86	6	159
37	2	281	87	6	186
38	2	308	88	6	213
39	2	336	89	6	241
40	2	363	90	6	268
41	3	25	91	6	295
42	3	53	92	6	323
43	3	80	93	6	350
44	3	107	94	7	12
45	3	134	95	7	40
46	3	162	96	7	67
47	3	189	97	7	94
48	3	216	98	7	122
49	3	244	99	7	149
50	3	271	100	7	176

APPENDIX FOUR
THE EXAMPLE HOROSCOPES

It was my original intention to employ the same set of example nativities as those used in *The Technique of Prediction* to illustrate the working of secondary directions. In the event, it was found that this was not a practical proposition. Firstly, that set of horoscopes contained several dating from the early part of the nineteenth century, so that the calculation of many of the antenatal revolutional figures deriving from these nativities would have made it necessary to consult ephemerides for years in the eighteenth century. Not only are these tables hard to come by but the solar and lunar positions are not given with sufficient precision. Secondly, among these nativities there was not enough varied material for the type of event analysis presented in Chapter 5. An attempt was then made to find enough material from my own private sources to furnish a reasonable number of examples for each type of event investigated, preference being given to those nativities which furnished examples of several different types of event. Because, in nearly every case, the natives are still living, it has been necessary to augment the collection of example horoscopes to cover cases of death. Also, because of the age-group of most of the natives, it has been necessary to widen the original field to include one or two grandparents of sufficiently recent birth to allow the easy calculation of the relevant antenatal Solar Revolutions. For these reasons a few horoscopes of the illustrious and sometimes the less illustrious, have also been included. Needless to say the example horoscopes published here only represent a small fraction of the total number studied.

Below will be found the data relating to the natal and revolutional figures dealt with in Chapters 5 and 7. The relevant data for the various solar and lunar figures referred to in other chapters are included in the actual chapters concerned. It will be observed that in some cases the revolution is not cast for the same locality as the nativity. This is because the revolutional figure must be cast for the place where the native is actually living at the time of the solar or lunar return. If he should be absent from that place on the day of the actual return although he would normally be residing there, such temporary absence is best disregarded. In all cases the time given is GMT.

Nativity No.	Case No.	Solar Revolution	Data
1	1		Male
			17 September 1918, London, 4.37 a.m.
		1a	16 September 1944, London, 11.58 a.m.
		1b	16 September 1944, London, 8.53 p.m.
		1c	15 September 1892, London, 10.00 p.m.
		1d	15 September 1892, London, 1.04 p.m.
	10	1e	16 September 1949, London, 5.02 p.m.
		1f	17 September 1949, London, 3.39 a.m.
		1g	16 September 1887, London, 4.55 p.m.
		1h	16 September 1887, London, 6.17 a.m.
	15	1i	16 September 1946, London, 11.36 p.m.
		1j	17 September 1946, London, 9.12 a.m.
		1k	16 September 1890, London, 10.21 a.m.
		1l	16 September 1890, London, 12.44 a.m.
	23	1m	16 September 1940, London, 12.36 p.m.
		1n	16 September 1940, London, 8.10 p.m.
		1o	15 September 1896, London, 8.57 p.m.
		1p	15 September 1896, London, 1.24 p.m.
	35	1q	16 September 1921, London, 10.38 p.m.
		1r	16 September 1921, London, 11.16 p.m.
		1s	17 September 1915, London, 11.16 a.m.
		1t	17 September 1915, London, 10.14 a.m.
2			Male
			19 January 1916, Bristol, 12.29 p.m.
		2a	18 January 1941, Bristol, 2.10 p.m.
		2b	18 January 1941, Bristol, 10.25 p.m.
		2c	18 January 1891, Bristol, 10.56 a.m.
		2d	18 January 1891, Bristol, 2.42 a.m.
	17	2e	19 January 1939, Bristol, 2.28 a.m.
		2f	19 January 1939, Bristol, 10.02 a.m.
		2g	17 January 1893, Bristol, 10.33 p.m.
		2h	17 January 1893, Bristol, 3.00 p.m.
	21	2i	18 January 1930, Bristol, 10.09 p.m.
		2j	19 January 1930, Bristol, 2.45 a.m.
		2k	19 January 1902, Bristol, 2.47 a.m.
		2l	18 January 1902, Bristol, 10.10 p.m.
	31	2m	19 January 1924, Bristol, 11.03 a.m.
		2n	19 January 1924, Bristol, 1.45 p.m.
		2o	19 January 1908, Bristol, 2.04 p.m.
		2p	19 January 1908, Bristol, 11.26 a.m.
	38	2q	19 January 1932, Bristol, 9.34 a.m.
		2r	19 January 1932, Bristol, 2.51 p.m.
		2s	18 January 1900, Bristol, 3.07 p.m.
		2t	18 January 1900, Bristol, 9.51 a.m.

Nativity No.	Case No.	Solar Revolution	Data
3			Female
			1 November 1903, Southport, 12.02 a.m.
	3	3a	31 October 1928, Southport, 2.40 a.m.
		3b	31 October 1928, Southport, 10.03 a.m.
		3c	30 October 1878, Southport, 10.31 p.m.
		3d	30 October 1878, Southport, 2.06 p.m.
	28	3e	31 October 1937, Southport, 5.49 a.m.
		3f	31 October 1937, Southport, 5.11 p.m.
		3g	30 October 1869, Southport, 6.26 p.m.
		3h	30 October 1869, Southport, 7.02 a.m.
	30	3i	31 October 1938, Southport, 11.34 a.m.
		3j	31 October 1938, Southport, 11.17 p.m.
		3k	30 October 1868, Southport, 12.30 p.m.
		3l	30 October 1868, Southport, 12.47 a.m.
4			Female
			7 February 1917, Hull, 8.37 p.m.
	4	4a	8 February 1940, Hull, 10.43 a.m.
		4b	8 February 1940, Hull, 6.26 p.m.
		4c	7 February 1894, Hull, 5.16 p.m.
		4d	6 February 1894, Hull, 11.11 p.m.
	37	4e	7 February 1921, Hull, 7.56 p.m.
		4f	7 February 1921, Hull, 9.16 p.m.
		4g	7 February 1913, Hull, 9.18 a.m.
		4h	7 February 1913, Hull, 7.59 p.m.
5			Male
			9 June 1926, London, 5.37 p.m.
	5	5a	9 June 1951, London, 6.29 p.m.
		5b	10 June 1951, London, 3.14 p.m.
		5c	9 June 1901, London, 4.34 p.m.
		5d	9 June 1901, London, 7.50 a.m.
6			Female
			2 May 1933, London, 7.58 p.m.
	6	6a	3 May 1951, London, 4.30 a.m.
		6b	3 May 1951, London, 10.42 a.m.
		6c	3 May 1915, London, 11.18 a.m.
		6d	3 May 1915, London, 5.03 a.m.
7			Female
			20 March 1920, London, 11.53 a.m.
	7	7a	21 March 1947, London, 1.08 a.m.
		7b	21 March 1947, London, 10.14 a.m.
		7c	19 March 1893, London, 11.03 p.m.
		7d	19 March 1893, London, 1.55 p.m.

Nativity No.	Case No.	Solar Revolution	Data
	33	7e	20 March 1924, London, 11.15 a.m.
		7f	20 March 1924, London, 12.35 p.m.
		7g	20 March 1916, London, 12.40 p.m.
		7h	20 March 1916, London, 11.20 a.m.
8			Female
			27 June 1924, West Bromwich, 5.17 p.m.
	8	8a	27 June 1948, West Bromwich, 12.29 p.m.
		8b	27 June 1948, West Bromwich, 8.57 p.m.
		8c	27 June 1900, West Bromwich, 9.52 p.m.
		8d	27 June 1900, West Bromwich, 1.28 p.m.
	29	8e	28 June 1947, West Bromwich, 6.36 a.m.
		8f	28 June 1947, West Bromwich, 2.40 p.m.
		8g	28 June 1901, West Bromwich, 3.46 a.m.
		8h	27 June 1901, West Bromwich, 7.40 p.m.
9			Male
			17 November 1913, Birmingham, 12.38 a.m.
	9	9a	17 November 1946, Birmingham, 12.51 a.m.
		9b	17 November 1946, Birmingham, 11.48 a.m.
		9c	16 November 1880, Birmingham, 12.28 a.m.
		9d	15 November 1880, Birmingham, 1.29 p.m.
	13	9e	17 November 1950, Birmingham, 12.02 a.m.
		9f	17 November 1950, Birmingham, 12.20 p.m.
		9g	16 November 1876, Birmingham, 1.15 a.m.
		9h	15 November 1876, Birmingham, 12.58 p.m.
	26	9i	16 November 1953, Birmingham, 5.20 p.m.
		9j	17 November 1953, Birmingham, 6.38 a.m.
		9k	16 November 1873, Birmingham, 7.49 a.m.
		9l	15 November 1873, Birmingham, 6.32 p.m.
10			Male
			10 February 1902, Berlin, 5.30 a.m.
	11	10a	9 February 1957, London, 1.48 p.m.
		10b	10 February 1957, London, 8.01 a.m.
		10c	9 February 1847, London, 9.24 p.m.
		10d	8 February 1847, London, 3.11 a.m.
		10e	10 February 1943, London, 4.32 a.m.
		10f	10 February 1943, London, 6.06 p.m.
		10g	9 February 1861, London, 6.45 a.m.
		10h	8 February 1861, London, 5.09 p.m.
11			Male
			8 January 1916, London, 9.34 p.m.
	12	11a	8 January 1928, London, 7.39 p.m.
		11b	8 January 1928, London, 11.36 p.m.
		11c	8 January 1904, London, 11.44 p.m.
		11d	8 January 1904, London, 7.48 p.m.

Nativity No.	Case No.	Solar Revolution	Data
	24	11e	7 January 1949, London, 10.12 p.m.
		11f	8 January 1949, London, 8.39 a.m.
		11g	7 January 1883, London, 9.15 p.m.
		11h	7 January 1883, London, 10.24 a.m.
12			Female
			22 June 1914, Birmingham, 10.01 p.m.
	14	12a	22 June 1930, Bristol, 6.59 p.m.
		12b	23 June 1930, Bristol, 12.36 a.m.
		12c	22 June 1898, Bristol, 1.13 a.m.
		12d	21 June 1898, Bristol, 7.36 p.m.
	16	12e	22 June 1940, Bristol, 4.44 a.m.
		12f	22 June 1940, Bristol, 1.52 p.m.
		12g	21 June 1888, Bristol, 3.21 p.m.
		12h	21 June 1888, Bristol, 6.25 a.m.
13			Female
			1 November 1923, Cheltenham, 9.13 p.m.
	18	13a	1 November 1941, Cheltenham, 5.43 a.m.
		13b	1 November 1941, Cheltenham, 11.45 a.m.
		13c	1 November 1905, Cheltenham, 12.15 p.m.
		13d	1 November 1905, Cheltenham, 6.14 a.m.
14			Male
			23 May 1915, Southampton, 11.32 p.m.
	19	14a	23 May 1955, Auckland, N.Z., 3.39 p.m.
		14b	24 May 1955, Auckland, N.Z., 5.42 a.m.
		14c	23 May 1875, Auckland, N.Z., 7.43 a.m.
		14d	22 May 1875, Auckland, N.Z., 5.45 p.m.
15			Female
			3 April 1917, Leicester, 1.19 a.m.
	20	15a	3 April 1946, Indianapolis, 2.11 a.m.
		15b	3 April 1946, Indianapolis, 12.02 p.m.
		15c	2 April 1888, Indianapolis, 12.51 a.m.
		15d	1 April 1888, Indianapolis, 2.59 p.m.
16			Female
			14 September 1890, London, 12.06 a.m.
	22	16a	14 September 1939, London, 8.26 a.m.
		16b	15 September 1939, London, 1.15 p.m.
		16c	14 September 1841, London, 3.25 a.m.
		16d	13 September 1841, London, 10.35 a.m.
	39	16e	14 September 1928, London, 4.45 a.m.
		16f	14 September 1928, London, 5.48 p.m.
		16g	13 September 1852, London, 7.29 p.m.
		16h	13 September 1852, London, 6.26 a.m.
	51	16i	14 September 1946, Capetown, 1.17 p.m.
		16j	15 September 1946, Capetown, 8.32 a.m.
		16k	14 September 1834, Capetown, 10.51 a.m.
		16l	13 September 1834, Capetown, 3.36 p.m.

Nativity No.	Case No.	Solar Revolution	Data
17			Tyrone Power 5 May 1914, Cincinnati, 12.24 p.m.
	25	17a	5 May 1933, Hollywood, Ca., 2.06 p.m.
		17b	5 May 1933, Hollywood, Ca., 8.40 p.m.
		17c	5 May 1895, Hollywood, Ca., 9.30 a.m.
		17d	5 May 1895, Hollywood, Ca., 2.56 a.m.
	50	17e	5 May 1947, Hollywood, Ca., 11.27 p.m.
		17f	6 May 1947, Hollywood, Ca., 10.52 a.m.
		17g	5 May 1881, Hollywood, Ca., 12.02 a.m.
		17h	4 May 1881, Hollywood, Ca., 12.37 p.m.
18			Male 3 January 1911, Aldershot, 6.00 a.m.
	27	18a	2 January 1957, London, 9.50 a.m.
		18b	3 January 1957, London, 1.00 a.m.
		18c	2 January 1865, London, 1.47 a.m.
		18d	1 January 1865, London, 10.41 a.m.
	34	18e	3 January 1924, Aldershot, 9.45 a.m.
		18f	3 January 1924, Aldershot, 2.02 p.m.
		18g	2 January 1898, Aldershot, 2.00 a.m.
		18h	1 January 1898, Aldershot, 9.44 p.m.
19			Female 17 January 1925, London, 9.57 p.m.
	32	19a	17 January 1953, London, 5.04 p.m.
		19b	18 January 1953, London, 2.12 a.m.
		19c	17 January 1897, London, 2.41 a.m.
		19d	16 January 1897, London, 5.28 p.m.
20			Adolf Hitler 20 April 1889, Braunau-am-Inn, 5.25 p.m.
	36	20a	21 April 1923, Munich, 10.44 p.m.
		20b	22 April 1923, Munich, 10.24 a.m.
		20c	21 April 1855, Munich, 11.53 a.m.
		20d	21 April 1855, Munich, 12.10 a.m.
	58	20e	21 April 1932, Berlin, 2.59 a.m.
		20f	21 April 1932, Berlin, 5.45 p.m.
		20g	21 April 1846, Berlin, 7.36 a.m.
		20h	20 April 1846, Berlin, 4.48 p.m.
21			Franklin D. Roosevelt 30 January 1882, New York City 1.05 a.m. (31 January)
	40	21a	1 February 1932, Washington, DC, 4.24 a.m.
		21b	1 February 1932, Washington, DC, 8.54 p.m.
		21c	30 January 1832, Washington, DC, 9.50 p.m.
		21d	30 January 1832, Washington, DC, 5.20 a.m.

Nativity No.	Case No.	Solar Revolution	Data
	44	21e	31 January 1933, Washington, DC, 10.10 a.m.
		21f	1 February 1933, Washington, DC, 3.00 a.m.
		21g	31 January 1831, Washington, DC, 4.02 p.m.
		21h	30 January 1831, Washington, DC, 11.11 p.m.
22			Male
			10 January 1885, Bognor, 10.27 p.m.
	41	22a	11 January 1938, Birmingham, 7.08 p.m.
		22b	12 January 1938, Birmingham, 12.34 p.m.
		22c	12 January 1832, Birmingham, 1.39 a.m.
		22d	11 January 1832, Birmingham, 8.13 a.m.
	45	22e	11 January 1942, Birmingham, 6.41 p.m.
		22f	12 January 1942, Birmingham, 1.26 p.m.
		22g	12 January 1828, Birmingham, 2.14 a.m.
		22h	11 January 1828, Birmingham, 7.30 a.m.
23			Female
			30 July 1884, London, 5.40 p.m.
	42	23a	1 August 1935, London, 1.23 a.m.
		23b	1 August 1935, London, 7.14 p.m.
		23c	31 July 1833, London, 9.57 a.m.
		23d	30 July 1833, London, 4.05 p.m.
24			Female
			28 October 1914, London, 7.11 a.m.
	43	24a	27 October 1953, London, 6.03 p.m.
		24b	28 October 1953, London, 7.08 a.m.
		24c	27 October 1875, London, 8.28 p.m.
		24d	27 October 1875, London, 7.24 a.m.
	47	24e	27 October 1954, London, 11.51 p.m.
		24f	28 October 1954, London, 1.14 p.m.
		24g	27 October 1874, London, 2.37 p.m.
		24h	27 October 1874, London, 12.51 a.m.
25			Eleanor Roosevelt
			11 October 1884, New York City, 3.01 p.m.
	46	25a	12 October 1932, Washington, DC, 5.53 a.m.
		25b	12 October 1932, Washington, DC, 10.18 p.m.
		25c	12 October 1836, Washington, DC, 12.01 a.m.
		25d	11 October 1836, Washington, DC, 7.48 a.m.
26			Female
			1 January 1926, Nairobi, Kenya, 1.59 p.m.
	49	26a	1 January 1954, London, 8.30 a.m.
		26b	1 January 1954, London, 5.42 p.m.
		26c	31 December 1897, London, 6.04 p.m.
		26d	31 December 1897, London, 8.52 a.m.

Nativity No.	Case No.	Solar Revolution	Data
27	52		Male 19 February 1914, London, 12.44 p.m.
		27a	19 February 1947, London, 12.58 p.m.
		27b	19 February 1947, London, 11.56 p.m.
		27c	18 February 1881, London, 12.36 p.m.
		27d	18 February 1881, London, 1.37 a.m.
28	53		Rodney Collin* 26 April 1909, Brighton, 9.18 a.m.
		28a	25 April 1956, Lima, Peru, 6.05 p.m.
		28b	26 April 1956, Lima, Peru, 10.15 a.m.
		28c	26 April 1862, Lima, Peru, 12.13 a.m.
		28d	25 April 1862, Lima, Peru, 8.01 a.m.
29	54		Carole Lombard 6 October 1908, Fort Wayne, Indiana, 9.30 p.m.
		29a	6 October 1941, Hollywood, Ca., 9.16 p.m.
		29b	7 October 1941, Hollywood, Ca., 8.30 a.m.
		29c	6 October 1875, Hollywood, Ca., 9.38 p.m.
		29d	6 October 1875, Hollywood, Ca., 10.26 a.m.
30	55		Eva Braun 6 February 1912, 48 N 09 11 E 33 11.05 p.m. (5 February)
		30a	4 February 1945, Berlin, 11.31 p.m.
		30b	5 February 1945, Berlin, 10.25 a.m.
		30c	4 February 1879, Berlin, 10.52 p.m.
		30d	4 February 1879, Berlin, 11.57 a.m.
31	56		Col. Charles Lindbergh 4 February 1902, Detroit, 8.04 a.m.
		31a	4 February 1927, St Louis, 9.56 a.m.
		31b	4 February 1927, St Louis, 6.13 p.m.
		31c	3 February 1877, St Louis, 6.24 a.m.
		31d	2 February 1877, St Louis, 10.08 p.m.
	57	31e	4 February 1932, Englewood, NJ, 2.49 p.m.
		31f	5 February, 1932, Englewood, NJ, 12.43 a.m.
		31g	4 February, 1872, Englewood, NJ, 1.31 a.m.
		31h	3 February, 1872, Englewood, NJ, 3.36 p.m.
32	59		Duke of Windsor 23 June 1894, Richmond, Surrey, 10.12 p.m.
		32a	24 June 1936, London, 1.37 a.m.
		32b	24 June 1936, London, 4.21 p.m.
		32c	23 June 1852, London, 6.44 p.m.
		32d	23 June 1852, London, 3.58 a.m.

*Author of *The Theory of Celestial Influence*.

INDEX

Also available in the Aquarian Astrology Handbook Series . . .

DARK STARS

Invisible Focal Points in Astrology

BERNARD FITZWALTER and RAYMOND HENRY

Twentieth-century astrology has a vocabulary of names and symbols which is widely held to be complete, yet astrologers are often frustrated by the limitations imposed by the traditional horoscope. Now Bernard Fitzwalter and Raymond Henry have resurrected elements of the star chart which have been lost in the mists of time:

Phaethon — the lost planet or binary sun of the solar system whose matter now comprises the asteroid belt;
Dark Suns — invisible gravity centres whose existence is proved by the elliptical orbits of the planets;
Planetary Nodes — where the plane of a planet's orbit intersects that of another.

This book describes the astronomical and astrological backgrounds to all these and provides interpretations based on historical and mythological research. A wealth of tables gives the calculated positions for all these points for the whole of the twentieth century, so astrologers can at last widen their vocabulary and restore the balance of the universe.

Bernard Fitzwalter has been teaching and writing about astrology for many years. He is the author of the Aquarian Sun Sign Guides *and* Sun Sign Secrets *series.*

Raymond Henry is an astrologer, an occult therapist and an ordained priest, with a particular interest in bringing astrology and astronomy closer together. He is a well-known member of the Astrological Lodge of London.